AN INTRODUCTION TO CONTEMPORARY AMERICAN FICTION

AN INTRODUCTION TO CONTEMPORARY AMERICAN FICTION

Alan Bilton

NEW YORK UNIVERSITY PRESS
Washington Square, New York

First published in the U.S.A. in 2003 by
New York University Press
Washington Square
New York, NY 10003

www.nyupress.org

First published in Great Britain in 2002 by
Edinburgh University Press
22 George Square
Edinburgh

A Cataloging-in-Publication record for this
book is available from the Library of Congress

ISBN 0-8147-9911-6 (hardback)
ISBN 0-8147-9912-4 (paperback)

Typeset in Palatino Light
by Pioneer Associates, Perthshire, and
printed and bound in Great Britain by
MPG Books Ltd, Bodmin, Cornwall

CONTENTS

PREFACE

This book offers a critical introduction to eight contemporary American novelists, all of whom can all be said to engage with the Postmodern condition, rather than necessarily being Postmodern writers. Certain key themes recur across the novels under consideration here – simulation, the mediascape, a questioning of the real and an exploration of the gap between words and things – which are central to the whole Postmodern debate. A number of more general but no less significant notions also appear throughout the book – space, borders, emptiness, issues of authenticity and individuality – and these too can be traced from chapter to chapter, providing important conceptual links as well as possibilities for further reading. Although some of these ideas might sound a little abstract, this book assumes no kind of prior theoretical knowledge and hopefully avoids the Postmodern symptom of self-validating (read: incomprehensible) jargon. A glossary of literary and critical terms appears at the end of the introduction (alongside an introductory guide to studies of Postmodernism) but I have tried my very best to employ as little 'terminology' as possible. The focus throughout is upon the actual act of writing – form, technique, stylistic invention, the vexed issue of realism – and how this relates to the wider US culture.

After the introduction, which explores the Postmodern as a metaphor for the spirit of our times, each chapter focuses on a specific writer and is followed by a biography (for those who are suspicious of Postmodern claims regarding the death of the author), a series of interesting and illuminating quotes culled from interviews and essays, extra information on lesser-known works, a guide to thematic links between authors, and an extensive, but by no means exhaustive, bibliography for each writer. The bibliographies include academic articles, interviews and reviews, and are intended to indicate both the main areas of critical interest and to provide a useful jumping-off point for further reading. The thematic links (nature, violence, technology, consumerism and so on) both bind the book together and provide a sense of clarification and continuity; they are also cross-referenced with the thematic index at the close of the book. The aim here is to explore provocative parallels, disagreements, comparisons and contrasts, rather than lumping such disparate and contentious writers together under the banner of some kind of Postmodern aesthetic. Throughout the book, the stress is upon the range of possible approaches rather than imposing dogmatic criteria; as such the book also plays a part in the ongoing debate between humanist and post-humanist ideas in the humanities.

In terms of the choice of authors, I've simply tried to choose writers whom I find interesting and who commonly appear on undergraduate American Literature courses; no conscious ideological intentions should thereby be impugned (although admittedly, as Post-Structuralist critics might point out, that doesn't mean they don't exist). This book is intended to be useful for students taking American Studies or English Literature courses, and seeks to spark discussion and debate rather than to provide a single interpretation (or plot-summary). For that much denigrated individual, 'the common reader', the book is intended to offer an introduction to the sheer range and diversity of contemporary American fiction. Ultimately, I would argue, the sheer quality and verve of current writing is itself a response and retort to the dilemma of the Postmodern condition.

Many thanks to all my colleagues at the University of Wales Swansea and the editorial team at Edinburgh University Press, for their encouragement and support. Special thanks to Rolando Hinojosa for so generously sharing his time and ideas. This book is dedicated, like everything else in my life, to Pamela.

SHORT GLOSSARY OF
CRITICAL AND LITERARY TERMS

Aleatory: the intrusion of the random into life; the messiness of existence, refuting claims that the world is ordered.

Atavism: regression back to a primitive state; the erasure of civilisation.

Cubism: the radical rejection of Renaissance notions of perspective and ordered space; a flattening of the subject so that different sides, angles and views can be perceived simultaneously. Turns space into a multitude of flat, depthless, plates.

Deconstruction: a breaking up of language into codes and systems, thereby revealing the institutionalised systems of power which underpin all signs and forms of knowledge.

Futurism: an attempt to represent movement, speed and noise; a crypto-fascist obsession with machine-made power, energy and dynamism.

Intertextuality: texts which reference other texts in an explicit manner; the relationship between books.

Local Colour: generally understood in terms of a tendency in nineteenth-century American literature to lionise idiosyncratic customs and manners as a kind of literary tourism. The term usually suggests a genteel obsession with quaint local peculiarities, and thus is much more sentimental than Regionalism, depending upon an old-fashioned, nostalgic faith in 'plain folks' and traditional ways of life.

Metafiction: fiction which draws attention to its own fictional state. A puncturing of the mimetic illusion.

Mimesis: Greek for 'imitation'. A mimetic piece of writing is founded upon a belief in a genuine reproduction of external reality.

Modernism: in literary or artistic terms, the revolutionary explosion of experimental art in the first half of the twentieth century, overturning previous aesthetic practices and conventions (including that of orthodox 'realism'). 'To be modern is to experience life as a maelstrom, to find one's world and one's self in perpetual ambiguity and contradiction' (Marshall Berman). Key terms are agitation, dizziness, drunkenness, chaos, speed and disintegration. Also seen as an aesthetic response to the machine age, urbanisation and the dawn of the mass media.

Naturalism: a literary movement (chiefly understood in terms of the mid to late nineteenth-century) which aimed to bring a pseudo-scientific objectivity to the art of fiction. Drawing upon post-Darwinian biology, it argued the case for a deterministic universe, wherein free-will is seen as considerably weaker than the brutal forces of heredity and one's environment. Although intended to be free from any distortion or authorial bias, naturalistic writing is frequently pessimistic, exaggerated and grotesque, exploring the seamier areas of perversion and violence. It is therefore linked at times with Expressionism, wherein reality is malformed by extreme mental and emotional states. Whilst the scientific trappings of the term have fallen away, a Naturalistic tendency can be traced throughout twentieth-century fiction.

Nihilism: the rejection of any kind of essential morality or meaning.

Numinous: supernatural, mysterious, ineffable; what cannot be put into words.

Pastiche: a knowing imitation of a pre-existing style, which doesn't parody or satirise the original, but merely repeats it in a deadpan manner.

Postmodernism: 'Postmodernism is what you have when the modernization process is complete and nature is gone for good' (Fredric Jameson). The triumph of the artificial and the end of the natural, original or authentic. An age in which reproduction overtakes production. Key terms are blankness, kitsch, repetition, and simulation. Also seen as an aesthetic response (and/or symptom) of the late-capitalist era of information overload and mass consumerism.

Post-Structuralism: philosophy which states that all linguistic meaning is a result of the relationship between signs, rather than between signs and the real world (the signified).

Quotidian: the everyday; in literary terms, what is often left out of realistic fiction (having to go to the toilet, getting stuck in traffic etc.) unless it is relevant to the plot.

Realism: on the surface this appears the most straightforward of literary terms, denoting the accurate reportage of the real world or actual life. Its virtues are honesty, exactness, sobriety and truth. The problem, of course, is that it presupposes an agreed-upon notion of reality – and therein lies the source of enormous theoretical difficulty. What might be to some self-evident common-sense, will be to others wholly false and dishonest; whether a thing is 'realistic' or not depends on shared assumptions and beliefs. In literary terms, realism suggests less an unproblematic reflection of the world than a mutual, communicable system of conventions; to some critics, verisimilitude (the appearance of being real) denotes a commitment to unadorned existential truth, whilst to others it is a mendacious illusion intended to convince the reader of the supposedly objective nature of the author's personal bias.

Regionalism: an emphasis upon specific geographical settings, via history, customs, dialect, manners and so on. The interests of regionalism are frequently sociological or even anthropological, and for many critics the term has rather negative connotations, suggesting something parochial, insular and small-minded, at least when compared with the great universal themes of High Art. Postmodernist thinking, which doesn't believe in such timeless universal definitions, has rekindled an interest in marginal or peripheral zones of experience, but is in turn suspicious of regionalism's links with what it sees as a discredited realism. Despite this, regionalism has achieved a new prominence in terms of an imaginative resistance to the standardising influence of global consumerism and homogeneous market-forces.

Romance: as an (extremely broad) genre, the romance denotes the creation of an imaginatively autonomous fictive world. Rather than transcribing reality, it uses events, characters and settings as allegorical symbols for abstract, spiritual properties, especially to do with the soul.

Self-reflexive: something that refers back to itself; self-reflective or self-validating.

Simulacrum: the identical copy of something for which no original has ever existed; a copy of a copy of a copy, until the prototype somehow disappers. Used as a description of the flow of images within the mass-media.

Solipsism: the philosophy that one can know nothing outside of one's own experience.

Sublime: awe-inspiring, elevated, beyond any means of description or any human scale.

Surrealism: an attempt to liberate the imagination from the constraints of reason or order via dreams, visions, hallucinations and madness.

Transcendentalism: a nineteenth-century philosophical tendency, which expresses a profoundly individualistic form of religious belief. Nature, rather than the church, acts as one's conduit to higher spiritual truth, the landscape a series of divine hieroglyphics intuitively translated by the imagination.

INTRODUCTION

The subject of this book is the astonishing vitality and energy of contemporary American writing, a rude health all the more remarkable given the number of pessimistic readings of the current cultural scene. After all, who would choose to be a novelist in the Postmodern age? Postmodernism tells us that ours is the age of the sequel, the remake, the copy, preoccupied with a kind of manic recycling and rebranding, desperately trying to disguise the fact that notions of originality or authenticity have been used up. As Steven Connor has noted, even the term, *Post*-Modern, sounds negative, like turning up to a party just as the bottles and cigarette butts are being swept away.[1] Instead of Ezra Pound's revolutionary injunction to 'Make it new', we must content ourselves with pastiche, quotation and parody – a kind of decadent knowingness. The age of artistic revolution is over, and in its place we face a sense of cultural exhaustion and glazed indifference, the endless repetition of earlier styles and fashions – a culture of déjà-vu.

We live, writes Umberto Eco, in a time of lost innocence, haunted by the fear that everything has already been said.[2] How does one go about writing a new love song, a fresh nature poem, an original coming-of-age novel? Both author and audience cannot help but recognise that the very terms seem hackneyed, clichéd, their language all but used up; all that remain are echoes, repetitions, a compulsory plagiarism which threatens any last remaining traces of sincerity. The only honest response then seems to be to acknowledge one's sources, to accept that even one's most earnest declarations of feeling are cribbed from bad pop songs or romantic comedies. But this inescapable self-consciousness – everything a reference, just like a movie, just like something on TV – inevitably turns to cynicism. By the time we have reached adolescence we have already experienced (and many times over) all the possible permutations of adult life in soap-operas and made-for-TV movies; life itself becomes a kind of rerun, our response a mixture of boredom and

1

irony. In essence, we have all been here before. Contemporary life seems ringed by quotation marks, and for that reason, impossible to take seriously. If one imagines Postmodern culture as an endlessly Xeroxed copy of itself, then with each generation the lines seem a little fainter, the shapes blurred, the image corrupted. Little wonder then that Andy Warhol is its patron saint.

Another way of thinking about the transition from the Modern to the Postmodern is to view it in terms of a shift from Art (with a capital 'A') to culture. Modernism was essentially an affair of the avant-garde who regarded their work as a deliberate provocation to philistine, bourgeois sensibilities. Modern Art was antagonistic, elitist and scandalous, the creation of bohemian genii beyond one's mortal ken. In the Postmodern age however, this elevated 'aura' has dissipated; corporate offices now buy contemporary art-works by the yard, reproductions of famous prints form part of interior decorating, and 'serious' novelists must fight for space on airport bookstands like everybody else. And yet in a sense our entire environment has been aestheticised; what once belonged to the elevated sphere of art (heightened reality, a rush of stimulation) has, in the age of mass information, become the mediascape we all now occupy.

To a large extent, we live in a wholly manmade world, surrounded by screens, images, monitors and advertisements, rather than by real or natural things. Nature has been relegated to a kind of leisure activity, 'views' plucked out of the landscape to be hermetically sealed off by car-parks, public amenities and gift-shops. For most of us, our environment is almost wholly artificial. The freeway, the shopping-mall, and the VDU screen constitute our everyday living space, our senses bombarded by a constant flow of mediated information, messages and commercials. Postmodern America represents a kind of merger between the hypermarket and the TV screen (think Disneyland or Las Vegas), sightseeing modelled upon camera-angles, images scored to a ubiquitous soundtrack. This is where the Postmodern populace makes its home: the heightened sphere of the aesthetic harnessed to the glut of the consumer market. But who wouldn't like to live their life as if it were a movie? Why not pump your food through with chemicals to make it taste better, take Prozac to make yourself happier, recreate your surroundings in the shape of your wildest dreams? If one could pluck one's brain out from its poor mortal shell, plug it into an endless virtual reality system, leave behind the ordinary and mundane to experience an endlessly stimulating simulation: well, who could resist?[3] Only those who still harbour some nostalgia for notions of the authentic, the natural or the real. Postmodernity, however, is the hyper-real, air-brushed, computer-generated and strategically-doctored, a kind of cartoon dream. Indeed, in a profoundly non-revolutionary age, only the technocrats are still talking about the possibility of a (virtual) utopia. As one character puts it in Don DeLillo's 1984 novel, *White Noise*:

> You have to open yourself up to the data. TV offers incredible amounts of psychic data. It opens ancient memories of world birth, it welcomes us into the grid, the network of little buzzing dots that make up the picture pattern. There is light, there is sound. I ask my students, 'What more do you want?' Look at the wealth of data concealed in the grid, in the bright packaging, the jingles, the slice-of-life commercials, the products hurtling out of darkness, the coded messages and endless repetitions, like chants, like mantras.'Coke is it, Coke is it, Coke is it.' The medium practically overflows with sacred formulas if we can remember how to respond innocently and get past our irritation, weariness and disgust.[4]

This in turn suggests one of the central tenets of Postmodernism, the Simulacrum, defined by Fredric Jameson (by way of Plato) as 'the identical copy for which no original has ever existed'.[5] It is not so much that the images being offered up by mass culture are somehow false or misleading – rather they bear no relation to any kind of lived experience at all. Images seem to be breeding in a wild state, a copy of a copy of a copy, until the original source eventually disappears; this then is where the originality of the Postmodern lies, in reproduction rather than production, dissemination rather than creation. Who needs artists? It's the system which represents the new avant-garde, making demands upon our senses and powers of comprehension far in excess of anything Modern Art required. Technology is rewiring consciousness in ways the Futurists could only dream of.

But is any of this true? And if it is, what should be the response of the contemporary novelist? Does the novel stake its claim to relevance by competing with the age, taking its place amongst the other products of the mediascape? But how can fiction compete with simulation, or its language capture the bewildering complexity of the flow of data, images and information? Moreover, will this way literature somehow succumb to the cultural logic of the day: empty spectacle, dumbed-down consumption, instant gratification? Shorn of its claims to high literary seriousness, reading fiction becomes just another leisure-time activity or a particularly old-fashioned sector of the entertainment industry. Or is the novel (at least, as we understand it to date) inherently inimical to the Postmodern spirit, in permanent opposition to the glut and glare of the information age – a position which also brings with it the risk of irrelevancy and redundancy? The author who tries to represent the society of the spectacle merely ends up reproducing its hollow parade of distractions; the writer who shuts his eyes risks the charge of naïve denial.[6]

At this point however, it is important that we draw a distinction between two very different uses of the word 'Postmodern'. In the context of the above, Postmodernism acts as a kind of shorthand for approaching the general state of contemporary culture, dominated by consumerism, the mass media and the reduplication of images. In literary terms, however, Postmodernist fiction is frequently used to describe a specific set of formal practices which draw attention to the novel as a work of fiction, thereby ultimately exploring language itself. Hence, these two uses are by no means interchangeable. Postmodernist writing shouldn't simply be seen as a symptom of the dominant culture, or necessarily sympathetic toward it – in fact generally, just the opposite is the case. And of course, the same is true of Modernism. T. S. Eliot's *The Wasteland* (1922), is often cited as *the* great Modern poem, but it is wholly anti-Modern with regard to its judgement of twentieth-century culture. Indeed, if we want to understand Modernism – that incredible outpouring of experimentation, creation and imaginative discovery which took place across the arts in the early part of the twentieth century – then two very different accounts suggest themselves: accounts which in turn provide us with the means to talk about the Postmodern in more detail.

The first reads Modernism in terms of a declaration of aesthetic independence – art for the first time unrestrained by the requirement to represent the real world ('mimesis') but free to explore its own, purely formal, characteristics. In this sense, abstract paintings are about nothing else but shape, colour and line; the act of painting rather than any ostensible subject. Similarly, Modernist literature could be seen to have turned inwards to explore the nature of consciousness, the ways by which we order (or narrate) the world, and ultimately that primary matter of fiction, language itself. A second interpretation of Modernism, however, places the movement within the context of the sweeping social and economic changes radically transforming America in the first part of the twentieth century: industrialisation, technological invention, urban growth, the emergence of mass consumerism. Whether writers or artists celebrated or condemned this new machine age, they were linked by the conviction that it was impossible to employ traditional artistic forms to record this new reality. A new world required a new art; generic forms of 'realism' no longer seemed to hold up.

The transplantation of European Modernism to an American idiom therefore created an unusual effect: what had seemed to be European abstraction now appeared as American realism. The geometric skyline of the American metropolis, with its giant blocks of steel and glass, seemed already Cubist; the kinetic rush of the city streets, the confusion of foreground and background, the kaleidoscopic rush of stimulation, somehow inherently Futurist. Indeed, this clash between artistic daring and accelerated social change provided the central dynamic of Modernity. As Robert Hughes writes, Modernism believed that it 'could find the necessary metaphors by which a radically changing culture could explain itself';[7] chaos, flux, disintegration, speed.

The missing term in all of this is capitalism. As Marshall Berman has argued, everyone within the capitalist economy is under constant pressure from relentless competition, and in order to survive one must constantly revolutionise the means of production – offering new products, speeding up production, cutting costs, working out more efficient production methods, testing new technology.[8] This constant upheaval spills over into the social fabric of the times: workers must be flexible, fluid, able to adapt to constantly changing conditions, locations and practices. Hence, Berman argues, constant change is itself a characteristic of capitalism – whatever stands still is swiftly obsolete, whilst the market functions via struggle, competition and disturbance – a sense of agitation and chaos also central to Modernism.

But if capitalism is the key to Modernism's vivacity, how have we become becalmed in the shallows of the Postmodern? One answer is that Berman's account assumes a laissez-faire model of capitalism, grounded in the principle of unrestrained competition. Postmodern culture, however, appears as a product of monopoly capitalism, the manifestation of a corporately managed, bureaucratically-controlled world. True, there is still constant change, but it denotes a revolution in marketing rather than a revolution in society; the same companies pumping out the same products, but repackaged and rebranded for the new season. Consumerism, or the gloss of media images, no longer threaten our most deeply held traditions; they *are* our traditions, and any sense of upheaval has been replaced by an impatient wait for new products. In this sense, we still live in an accelerated culture, but the future-shock is gone, change a function of merchandising, promotion and market-spin. In the place of Modernist disintegration (as in *The Wasteland*), we are witness to the closure of a vast interlocking system of administration and information, everything co-opted and absorbed by the global market-place. As long as it sells, everything is permitted, and thus the adversarial nature of Modernism collapses into a form of universal assimilation. If everything is a product, then anything can be used to fuel the system. In DeLillo's *Mao II* (1991), novelist Bill Gray's assertion that writing is dangerous, that 'every government that holds power or aspires to power should feel so threatened by writers that they hunt them down everywhere', is ridiculed by his editor, who says of his clients:

> I say, Coochy, coochy, coo . . . I tell them the reprint bidders are howling in the commodity pits. There is miniseries interest, there is audiocassette interest, the White House wants a copy for the den. I say, The Publicity people are setting up tours. The Italians love the book completely. The Germans are groping for levels of rapture. Oh my oh my oh my.[9,10]

In the market-place, even the most recalcitrant of novelists seem house-trained; the days of spitting in the face of bourgeois respectability are long gone (everyone knows that controversy sells). And with it, perhaps, a sense of idealism and confidence also departs. That Hart Crane was willing to stake his life on his poetry, or that the Surrealists believed in unsettling the very seat of reason now seems unimaginable. Surrealism has been co-opted by advertising, Futurism recalled with nostalgia, subversion and moral transgression, available now in a store near you. Does the novel possess any power to influence society? Once literature might have hoped to appeal to an elite of learned individuals; but, in an age of mass-communication, power at once seems more dispersed and further away than ever. Only the famous get their voices heard above the hum of journalistic muzak, but the mechanisms of celebrity in turn tame and neuter dissent. The result is rather like psychiatric rest-cures at the turn of the last century; isolate the hysteric from his family, then feed and stupefy the patient until his nerves are passive once more. The endless cycle of readings, lectures, book-sign- ings, promotional interviews, book fairs and festivals not only prevents writers from writing, but binds them ever more securely to the logic of the entertainment industry, a kind of gelded fame.[11] Why would an industry market a product harmful to its profit? The financial rewards and media celebrity allotted to 'name' authors are a badge of their harmlessness. And if you're not famous then nobody will listen at all.

Alongside this, we seem to have gone beyond the point of any conceivable aesthetic revolution. In both art and literature, the 'shock of the new' relies upon a struggle between traditional notions of realism and new modes of perception. The heroic age of Modernism is founded upon a perceived failure of existing forms, and a desperate search for the new. But we are now so far beyond the distant shores of abstraction, that this struggle appears as merely a distant speck on the horizon. The 'new' will never be so shocking again. When fine art has removed every last speck of paint from the canvas and drawn our attention to the space where it no longer hangs, when Joyce has put every possible word into a book and Beckett then erased them, where else is there to go? The result is rather like the closing of the frontier; there's no more untouched territory to light out for. In his famous essay, 'The Literature of Exhaustion', John Barth admits that 'it may well be that the novel's time as a major art form is up, as the times of classical tragedy, grand opera, or the sonnet sequence came to be'.[12] The family saga, the historical chronicle, the coming-of-age tale, affairs of the heart; all told now, worn out, irrelevant to our accelerated culture. Why not wait for the movie, instead? And even then, the trailer is often enough.

Underpinning such a position is the perceived redundancy of the humanist ideals the novel most warmly cherishes – individualism, self- expression, the realm of the personal. Fredric Jameson, for example, speaks glibly of the passing of any kind of unique writerly style, that idiosyncratic voice 'as unmistakable as your fingerprint', now a thing of the past for the simple reason that 'there is no longer a self present to do the feeling'.[13,14] In terms of Postmodern theory, the self has gone the same way as the soul; held up to be a mirage, an ideological trick of the light, a bourgeois illusion. The self has been decentred. We no longer possess any kind of inner core or essential us (we never did; the self was a fiction born of a specific stage of economic development, the beginnings of consumerism and the era of the artisan), but rather are simply a nexus for all the thoughts, words and feelings existing out there in culture. There is no interior life in Postmodernism; emotions are free-floating and impersonal, triggered by external stimuli. At the end of Bret Easton Ellis's *The Rules of Attraction* (1987), for example, one character races after his departing lover, 'because it felt like the "right" thing' to do. It was a chance to show some emotion. I wasn't acting on passion. I was only acting . . . It seemed like something I'd been told to do. By who or what was vague.'[15] Rather like a TV audience responding to cue cards, our emotions are no longer governed by internal desires, but simply triggered by generic recognition: if this was a movie, then this is when I would laugh or cry. With no essential I, we simply act as a fragmented channel for cultural discourse. We don't say words, words say us. Identity becomes merely a matter of media-reception, jumping from channel to channel schizophrenically; ultimately, consciousness appears as a strange kind of self-awareness within language rather than inside me.

But at this point the humanist in us may well bridle. After all, who says that the sociologists or the semioticians are right? One might quote the poet e. e. cummings at this point: 'When men are thought of in terms of statistics, numbers or manipulative digits, and treated the same way, then there is a corresponding lack of that humane vision which regards them as human beings.'[16] The wisdom of the novel has always stressed the essential specificity of human identity, as something inimitable, unique, and inexhaustible: everyone has their reasons, desires, depths unfathomable. Good Marxist that he is, Jameson seems quite content with the idea of an end to the autonomous bourgeois ego, but who would be prepared to declare the extinction of the personal in their own lives? Are we really just an effect of language, or is this just a way of reworking the old party line that all consciousness is class consciousness? Moreover, is the idea of the erasure of the individual voice actually true? DeLillo might mimic the banalities of jargon-ridden America, Paul Auster draw upon the writings of nineteenth-century Transcendentalism, or Rolando Hinojosa appropriate legal documents, newspaper cuttings, and bar-room jokes, but one page of any of the writers considered in this volume is immediately identifiable, and in a sense, inimitable – even those writers, like Ellis, who take the extinction of individuality as their central theme.

Moreover, Jameson's Marxist critique of bourgeois individualism is oddly similar to the language of Postmodern consumerism. In Douglas Coupland's *Microserfs* (1994), the author writes of a species of catfish which can be fed with grain to produce a white fish fillet with absolutely no discernible flavour or texture – ready, then, to be injected with chemicals to produce any food product which manufacturers may wish.[17] Such a notion is close to the Postmodern view of individuality (all of us McHumans or Filet O' Flesh) as something to be purchased and consumed, selected from the rack – who we are defined by our clothes, music, car or decorating-style, the logos and labels of consumer culture. In a sense, the fashion industry's narcissism hides the fact that there is no essential self any more – one's identity is as interchangeable as one's wardrobe. The secret of who we are is no longer about depth or mystery (as it is for, say, Freud) but surfaces and signs, a flattening out of personality. But is one's selfhood so easily evaded – can one actually choose to be someone else? We might all contain multitudes, but is there no core? Is this all there is, merely a meeting of various kinds of discourse, not selfhood but a kind of bibliographical nexus?

Accompanying the death of any kind of individual style for Jameson, is the passing of the age of great authors. 'Such figures no longer hold any charm or magic for the subjects of a corporate, collectivized, post-individualistic age: in that case, goodbye to them without regret'[18], he writes. But whilst this claim is made in the name of democracy (an end to literary aristocracy!) there seems a slightly sinister edge to this collective disdain for the individual talent, its denial of the fact that, alas, some writers may be better than others. Of course, such a rebuttal itself begs the question of who decides matters of literary worth, ultimately ennobling those worthy of canonization in the first place. Jay Clayton in *The Pleasures of Babel* (1993) believes that 'we are in a great age for literature . . . but a feature of that greatness is the disappearance of the old Romantic notion of the masterpiece'.[19] Multicultural America is too fragmented for any kind of common consensus as to worth; instead 'particular communities of readers' construct their own enclaves, the general public replaced by specific interest groups – generally defined along ethnic or gender lines.[20] Consensus, he argues, is just an ideological mirage masking the interests of the dominant group; any idea of a shared canon of great works will always exclude the marginal. But there is also a loss of faith in communication or empathy in Clayton's model; the belief that fiction can tell us about lives other than our own. If there can be no kind of mutual understanding between groups, no shared common ground, then literature becomes simply retelling each of us what we already know. But do all definitions of common ground eventually ostracise the uncommon? And does fiction talk about 'the real world' anyway?

Freedom from the responsibility to represent the real was one of the first demands of Modernism, but much Postmodernist thinking rejects entirely any commonsensical notion of truth or fidelity to lived experience. What the layman might call 'realistic' is in fact, just a series of generic conventions labelled as such, its illusion of objectivity or verisimilitude serving to disguise its central, authoritarian message: this is the way things are – don't touch. Leo Bersani argues that far from being neutral, realism always serves the interests of the status quo, sustaining existing networks of power.[21] According to Bersani, realism is single-minded, brooking no opposition (Who can argue with common sense? We all know what's real), encouraging passivity in the reader by suggesting that the world is ordered and causal – all counter-revolutionary properties in Bersani's view. Only works which subvert or disrupt this appearance of cohesion can be classed as truly progressive; everything else just serves the authorities.[22] But is conventional realism really so conservative? Is, say, a straightforward narrative involving workers' rights in the third world supporting the capitalist system whilst an experimental poem, deconstructing semantic logic serving the Marxist cause? Moreover, the demand that (in political terms) literature supports what could be rather than what really is, sounds, to my ears at least, uncomfortably close to Stalinist dogma; as Rolando Hinojosa is fond of quoting, 'facts are bothersome things in that they refuse to go away'. Would any 'realistic' writers claim that truth was straightforward and untroubling anyway?

Aside from politics, Post-Structuralism provides a philosophical position from which realism no longer appears realistic. Post-Structuralism argues that meaning in language is constructed from the connections between words rather than by the naïve notion that words refer to anything outside of themselves. Words and things are thus totally different entities; the former general, abstract and arbitrary (like the word

'Cat'); the latter, specific (no two cats are entirely alike), physical (it is impossible to translate perfectly the feel, smell or sound of cats into words), and bearing no necessary connection to its sign (there is nothing inherently catlike about the word 'cat'). Words don't refer to the 'real' but to other words; meaning is always internal. As Jerome Klinkowitz puts it, 'Deconstructive philosophy teaches us that we are never really talking about things, only the relationship between them – specifically those relations that indicate what a thing is not.'[23] In terms of language, Klinkowitz argues, the real is a kind of absence forever beyond its reach; words straddle this void and create their own kind of internal coherence, but without ever touching what lies below.[24] The subject of fiction is therefore not the real world, but the ways in which we structure its absence, which is to say, the ways in which we construct and narrate fiction – including the common sense fictions we rely upon in our everyday lives. One ideal of Post-Structuralism thus sounds like a hangover from high-Modernism – the creation of a purely self-contained system, reliant upon nothing outside of itself; not a reflection or second-hand copy of something else but self-constitutive, independent, wholly abstract. The other approach of Post-Structuralism is to discredit those systems which do claim access to the real, revealing their meaning to be wholly arbitrary; either way, all books are purely about other books, with no way out of this linguistic short-circuit. An airless library, a labyrinth of mirrors, one's own reflection infinitely refracted; is this what language is? Not a mirror upon the real, but an artificial attempt to impose order upon the formless (and thereby disguise its own arbitrariness)?

But need one worry about all of this? Such an academic programme bears little relation to the reason why most books are read or most book are written – not that this in itself discredits the idea, of course. But can fiction survive without any relevance beyond its own composition? After all, what might be true for painting or music, doesn't necessarily hold true for language. Whilst the novel can never produce a perfect correspondence between fiction and actual experience, when has it ever claimed it could? Fiction offers conditional understandings, contingent suggestions, ironic possibilities, even in its most realistic modes; oddly, the last people in the humanities who are still talking about 'absolute truth' are the Post-Structuralists in the business of demolishing it. As André Brink has pointed out 'in retrospect, this has always been the case: language in the novel did not only tell a story but reflected on itself in the act of telling.'[25] All novels are to a greater or lesser degree, metafictional; the writer of a realist text knows only too well about the constructed nature of her fictional world, its reliance upon other works, and its stylised distance from whatever we might call real life.

Moreover, it is possible once again to draw parallels between academic theory and the logic of the wider culture. As Gerald Graff has pointed out, a denial of the realm, an obsession with simulation, and a concern with structure and code are all characteristics of the mediascape itself.[26] Indeed, the impenetrable prose of much theoretical writing ('mounting obscurity upon obscurity in endless spirals of self-validation') resembles the bureaucratic terminology satirised in many of the novels studied in this book; theory, in this sense closer to symptom than cure.[27] Our exile from the real, the creation of a wholly artificial world, the loss of the authentic, the end of individuality – these motifs occur again and again in both fiction and theory, and lie at the heart of our understanding of the Postmodern.

But do we have to accept the Postmodern at all? For many people, slogans such as 'the death of the real' or 'the end of nature' simply make no sense at all. Certainly, there are times, on cold, wet, windy days, wandering through the mud, when the simulacrum seems very far away indeed. In philosophical terms, 'the real' has always been a problematic entity, and notions of some kind of separation between words and objects can be traced back to Plato at least. What's so different, one might ask, about today? Indeed, in the context of the Postmodern dilemma (the fear that everything has already been said, that all writers have been incorporated by the system, that our age expresses a loss of creative verve and ambition), it might be instructive to read jeremiads expressing identical fears but written in the 1920s – a period which in retrospect appears as the most vital and adventurous in American literary history.[28]

Such doubts are always with us; but at the very least, such sentiments do serve to express the spirit of the age. Empty spectacle, blank repetition, a declining faith in humanism; these symptoms of Post-modernity can be observed across the arts, although admittedly perhaps less in fiction than elsewhere. In a sense, the Postmodern logic of reproduction and repetition is simply built into the market-place. Our culture is market-tested, consumer-orientated and pre-packaged, the result of demographic research, consumer surveys and target-audience analysis.

The turnover is so fast, the technology so expensive, the demand for new products so overwhelming, that the end result is a paradoxical over-inflation of signs and their almost instantaneous exhaustion. What remains untouched by this logic? What images, stories or emotions, haven't been fed into the culture machine, to be reproduced as consumer goods, life-style choices, magazine articles? What exists outside of the system?

It is interesting to note how many of the novels studied in the following chapters are concerned with maps, exploration and representation, the search for some kind of redemptive space. The wilderness has always functioned in American literature as a trope of possibility or salvation, liberation from a corrupt and mercantile civilisation; even with nature tamed and the wilderness crisscrossed by freeways and shopping-malls, this motif still doesn't seem finished with. The search for some kind of virgin territory underpins much of the writing explored in this book; some kind of fictive (rather than literal) space uncontaminated by the dominant logic of endless replication. Of course the search for the real, rather like the search for God, is unlikely to be conclusive, and notions of the real, the elemental or the authentic are notoriously unsupportable. In Paul Auster's *Moon Palace* (1989), the hero's search for the cave in the deserts of Utah containing his grandfather's (Modernist!) paintings – strange, visionary works, evidence of some kind of epiphanic union with nature – ends bathetically, when he discovers that the cave has been flooded to make way for a dam. But in his written record of events – in his struggle to represent the real, rather than his success – the novel nevertheless grants the narrator some sense of absolution. The writers under consideration in this study explore the border between the subjective and the objective, words and things, personal identity and imposed role; little wonder then that the primary metaphors are spatial ones of cartography and discovery.

Ultimately, the idea of a space outside of culture is a paradoxical one. How can one even imagine such a thing, given that our very thoughts are culturally determined? Doesn't the struggle to represent such a site thereby despoil and incorporate it? How can fiction, of all things, oppose the law of simulation and address the real? And isn't the notion of the wilderness a cultural myth in the first place? Nevertheless, the idea of aesthetic territory left to explore, things still unsaid, visions not yet witnessed, remains central to contemporary fiction, even in its apparent denial. This space – at once within language and out there – perhaps accounts for the otherwise incomprehensible vitality of the novel in an age of ostensible exhaustion. The struggle to represent suggests that there are still things left to say and still a voice to say them with; ultimately, such a struggle cannot help but go against the temper of the times.

NOTES

1. Steven Connor (1997), *Postmodernist Culture* (2nd edn), Oxford: Blackwell, p. 74.
2. Umberto Eco (1985), *Reflections on The Name of the Rose*, translated by William Weaver, London: Secker & Warburg, pp. 65–81.
3. Indeed, isn't this the central paradox of the Wachowski Brothers' *The Matrix* (1999)? The film warns us of the dangers of technology, of succumbing to simulated illusion on a mass scale, but the appeal of the film is in turn dependent upon its special effects and computer-game imagery, the idea of escaping the mundane and plugging into a fantastical sphere where everything is possible.
4. Don DeLillo (1986), *White Noise*, London: Picador, p. 51.
5. Fredric Jameson (1993), *Postmodernism, or the Cultural Logic of Late Capitalism*, London: Verso, p. 18.
6. The phrase is Guy Debord's, the French philosopher and sociologist, father of Situationism.
7. Robert Hughes (1991), *The Shock of the New* (2nd edn), London: Thames & Hudson, p. 9.
8. Marshall Berman (1983), *All that is Solid Melts into Air*, London: Verso, pp. 90–105.
9. Don DeLillo (1991), *Mao II*, London: Jonathan Cape, p. 97.
10. Ibid., p. 101.
11. For a stimulating study of this question see Joe Moran (2000), *Star Authors: Literary Celebrity in America*, London: Pluto Press.
12. John Barth (1967), 'The Literature of exhaustion', *Atlantic Monthly*, 220, 2 Aug., pp. 29–34.
13. Jameson, p. 15.
14. Ibid.
15. Bret Easton Ellis (1988), *The Rules of Attraction*, London: Picador, p. 281.
16. e. e. cummings (1962), *six non-lectures*, New York: Atheneum, p. 56.
17. Douglas Coupland (1994), *Microserfs*, London: Flamingo, p. 128.
18. Jameson, p. 306.
19. Jay Clayton (1993), *The Pleasures of Babel*, New York: Oxford University Press, p. 30.
20. Ibid.

21. See generally Leo Bersani & Ulysse Dutoit (1981), *The Forms of Violence*, New York: Schocken Books.
22. Ibid., p. 73.
23. Jerome Klinkowitz (1992), *Structuring the Void*, Durham: Duke University Press, p. 1.
24. Ibid., p. 3.
25. André Brink (1998), *The Novel*, London/Basingstoke: Macmillan, p. 6.
26. Gerald Graff (1979), *Literature Against Itself*, Chicago: University of Chicago Press, p. 6.
27. Charles Newman, quoted by Connor, p. 7.
28. See for example, Harold Stearns (1922), *Civilization in the United States*, New York: Harcourt.

POSTMODERNISM AND CONTEMPORARY FICTION:
AN INTRODUCTORY BIBLIOGRAPHY

Alexander, Marguerite (1990), *Flights from Realism*, London: Edward Arnold (interesting study of the relationship between Postmodernism and realism).
Alter, Robert (1984), *Motives for Fiction*, Harvard: Harvard University Press (explores Postmodernity in the light of why authors actually write and why readers really read).
Baker, Stephen (2000), *The Fiction of Postmodernity*, Edinburgh: Edinburgh University Press (fairly dense, but excellent on DeLillo and Pynchon).
Baudrillard, Jean (1988), *America*, London: Verso (witty, cranky and frequently crazy jottings of the French intellectual on a road trip across the States; best read as a strange mixture of science fiction and linguistic satire, nonsensical in parts, brilliant in others. Approach with extreme caution).
— (1990), *Cool Memories*, London: Verso (more of the same: playful, provocative, frequently exasperating).
Brink, André (1998), *The Novel*, London/Basingstoke: Macmillan (very interesting discussion of the relationship between realism and self-conscious fiction by the well-respected author).
Bukatman, Scott (1993), *Terminal Identity*, Durham: Duke University Press (mind-boggling trip through both science-fiction and contemporary technology).
Burke, Sean (1995), *Authorship: A Reader*, Edinburgh: Edinburgh University Press (indispensible collection of essays on authorship, starting with Plato and on through Barthes).
Cassedy, Steven (1990), *Flight from Eden*, Los Angeles: University of Calfornia Press (draws parallels between Postmodern theory and ancient myth: weird but brilliant).
Clayton, Jay (1993), *The Pleasures of Babel*, New York: Oxford University Press

(energetic advertisement for literary multiculturism: plenty to argue over in places).

Connor, Steven (1997), *Postmodernist Culture*, Oxford: Blackwell (clear and concise introduction to theoretical issues).

Eagleton, Terry (1996), *The Illusions of Postmodernism*, Oxford: Blackwell (polemical, Marxist, critique of the issue – never less than stimulating and contentious).

Etlin, Richard (1996), *In Defence of Humanism*, New York: Cambridge University Press (the old guard strikes back).

Foster, Hal (ed.) (1983), *Postmodern Culture*, London: Pluto (collects key essays on the topic).

Graff, Gerald (1979), *Literature Againts Itself*, Chicago: University of Chicago Press (much cited defence of realism).

Harvey, David (1990), *The Condition of Postmodernity*, Oxford: Blackwell (excellent on the information age and the strange non-spaces of advanced technology).

Hughes, Robert (1997), *American Visions*, London: Harvill (lively and opinionated introduction to American art).

Hutcheon, Linda (1989), *The Politics of Postmodernism*, London: Routledge (difficult but worthwhile).

Jackson, Leonard (1991), *The Poverty of Structuralism*, New York: Longman (good anti-theory tract).

Jameson, Fredric (1993), *Postmodernism, or the Cultural Logic of Late Capitalism*, London: Verso (pretty much the key study of the area. If you're interested in Postmodernism, you really should read this. Keep a dictionary to hand at all times.)

Klinkowitz, Jerome (1992), *Structuring the Void*, Durham: Duke University Press (probably the best book on Structuralism and self-conscious fiction).

Levine, George (ed.) (1993), *Realism and Representation*, University of Wisconsin Press (wide range of essays on the topic).

McHale, Brian (1992), *Constructing Postmodernism*, London: Routledge (Structuralist readings of key novels).

Millard, Kenneth (2000), *Contemporary American Fiction*, Oxford: Oxford University Press (good on gender, race and cultural identity).

Moran, Joe (2000), *Star Authors: Literary Celebrity in America*, London: Pluto (explores the role and influence of contemporary writers).

Norris, Christopher (1993), *The Truth about Postmodernism*, Oxford: Blackwell (good heated debate about politics and philosophy: not necessarily the best place for beginners, though).

Woods, Tim (1999), *Beginning Postmodernism*, Manchester: Manchester University Press (student-friendly starting point).

DON DeLILLO[1]

Given the academic and inward-tending nature of much of the writing on Postmodernism, it is interesting that the writer who in many ways articulates and dramatises its concerns most clearly, has scrupulously distanced himself from either campus life or theoretical discourse. Whilst DeLillo's novels are concerned with, in his own words, language 'as a subject as well as an instrument in my work', he has been quick to assert the caveat that he approaches language 'from street level', any degree of abstraction in his work already present in the texture and fabric of contemporary America.[2,3]

Indeed, in many ways, DeLillo's central literary talent is that of mimicry. Over the course of twelve novels and numerous shorter works, plays and essays, DeLillo has developed a characteristic literary voice which blends bureaucratic slapstick with occult intimation, his prose-style ranging freely from a parody of the cliches and banalities of terminology-ridden America, to a kind of portentous incantation, somewhere between a corporate mission statement and the Book of Revelations. DeLillo's world is always slightly out of focus, perpetually breaking up into static or dissolving into electronic dots and signals. The creeping elements of abstraction in his work thus appear both threatening and mysterious – pieces of corporate jargon insidiously infiltrating everyday speech, streams of electronic data scorching the sit-com imagery of his work – a Pop Art world whose imagery is repeated and repeated until it becomes something stranger, less identifiable.

Indeed, Andy Warhol's prints provide one way of approaching DeLillo's work and the Postmodern logic of endless replication. One lurid reproduction (of a movie star, an electric chair, a car accident) still provides a recogllisable image: but what of ten, a hundred, and onwards into infinity? Warhol's art suggests that if one reproduces indefinitely, then eventually the way back to the original will be lost, the image no longer signifying anything beyond its own duplication. What was once a face becomes blurred, merely shapes, smudges, shadows; even when one can still recognise the subject matter it no longer elicits any kind of emotional response. One image of an electric chair still says something about capital punishment; a dozen replicated copies signify only numb repetition. This then is the starting line for DeLillo's fiction: the transformation of the familiar into the alien; the vanishing point at which the original disappears. On the one hand, his work takes place within an overwhelmingly cinematic and televisual setting, an optical landscape comprising ubiquitous TV screens, billboards and monitors, a continuous bombardment of dazzling electronic imagery. But there is also an unsettling sense of invisibly about his work, as if somehow this degree of sensory stimulation leaves the age paradoxically less easy to visualise.

Indeed, the dominant feeling in DeLillo's fiction, is that contemporary reality has outdistanced any language with which to describe it, one's conventional vocabulary no longer able to cope with the linguistic surroundings in which it now finds itself. DeLillo's writing is concerned with the emergence of a technological and bureaucratic space which we cannot even begin to describe – precisely because we lack the correct terms with which to do so.

Elsewhere, Fredric Jameson has demonstrated how inadequate our usual terms seem when attempting to deal with, say, the flow of capital within the multinational money markets, the electronic codes employed by interlocking information agencies, or the vast weight of data circulating within bureaucratic channels.[4] In the strange new world of information-technology, credit card details, bar codes, fax numbers, and endless waves of incognisable statistics are beamed from satellite to satellite as electronic signals no longer resembling words at all: invisible, intangible, unimaginably abstract.[5]

In DeLillo's fifth novel, *Players* (1977) Lyle Wynant, a financial consultant, notes that: 'He'd seen the encoding rooms, the micro-filming of checks, money moving, shrinking as it moved, beginning to elude visualization, to pass from a paper existence to electronic sequences, its meaning increasingly complex, harder to name' (*Players*, 110).

Critics of this non-space of information-technology, argue that since we lack the correct terminology even to picture its immaterial dimensions (which are closer to abstract mathematics than conventional modes of description), we cannot even begin to analyse or criticise its processes. Instead, the abstract codes through which it operates are closed to us, deliberately rendered private and inaccessible, so that our technological illiteracy becomes a means of passivity and control.

Mudger, the head of the mysterious information-junta in DeLillo's *Running Dog* (1978), explains that:

> The facts about you and your existence have been collected or are being collected. Banks, insurance companies, credit organisations, tax examiners, passport offices, reporting services, police agencies, intelligence gatherers. It's a little like what I was saying before. Devices make us pliant. If *they* issue a print-out saying we're guilty, then we're guilty: (*Running Dog*, 93)

This inability to quarrel with our accumulated data makes us obsequious, subservient towards those who have access to our numbers, the technocrats who can translate the electronic codes. Who can argue with one's bank account, credit-rating or governmental file? In DeLillo's novels, the whole terminology through which the system functions – the cryptography, passwords and bits of jargon – take on the status of secret, esoteric knowledge, jealously guarded over by stenographer-cabbalists. Bureaucratic language appears as the property of other people, copyrighted by shadowy agencies and corporations: alien, untrustworthy and untranslatable, open to manipulation by those whom DeLillo calls 'the king's linguists' (*Great Jones Street*, 68).

Whilst ordinary, demotic speech at least permits a shared sense of argument and dissent, terminology is specifically designed to block understanding, excluding those who have yet to be initiated into its hermetic secrets. Worse still, these codes seem to infiltrate insidiously everyday speech, one's vocabulary colonised by acronyms and ciphers, brand-names and jargon, impossible to connect to any familiar meaning.

In DeLillo's novels, language seems annexed by monopoly capitalism, thought itself franchised by the anonymous signatories of state power. Characters are possessed by a strange kind of babbling or speaking in tongues, their dialogue privatised by signs they cannot understand and symbols they can no longer decipher. At times the text itself displays odd symptoms of this bizarre *logorrhoea*; the roll-call of players in DeLillo's football novel, *End Zone* (1972), is constantly mutating and rewriting itself, with no fewer than fifty-four different team-names mentioned at some time, a number inflated still further

by the nicknames, insults, and mispronunciations employed throughout the book. Characters seem to blend into one another, to speak
under various different pseudonyms or vanish entirely as new and
ever stranger appellations are coined. This process is taken still further in DeLillo's surreal science-fiction work, *Ratner's Star* (1976),
where the disembodied voices of the various scientists, technicians
and mathematicians, decompose and recombine like the mathematical
formulae which they sprout, any kind of sovereign voice or consistent
identity displaced by the continuous proliferation and transformation
of sign.[6]

As this inexplicable nomenclature escalates and expands, familiar
words seem to fade, erased by emergent alien symbols. It is as if parts
of characters' dialogue or vocabulary are missing, the simplest of nouns
deleted and replaced by incomprehensible codes or a kind of neural
static which no longer resembles any kind of language at all.
Characters name of a friend, or the word for 'sunset', only to find it
replaced by an ad for *Mastercard*, or a string of encoded data. Likewise,
whole swathes of memory seem effaced, as if the very words which
structure thought or identity are breaking down, obliterated by the
influx of mysterious new material.

'Everything was a shape, a fate, information flowing.'

(Mao II, 126)

Whilst DeLillo's early work suggests a dismantling of language, a
necessary 'unmaking' of bureaucratic codes, his later novels chart the
erasure of *all* language, words replaced by the apparent oxymoron
'invisible images', a blinding blankness which is itself a metaphor for
the strange new world of information-technology. Hence, whilst his
early work attacks language, his later books seek to preserve it. What is
perhaps most interesting about this development is the way in which
it bridges the schism between 'experimental' and 'realistic' fiction which
bedevils so much of the writing on contemporary fiction. DeLillo's first
four novels, for example, from *Americana* in 1971, through *End Zone*
(1972), and *Ratner's Star* (1976), appear as prime examples of the self-
consciously difficult, 'metafictional' writing which flourished in
American letters from the late '60s through to the early '70s, part of a
radical project intended to deconstruct conventional modes of language
and substitute some kind of revolutionary alternative in its place. What
links all four novels is an attempt to escape the machinations and

deceptions of ordinary language, to hint at 'the word beyond speech', some notion of the real or the elemental existing beyond the reach of linguistic corruption.[7] But even at this stage in DeLillo's career, one can detect a self-parodic edge to these artistic guerrilla tactics, what DeLillo called 'the pull of crazed prose', with its over-extended digressions and puzzling omissions.[8] Indeed, rather than supporting any kind of radical agenda, these textual games instead seem to hint at some kind of terrible linguistic or communicative collapse, which is ultimately the central theme of all his work.

Hence, the first half of his début novel, *Americana* can be read as a kind of surrealist satire on office politics, exploring bizarre manifestations of bureaucratic paranoia within the corridors of an unnamed corporate TV network. Initially, DeLillo seems to employ the banal emptiness of the TV executives' dialogue as a rather blunt satire on media double-speak and corporate jargon. Always a superb mimic of the inanities of modern speech, he records the employees' discourse as a mixture of corporate clichés and managerial platitudes, the same meaningless verbiage repeated by indistinguishable speakers in an endless series of pointless meetings:

> 'Let's come back to this,' Weede said. 'I want to generate a
>   little heat on the Morgenthau thing.'
> 'The Morgenthau thing is just absolutely fine,' Jones Perkins said.
> 'What about Morgenthau himself?'
> 'What about Morgenthau himself,' Jones said. 'Well, he has just
>   about made up his mind to do it and get it done and the hell
>   with the haircream people.'
> 'But has he definitely committed?'
> 'I would say he has just about definitely committed.'
> 'In other words we have rounded the buoy.'
> 'Weede, I would go even further than that. I would say that he
>   has just about committed.' (*Americana*, 64–5)

David Bell, the somewhat asinine protagonist of the novel, worries about his own toneless repetiton of such nonsense. 'My whole life was a lesson in the effect of echoes,' he laments. 'I was living in the third person' (*Americana*, 58). Whilst Bell can at least console himself with his own proficiency at manipulating these terms, he feels that his life is

Xeroxed; that, like Patrick Bateman in Ellis's *American Psycho* (1991), he is turning into an indistinguishable copy. Like other practitioners of the 'office arts' in the novel, Bell is both drawn towards, and suspicious of, the 'linguistic free-fall' of officialese (*Americana*, 59), spending his time engaged in the decipherment of the endless flow of documents, memoranda and dicta, which are circulated through the network in lieu of any actual work. These dispatches are believed to relate to the cycles of hirings and firings which periodically shake the company, but their jargon is so impenetrably opaque, a paranoid incomprehension and uncertainty inevitably ensues, the circulars growing increasingly elliptical and surreal. 'Words did not mean what was being said, nor even the reverse' notes Bell (*Americana*, 36), and with the messages transmitted immune to interpretation, he too is forced to turn to ever more eccentric means of unlocking the Xeroxed omens and portents. Gathering in hushed clusters in corridors or deserted offices, the staff divine occult connections between doors left open and salaries allotted, the colour of office sofas and promotion opportunities. 'Hidden energies filled the air, small secret currents' (*Americana*, 13) DeLillo writes, and as the messages on Bell's answering machine become ever more elusive, superstitious theories continue to escalate. Soon strange runic symbols are being concocted from the contents of the stationey cupboard ('nine pencils in each circle, arranging them in three triangles of three pencils each. I put an eraser inside each triangle' (*Americana*, 77)), as Bell's fellow execs resort to primitive diabolism in an attempt to penetrate the mysteries of the station, the secret meanings of coffee orders, the role of the enigmatic employee who deals only with fashion coordination.

Whilst Bell dabbles in dream interpretation ('There's some kind of valuable clue in there, somewhere,' he tells his ex-wife (*Americana*, 57)), and struggles to uncover the true identity of the mysterious memo-writer dubbed Trotsky, the wave of rumours, sackings, and promotions continue unabated, orchestrated more by the internal movement of paperwork than by any managerial decisions. Signals seem to emanate from some place deep within the bureaucratic system itself, autonomously rewriting themselves and in the process becoming increasingly untranslatable. 'We seemed to be no more than electronic signals and we moved through time and space with the stutter and shadowed insanity of a TV commercial,' admits Bell (*Americana*, 24), the familiar environs of the office 'tilted and warped', as if entering an alien, electronic zone, 'all the screens snowy and the airwaves bent with static' (*Americana*, 68).

Significantly, as terminology proliferates in DeLillo's novels, ordinary speech appears to contract, the media clichés his characters exchange evacuated of all meaning to become a kind of garbled drool. DeLillo's dialogue is frequently mangled and mispronounced, full of odd omissions and blanks, as if the stock-phrases which his characters attempt to recite have themselves somehow become scrambled. Bell attempts to model his marriage in *Americana* on the screenplay of some sentimental romantic comedy, scenes of 'soft focus tenderness' choreographed to a series of 'cuts and slow dissolves' (*Americana*, 37), but this shared fantasy swiftly seems to break down, as Bell fumbles his lines, replays his memories at the wrong speed, or can no longer picture the camera angles in his head. Ultimately their mutual script becomes unreliable and bizarre, Bell returning home late to find his wife sitting on the floor of their apartment, wearing a sombrero and trying to write a haiku (*Americana*, 37). Similarly, when Bell attempts to arrange his memoirs and write the *Bildungsroman* which forms the middle section of the novel, his reminiscences also seem oddly out of synch, shot through with eerie gaps and absences, a repeated image of falling snow suggesting an ever more threatening emptiness. It is as if a textual cancer is at work within his inbuilt dictionary, wiping out the familiar terms which define a stable sense of memory and identity, replacing them with signals from some abstract, electronic realm.

'There is nothing more mysterious than a TV set left on in an empty room ... It is as if another planet is communicating with you. Suddenly the TV reveals itself for what it really is: a video of another world, ultimately addressed to no one at all, delivering its messages indifferently, indifferent to its own messages (you can easily imagine it functioning after humanity has disappeared).'

(Jean Baudrillard[9])

This collapse of comforting clichés, and sudden lurch from the generic into the alien or hallucinatory, is central to DeLillo's fiction. His best known novel, *White Noise* (1984) is set in a small-town America not dissimilar to that of Bell's memoirs, the community of Blacksmith founded upon the same kitsch signifiers (white picket fences and chocolate box houses) as a TV sitcom. DeLillo's descriptions suggest a day-glo Norman Rockwell print, the town exuding an artificial wholesomeness which makes its inhabitants feel as if they're part of a permanent soup commercial; Blacksmith is portrayed as suburbia by way of Disneyland, *The Truman Show* (1998) captured in print a decade before the movie. The novel's professor hero, Jack Gladney, lives with his family in a leafy suburb indistinguishable from a film-set or merchandising campaign, part of a plastic community founded upon TV clichés and brand-names. One can hear the laughter-track, imagine the establishing shots or the ad-breaks; DeLillo, however, appears less concerned with the absolute artificiality of the setting (the grass too green, the sky too blue) than with the notion that such clichés allow us to recognise ourselves. Advertising, TV, and life-style packaging provide the mutually under-stood glossary from which a commercialised sense of clannishness and belonging is fashioned – identity bought off the peg, the images of both who we are and who we want to be.[10] From the hieroglyphics of cereal boxes to advertising jingles and tabloid slogans, consumer-culture provides the quotations and references which make up the shared vocabulary of our lives, a kind of consensual hologram which we all inhabit. As the critic John Frow has pointed out, when DeLillo describes an intimate domestic scene (watching a sleeping child, for example) in terms of the soft lighting and intimate close-ups of a soapy telemovie, he does so less to question the *validity* of the moment (or the emotions involved) than to stress how TV frames the experi-ence, the medium itself establishing the terms of reference.[11] In the novel everything appears irradiated by the ubiquitous glow of the screen – one's memories, sense of self, modes of perception, a culture's shared assumptions and expectations – the TV set the totem around which the tribe gathers and knows itself to be 'like minded . . . spiritu-ally akin' (*White Noise*, 4).

As the novel progresses, however, something seems to interfere with the reception and this generic picture begins to flicker. The residents of Blacksmith experience an eerie sense of foreboding, nervously contem-plating what other particles, aside from cathode rays, may be floating in the air – invisible fumes from the local chemical plant, radiation emenating from household appliances, trace elements somehow finding their way into the town's water supply. Invisible energies seem to permeate the town, teetering on the edge of perception, 'just beyond our reach and just beyond our vision':[12] a blurred glimpse out of the corner of one eye, a metallic trace on one's tongue, a word which refuses to come to mind.

Once again, DeLillo stresses how technology serves to manufacture a sense of unaccountability and uncertainty, the citizens of the nostalgically titled Blacksmith unable to name the products produced in the factories which ring their Legoland enclave, or to identify the chemicals in the pre-packaged food which they eat. Anxiously recording his son's receding hairline, Gladney asks:

> Did his mother consume some kind of gene-piercing substance when she was pregnant? Am I somehow at fault? Have l raised him, unwittingly, in the vicinity of a chemical dump-site, in the path of air-currents that carry industrial wastes capable of scalp degeneration, glorious sunsets? (People say the sunsets around here were not nearly so glorious thirty or forty years ago). (*White Noise*, 23)

Technical processes seem both immaterial and imperceptible, impossible to describe or define. Before the emission of invisible cancers and incognisable data, the town-folk appear ignorant and illiterate, the wordless energies charged with superstitious dread and mystery. Suddenly the picture jumps and the Gladneys are caught up in a disaster movie, the script dictated by news broadcasts and official announcements; later the picture is scrambled once more and Jack finds himself in the *noirish* black and white German Town, gun in hand and murder in mind. But the most threatening setting of all is not generic, but profoundly unimaginable; a strange electronic dimension which foreshadows the collapse of all the familiar scenarios which Blacksmith's citizens have depended upon. It is as if the channel has been changed one time too many, the remote-control only picking up static (the *White Noise* of the novel's title).

DeLillo develops this sense of the alien and the abstract impinging upon the everyday through the Gladney's trips to the local hypermarket, the shopping mall marking the frontier between suburbia and a dazzlingly unfamiliar, technological realm. Initially, these shopping expeditions are joyous and sustaining, the packaging and advertising surrounding each product reinforcing the particular image of the person they would like to be. The clan returns refreshed and invigorated, with a heightened sense of togetherness and shared identity; I shop therefore I am. Slowly, however, the mall begins to appear ever more ominous and unfamiliar, as if the family had suddenly stepped down from the screen and wandered into the circuitry behind it.

DeLillo describes its interior as a strange, abstract, immaterial dimension, scrambling any sense of orientation or time to occupy its own inclusive sphere. Shoppers wander dazed amongst a hallucinogenic flow of vivid but insubstantial images, their features distorted and refracted across endless banks of video monitors, mirrored corridors, and merchandising displays, so that the crowds are no longer certain of where they end and the spectral projections begin. Critic William Kowinski has described malls as 'liquid TV', consumers drifting from store to store as if switching channels, their surroundings increasingly dematerialised as they follow their credit-card details into the grid.[13] Estrangement and alienation replace the 'psychic replenishment' (*White Noise*, 20) of earlier jaunts, as familiar products vanish from the shelves to be replaced by unknown, blank goods. The packaging the family relies upon is erased by 'smeared print [and] ghost images' (*White Noise*, 326), the life-style connotations and idealised identities obliterated and effaced. Voices echo around the hall which the narrator cannot identify, much less understand, an aural static midway between electronic muzak and unheard-of brand-names, whilst at the exit to the hypermarket, eerie-looking bagging staff wait next to the check-out, conversing in a strange and unknown tongue.

Unlike the happy shoppers of yore, the patrons at the end of the novel stagger lost and confused amongst the ever-shifting aisles which reconstitute themselves like liquid circuitry, following signs they cannot understand, deafened by the 'ambient roar' (*White Noise*, 326) of electronic signals (instructions? codes? messages?) which disrupt any attempts at thought or concentration. Only the computer terminals at the check-out proffer comprehension, scanning each bar-code to validate the purchase and inform each shopper as to what it is they have actually purchased. As Gladney admits, the people have no choice but to queue up obediently, passively submitting to the technological authority:

> They walk in a fragmented trance, stop and go, clusters of well dressed figures frozen in the aisles, trying to figure out the pattern, discern the underlying logic, trying to remember where they'd seen the Cream of Wheat. They see no reason for it, find no sense in it. The scouring pads are with hand-soap now, the condiments are scattered . . . But in the end it doesn't matter what they see or think they see. The terminals are equipped with holographic

scanners, which decode the binary secrets of every item, infallibly. This is the language of waves and radiation, or how the dead speak to the living. (*White Noise*, 325–6)

As the narrator notes earlier, in a world where disembodied information passes between computers as ethereal patterns of data, changing and growing every second of the day, 'nobody knows anything' (*White Noise*, 149). Like Stone Age man trying to interpret the mysteries of nature via preternatural signs and divine supplication, the inhabitants of Blacksmith regress into archaic patterns of mythic belief, seeking desperately to appease the *numinous*, the fields of data which lie beyond cognate representation, and which are therefore invested with a strange and awful power. Indeed the novel is steeped in a kind of tabloid mysticism, whereby ancient beliefs are reinvented via modern appliances, reincarnation through insurance sales or the transmigration of souls occurring along phone-lines. With a disarming lack of irony, Gladney's fellow lecturer at 'The College-on-the-Hill', Murray Jay Siskind, compares the mall to an ancient Tibetan lamesery, a 'portal', or 'transitional state' between this world and the next, its aisles an electronic afterlife populated by disincarnate voices, eldritch energies, and occult symbolism, wherein one exchanges one's old sense of self for immaterial circulation within the 'psychic data' of the grid (*White Noise*, 37).

Whilst DeLillo's metaphysical leanings rarely appear as uniformly parodic, his novels nevertheless suggest that such superstition is a sign of his characters' failure to map the strange non-spaces of the contemporary environment. As John A. McClure has argued, DeLillo's novels project fantasies of demonic conspiracies onto the mundane facts of financial corruption and bureaucratic manipulation, but at the same time foreground the delusional nature of his protagonists' obsessions, illuminating the way in which supernatural intimations are inscribed upon the blank spaces we fail to comprehend.[14] DeLillo's novels visualise the unimaginable flow of data via a kind descriptive negativity. He illuminates the spectral contours of technology precisely through the collapse of familiar terms or forms of representation, the limitations of language indicative of the ghostly shape of the information network itself. It is as if he seeks to trace the pattern of data via the silhouette it burns into our familiar understanding, the evacuation of language a key idea in his attempt to approach the Postmodern condition.

The novel ends with Gladney staring up at another lurid, War-holesque sunset (*White Noise*, 321), the colours too vivid, the sky a vast screen-saver, the 'view'seeming to spill out of the borders of the frame. Night after night, the technicolour sunsets, shot through with chemical waste, have been growing more spectacular; the event now has nothing to do with nature and everything to do with reproduction. Slowly the sunset is passing beyond all means of representation, no longer recognisable in any conventional sense. It appears as an invisible vision, symbol of the strange, new, technological world.

'Technology evolves, language changes, the voice breaks, fate overtakes us.'

(Jean Baudrillard[15])

DeLillo's subsequent novel, *Libra* (1988), applies these ideas to a specific historical event – the assassination of John F. Kennedy – and in doing so makes explicit the political and cultural sensibility which informs and underpins all of his previous work. For DeLillo, the events of November 22 1963 signal the demise of 'manageable reality', 'an aberration in the heartland of the real' (*Libra*, 15), which has irrevocably marked him as an American citizen and as a writer, indeed in some sense determining his very vocation.[16]

For DeLillo, the general scepticism felt about the official interpretation of events, a gnawing sense of history as manipulated fiction, undercuts the apocryphal clarity of the day, clouding the murder in uncertainty and ambiguity. In *Libra* the true sequence of events is eerily erased by the blur of TV footage and the theory and counter-theory, and it is this sense of drowning in (dis)information, of being unable to differentiate paranoid fantasy and authentic documentation, which the novel self-consciously seeks to salve, if not solve.

In an interview with *Rolling Stone*, DeLillo argued that:

> the fiction writer tries to redeem this despair. Stories can be a consolation – at least in theory. The novelist can try to leap across the barrier of fact, and the reader is willing to take that leap with him as long as there's some kind of redemptive truth waiting on the other side, a sense that we've arrived at a resolution.[17]

Thus, the novel doesn't set out to resolve events in any historically accountable fashion (although, of course, the novel has been frequently appraised – and criticised – in just these terms), but rather seeks to impose some sense of order and form, 'correcting, clearing up, and perhaps most important of all, finding rhythms we just don't encounter anywhere'.[18] 'Fiction rescues history from its confusion,' argues DeLillo, constructing a coherent space which, if taken on its own fictional terms, can be seen to make sense.[19] Even if the truth is utterly unattainable, compromised by doubt and paranoia, art provides a workable sense of meaning, a correlative to the chaos and ambiguity pandemic elsewhere.

And yet, in many ways, the novel itself is less explicable than DeLillo's own criteria might suggest. After all, the novel is constructed around a series of surrogate author figures, all of whose attempts to script some kind of coherent plot or generic narrative ultimately collapse into uncertainty and textual confusion. The original conspirator, for example, pensioned CIA operative Win Everett, conceives of the 'plot' to kill Kennedy as possessing 'art and meaning' (*Libra*, 264), his beautifully crafted scenario destined to be studied by intelligence experts in terms of its dramatic structure and vivid narrative. Decommissioned following his role in the Bay of Pigs fiasco, Everett, like the other 'author' figures in the novel, feels himself to be isolated, impotent, peripheral to the centralised sources of power. At the start of the novel he has been exiled to a girls' high-school in Texas, and denied any role in determining intelligence policy. His response is to embark upon a complex campaign of disinformation, manipulating textual material (visa applications, altered signatures, pseudonyms) within the administrative channels of the CIA so as to construct a bizarre simulated conspiracy which implicates Castro in a (wholly fictitious) plot to kill Kennedy. The 'plot' is thus initially engineered as a textual illusion, whereby Everett fashions a bureaucratic hit-man from doctored photographs, mismatched fingerprints and falsified paper-work, a mimeographed assassin let loose in the agency's files. Everett works out this material in terms of script, plot, character, sketching out a generic espionage yarn with scissors and tape; the fore-runner to this operation is the virtual revolution staged by the CIA in Guatemala, where Everett's team transmitted false news-broadcasts, faked communiqués and invented codes, the conflict staged on a textual, rather than military, front. However, when the agency attempts to duplicate this fictional *coup d'état* in Cuba, something goes mysteriously awry. The signals (rumours, speeches, non-existent orders and codes) seem to break down and mutate, delirious surrealistic messages ('the sound of a mind unraveling' (*Libra*, 127)) becoming confused with the agency's own transmission band, as real manoeuvres are mixed up with discontinuous frames of radio static and illusory explosions.

This fiasco provides the subtext to the conspirators' plot, their composition intended to restore some sense of order to this bizarre information collapse. However, as Everett's plans hatch and grow, his fellow schemers sense that 'There's something else that's generating this event. A pattern outside experience' (*Libra*, 304), to which they respond with superstitious awe and dread. Everett again starts to lose control of his material and, as with Cuba, the ersatz assassination becomes conflated with a genuine murder attempt as the distinction between the textual and the actual begins to blur and fade.

The espionage genre – in its most bureaucratic form as the exchange of classified information – functions in DeLillo's fiction as a metaphor for the manipulation of language, the passwords, cryptograms and jargon constantly metamorphosing as they pass through ever more shadowy networks of anonymous operators and clerical factions, becoming progressively more unreadable and uninterpretable in the process. As DeLillo notes:

> 'There were complexities of speech. A man needed special experience and insight to work true meanings out of certain murky remarks . . . Brilliant riddles floated up and down the echelons, to be pondered, solved, ignored.' (*Libra*, 21)

Realising that his own subject matter is slipping away from him, Everett dreams of being strapped to a polygraph device, excavating some sense of truth from beneath the impenetrable code-words and forged documents. Slowly it becomes apparent that Everett's photocopied character has become confused with the files of a real individual – Lee Harvey Oswald – and it is as if in a moment of alchemical reaction, the papers are transubstantiated; Everett's fiction made real.

DeLillo's Oswald is a nobody, a social loner and private misfit perpetually on the outside of life, dreaming of admittance into history. His biography is sketched in through vignettes of suburban poverty and domestic anomie, an aimless adolescence spent drifting through increasingly cramped residences; like Everett, Oswald feels exiled to the periphery of affairs, and he too plots a kind of textual admittance, a way into the network of subterranean power which will take him out of his skin and into the channels of 'something vast and sweeping' (*Libra*, 41). Believing that only a man with papers is substantial, Oswald slowly worms his way into the bureaucratic network, deliberately getting himself photographed by spy-cameras, registered by consulates or recorded by census takers, his misdemeanours noted in secret files. Oswald turns himself into a bit-player in minor CIA dispatches, finger-printed into history as his fictional alter-ego (a composite of spy and gangster fantasies) gathers (paper)weight and mass. Passing on information to faceless agencies in Japan, he feels himself 'entering the stream of things' (*Libra*, 84), Tokyo transformed into a dislocated zone of floating neon signs and whispered, foreign, code-words. Likewise, the bureaucratic apparatus of the Soviet Union feels like the border of some strange textual dimension; Oswald's dossier proof of his steno-graphical existence.

As Oswald nears his goal however, this dossier seems to shift and transform, his data increasingly confused with the photo-fit composite manufactured by Everett. Unable to differentiate his own thoughts from external signals, to seperate his sense of self from that of his pseudonym, Oswald's 'Historic Diary' is increasingly marked by gaps and omissions, his 'character' oddly random and disjointed. This inability to distinguish between the textual and the actual, between Oswald's own decisions and the script produced by other parties, is finally framed in terms of a cruel metafictional joke. In the key scene in the book, DeLillo portrays Oswald, rifle in hand, sequestered in the Texas Book Repository on Dealy Plaza, hidden behind a wall of books and firing through an opening in the leaf cover (*Libra*, 395). Thus is Everett's bureaucratic assassination made literal.

Lee experiences the shot as a sudden tear in the movie images running inside his head, 'the light so clear it was heart breaking . . . a white burst in the middle of the frame' (*Libra*, 400). Even DeLillo's description seems scrambled and distorted, the very text of the novel scattered across the page as sentences deteriorate into a shower of syn-tactical static. Indeed, for onlookers, the event seems to lack any kind of rational framework on which to agree, the shot distorting time and space to leave only random, arbitrary frames (a hoarding advertising roller-skates or shoes abandoned on a car-bonnet) impossible to connect or interpret.

Crucially, this sense of mental disconnection or incompleteness is accentuated and framed by the obsessive TV news coverage and the barrage of images jamming every channel. Endlessly repeated and played with numbing regularity by all the networks, the footage appears strangely fragmented, full of ambiguous fissures and missing cells of information, the screen a blur of random particles and convulsive flickers; with each compulsive screening the images seem to collapse into mere blur or glare, manufacturing a hallucinatory sense of absence and dazzle. Thus, once again, we are back to Andy Warhol's rule of Postmodern repetition. Indeed, DeLillo stages Kennedy's death in terms of a strange visual ricochet. At the moment of impact Kennedy is photographed by a figure in the crowd whose lens takes in a second photographer. A further onlooker snaps both of these spectators, whilst from a nearby vantage point, a cine-camera films the massed paparazzi; TV crews then track the camera-man. In this prism of self-reflecting images, the subject itself seems to vanish, Kennedy erased-from the frame in a burst of exploding flash-bulbs. The 'images' are thus no longer perceivable but rather act as shorthand for a flow of signals which no longer reflect anything other than their own existence.

Thus, for DeLillo it is not the actual assassination act, but rather its reporting, which signals a seismic shift in American life. In Fredric Jameson's words, 'suddenly, and for a brief moment, television showed what it could do and what it really meant'; the images of Kennedy's death, repeated and repeated and repeated again, becoming visual blurs and shadows, no longer a record of events but an absence at the heart of the event.[20,21] Ironically, the apotheosis Oswald sought to achieve via clerical means – shedding his old sense of self for absorption within the information networks and the intelligence channels – is finally enacted in the dens and living rooms of viewers across America. Staring at the bizarre, distorted material on the screen, the audience can no longer differentiate between figures and shapes, shadows and light, thoughts and signals. The event happens outside of language and manufactures a kind of wordless mass hallucination, a collectivity created by the erasure of conventional terms. What is left is amnesia, absence, a sense of mental vacumn. The novel portrays Kennedy's death as a gaping hole in language and therefore in historical memory, a void which the novel seeks to span.

The author-figure who most clearly corresponds to DeLillo's own role in the novel, is Nicholas Branch, the CIA activist commissioned to write the official, confidential history of events for the agency's own files. Branch's undertaking to uncover the actual sequence of events thus parallels the implicit premise behind the novel itself, but also suggests Everett's response to the information meltdown of Cuba, and his failed attempt to impose some scripted sense of order amidst the proliferating mass of data.

Indeed, as the agency furnishes Branch with ever more reams of information – statistical data, eye-witness reports, photographs, tape-recordings – Branch's belief in any clear chronology, or in his ability to produce any kind of coherent narrative record, diminishes. The sheer density of material ('baptismal records, report cards, divorce petitions, cancelled checks, daily time-sheets, box returns, property lists, post-operative X-rays, photos of knotted string' (*Libra*, 181)) overwhelms his ability to discriminate or weigh, each new mass of data superseding and cancelling out what came before. Rather than arranging events into some sort of narrative or explanation, Branch comes to resemble a faceless clerk no longer interpreting incoming material but rather disseminating data back to the anonymous curator from whom it originates in the first place. Information is endlessly regurgitated and recycled between nameless governmental units, manufacturing an end-less self-generating labyrinth of spiralling complexity and ambiguity, increasingly perforated with omissions, gaps, inconsistencies, untrans-latable jargon and over-exposed photographs. All this, of course, serves to complicate and contradict the more straightforward fictional biography of Oswald which DeLillo presents earlier in the novel, reducing everything to the same level of suspicion and solipsistic doubt (Oswald appears in the wrong place at the wrong time, several photographs show the same false mug-shot, the time-line is skewed and distorted). At the end of the novel, Branch finds himself trapped by mounds of paper in a tiny, cramped room (an echo of Oswald, Everett, and by extension of DeLillo too), feeling himself becoming bodiless as the solid walls of his study are replaced by flickering sheets of manuscrlpt, type-face replacing furniture, and inscrutable clearance-codes obscuring the exit to his office. Textual material is replaced by bursts of 'heat and light' (*Libra*, 14), information erasing itself, the material disintegrating before his very eyes. Branch, like the other authors in the novel, finds his 'plot' rewritten by the codes around him, his words vanishing, breaking up, turning into 'the history no one will read' (*Libra*, 60). For DeLillo, the Kennedy assassination marks the moment when words could no longer hold the world, signalling the breakdown of linguistic order and the substitution of an entirely new kind of logic in its place.

'The writer sets his pleasure, his eros, his creative delight in language and his sense of self-preservation against the vast and uniform Death that history tends to fashion as its most enduring work.'[22]

The TV audience in *Libra* presages the strange amorphous masses which haunt DeLillo's later work; an emergent, collective state of being, lacking the words that articulate what George Steiner calls our 'mechanisms of identity'.[23] 'The future belongs to crowds' warns DeLillo (*Mao II*, 16), heralding the extinction of intimacy, individuality, or any kind of original voice. The mass wedding conducted by the Reverend Moon in *Mao II* (1991) is again framed via the photographic image, 'instamatic' couples (*Mao II*, 183) with comic-book hair and airbrushed skin, 'filling picture frames with their microcosmic bodies' (*Mao II*, 10). 'They take a time-honored event and repeat it and repeat it until something new enters the world', notes one onlooker, the couples becoming an undifferentiated mass, a wave, 'lifted by the picture-taking, the framing of aura' (*Mao II*, 15), moving outside of representation entirely. In a sense, of course, DeLillo's virtuoso performance in such passages seems to contradict his central thesis here; indeed, in response to the diminution of the linguistic subject, his own prose can be seen to offer a kind of ethical and aesthetic retort.

Similarly, DeLillo's biggest novel, *Underworld* (1997), a massive work in terms of both its scale and ambition, also stands in monumental opposition to 'the evanescent spectacle of contemporary life', its historical depth and richly textured language inimical to the 'drama of white-hot consumption and instant waste'.[24,25] Critics have been swift to lionise the text in terms of its rebuttal of a perceived cultural mediocrity, the numbing repetition of recycled images and stereotypes, 'the re-run, the sequel, the theme-park', the whole logic of empty repetition.[26,27] *Underworld*, with its stress upon literary craft and skill, its assertion of language as the guarantor of memory, individuality and shared communication, and perhaps most of all, its faith in the ability of words to capture the warp and weave of lived reality, thus suggests a spirited denial of the tenor of the age, the very existence of the text testimony to the importance of writing in a self-erasing world.

At the same time, however, a sense of nostalgia and loss permeates the book, making the novel the most backward tending and wistfully retrospective of DeLillo's works. In an essay on the origins of the novel, DeLillo discusses its creation in terms of his personal excavation of 'a nearly lost language, the idiom and scrappy slang of the post-war period, the writer's own life-time':

> In *Underworld*, I sought out the word-relatedness of memory. The smatter language of old street games and the rhythms of a thousand street-corner conversations, adolescent and raw . . . And what rich rude tang in the Italian–American vulgate, all those unspellable dialect words and derivations of the Bronx, and what stealthy pleasure to work out spellings, and how surely this range of small personal recollection served to quicken and enlarge the language that ensued.

> Small tactics, minor maneuvers. I used lower-case letters for such trademarked, terms as Styrofoam, Velcro, Plexiglass, but why? I didn't realise until the book was nearly done that I wanted to *unincorporate* these words, subvert their official status. In a novel about conflict on many levels, this was the primal clash – the tendency of language to work in opposition to the enormous technology of war that threatened the era and shaped the book's themes.[28,29]

The novel thus juxtaposes the grimy physical textures (and DeLillo's redolent descriptions) of the Bronx in the 1950s, with the holographic emptiness of Phoenix in the 1990s, the palpably real contrasted with the abstract and the electronic, a dualism central to the book.

More problematic is the novel's implicit suggestion that events from the historical past (say, Bobby Thomson's home-run or footage of early nuclear tests) possesses a greater claim to permanence and solidity than the fast-forward nature of contemporary reality. For DeLillo, the notion that the past is free from 'the debasing process of frantic repetition that exhausts a contemporary event before it has moulded into coherence' underpins his very motivation for writing the book, suggesting a nostalgia for real things and retrieved memories (*Underworld* is by far the most autobiographical of DeLillo's novels) which does seem to border on the Postmodern truism that reality is somehow now a thing of the past.[30]

As with *Libra*, however, the novel is a more complex entity than such a manifesto might at first suggest. Central to the structure of the book is the baseball hit by Bobby Thomson in 1951, a mythical grail-object which exists as a trope of the absolute realities of the physical and the historical, 'a priceless thing somehow, that seems to recapitulate the whole history of the game every time it is thrown or hit or touched' (*Underworld*, 26). However, the quest for this sacred talisman is framed as a parody of both the philosophical search for 'real' things in DeLillo's early work, and the investigation into the truth surrounding Kennedy's assassination in *Libra*. Memorabilia-collector Martin Lundy's obsessive scouring of press photographs of the actual hit, his attempts to verify wind-direction, trajectory and strength of impact in order to determine who in the crowd might have caught the ball, thus simultaneously mirrors and satirises Branch's investigations in DeLillo's earlier work. Like Branch, Lundy collects 'Birth certificates, passports, affidavits, handwritten wills, detailed lists of peoples' possessions' (*Underworld*, 177), blowing up still photographs to reveal 'a universe of dots' (*Underworld*, 177) waiting to be analysed, measured, and recorded. And yet, once again, the truth remains elusive. Lundy's attempt to rewind to the very instant at which the ball is hit (a countdown which mirrors both the nuclear imagery and the wider narrative structure of the novel) fails because he can never make the final leap to a position of absolute certainty; there remain lost leads, unreliable testimonies, blank spaces, and Lundy, like Branch, has to turn to superstitious 'rumours and dreams' (*Underworld*, 179) to make the final imaginative link.

Thus, while baseball is certainly configured nostalgically in the novel (DeLillo's evocative description of the Giants/Dodgers clash contrasting with the vision of uniformity suggested by the ceremony in the same stadium in *Mao II*), it cannot be simply argued that the famous 1951 game was somehow 'real', while contemporary reality is hopelessly counterfeit and mediated. After all, the '50s crowd watch the visiting celebrities as much as the game, longing for Gleason to act out his stage routines, or waiting to see how Sinatra reacts to a hit before mimicking his responses with their own. Similarly, Russ Hodges' famous play-by-play account of the match is itself profoundly 'mediated', in the sense that it not only describes the game, but also frames and articulates events even for those watching in the stands, radios clasped to their ears, hanging on his every word. At the same time, however, Hodges' play-by-play also suggests an idealised version of the writer antithetical to the submissive fate assigned to authors in *Libra*.[31]

Ultimately, it is not a question of the degree to which Hodges' words perfectly relate to the reality of the event (he invents things, allows his emotions to show, coughs, sneezes and splutters, his voice profoundly human), but rather the breadth of expression involved, the range of his timbre, and his responsiveness to the human scale of events. Similarly, in a later scene when the small-time street-hustler Manx Martin attempts to sell the baseball, his pitch becomes a matter of trust, persuasion and shared-communication rather than verifiable truth, 'the logic of this argument about six times removed from the question of the ball's actual history' (*Underworld*, 246–7), as DeLillo puts it.

Indeed, a notion of art as a humanising agent lies at the very heart of the novel. The primitive daubing of paint onto deactivated nuclear aircraft by Klara Sax and her followers suggests an attempt to impose human characteristics upon the unimaginable, to introduce a human element into the mechanistic, electronic systems which terrify and dominate.

As Sax explains:

> See, we're painting, hand-painting in some cases, putting our puny hands to great weapons systems, to systems that came out of the factories and assembly halls as near alike as possible, millions of components stamped out, repeated endlessly, and we're trying to unrepeat, to find an element of felt life, and maybe there's a sort of survival instinct here, a graffiti instinct – to trespass and declare ourselves, show who we are. (*Underworld*, 77)

This conception of art is repeated throughout the novel – in Moonman's wildly expressionistic graffiti, in the angel-paintings on 'The Wall' in the Bronx, in Eisenstein's oddly humanist science-fiction film, even in Lenny Bruce's non-jokes and missed punch lines ('She never worked in a whore house at all ... Let's make her human. Let's give her a name' (*Underworld*, 632–3)). It is present in DeLillo's preference for the eccentric contours of the Watts Tower above the binary uniformity of the World Trade Centre, and it lies at the very heart of the novel's privileging of human memory above 'history's flat, thin, tight and relentless design'.[32,33]

Indeed, *Underworld* configures the Cold War as a war which didn't happen – an abstracted, textual conflict fought through propaganda footage, bureaucratic espionage and the abstract codes of intelligence agencies and nuclear simulations. The novel's central achievement is thus to articulate these enormous abstractions in strikingly human terms; in nocturnal dreams of spy-satellites, adolescent fumblings during bomb-drills, erotic fantasies stimulated by missile launches or the texture of plastic. DeLillo's response to the invisible complexities of the information-war is thus to reassert some sense of manageable perspective, to measure events according to a more human scale. This notion underpins the scatology of Lenny Bruce's routines in the novel, whereby the blockade of Cuba is articulated via the supply of toilet paper, or the degree of nuclear terror in the world measured through changes in the angle of the American male's erection. Similarly, the journey from Western Europe to the communist East is described in terms of the quality of toilet facilities, the consistency of stools and the pungency of fumes released, slowly changing as the travellers' digestive systems adjust. These base bodily functions are presented as the antithesis of the intangible flow of information elsewhere in the novel, the interlocking matrices of nuclear test-sites, the inaccessible store-rooms of data, and thus serve to set up the binary structuring device of the book; the palpable contrasted with the immaterial.

At times this idea borders on science fiction, with the unearthly realm of information floating ethereally above compacted pockets of dense matter and poverty – the wasteland of inner-city America or the irradiated horrors of Post-Chernobyl Russia; but even this material is redeemed by its stress upon ordinary life, the day-to-day practicalities of survival amongst the rubble. After all, even in the most extreme of circumstances, ordinary existence manages to reassert itself, and the underworlds of DeLillo's novel – the back-rooms, alleyways, store-houses and service tunnels – suggest a coarse grained texture and materiality implacably opposed to the intangible disappearance registered elsewhere.

In *White Noise*, an excavation of the Gladney family's rubbish bin unearths a bizarre collection of used and discarded objects: a scrawled obscene figure, 'a banana skin with a used tampon inside, ear-swabs, crushed roaches . . . sterile pads smeared with pus' (*White Noise*, 259), the effluvia of daily obsessions, daydreams and physical needs. For DeLillo, this unsavoury debris serves to suggest the quotidian, the humanly mundane, the very fabric of lived reality. In *Underworld*, the theft of J. Edgar Hoover's dustbins throws the agency into apoplexy, horrified that such mortifying material – evidence of bad hygeine, masturbatory fantasies, idle scribbles (*Underworld*, 558) – should be made public; the accumulated sediment of what it means to be human. In a sense the entire novel is composed from such material – the flotsam and jetsam of discarded matter, cultural daydreams and private fantasies, jingles and accents, the babble of private voices and unspoken lines which suggest the solitary acts and humbling needs deleted from the system, and also from history.'The novel does not want to tell you things you already know about the great, the brave, the powerless and the cruel,' DeLillo argues. 'It gives them sweaty palms and head colds and urine stained underwear' ... This is how consciousness is extended and human truth seen new.'[34]

If at times the sheer size and structural complexity of the book recalls Bill Gray's great unfinished novel in *Mao II*, the work a vast circuit-diagram of plot and sub-plot, DeLillo seems to raise this spectre only ultimately to reject it. Certainly, the book is held together by recurrent motifs, shapes, textures, structural repetitions and reflections, but DeLillo denies the presence of any over-arching master-plan or synthesis, the meta-narrative of conspiracy theorists or authoritarian information-gatherers. In the oddly ethereal and supernatural channels of cyberspace at the end of the novel, all plot lines converge, and the elements of the novel fuse into one transcendent, epiphanic, nuclear-vision; but DeLillo himself rejects such an apotheosis, his attention drawn instead to the plurality of events occurring 'offscreen, unwebbed ... the thick, lived tenor of things' (*Underworld*, 827), which informs the subject of his subsequent book, *The Body Artist* (2001). Ultimately then, such an ending suggests less a retreat from the novel's imaginative engagement with electronic reality, than the culmination of DeLillo's attempt to connect the data-stream to tangible objects and human reference.

What is perhaps most remarkable about the novel is DeLillo's recovered trust in his own ability to do, his faith in the ability of language to renew and reveal. Such a programme links DeLillo to the sense of ambition and possibility which characterises Modernism, rather than the defeated tenor of much Postmodern thinking. Indeed, in this sense, *Underworld* suggests less a colossal full stop to the twentieth century, than a passionate and eloquent argument for the importance of meaningful inscription in the twenty-first.

NOTES

1. Page references are to the following editions of DeLillo's novels: *Americana* (London: Penguin, 1990), *Players* (London: Vintage, 1991), *Running Dog* (London: Picador, 1992), *White Noise* (London: Picador, 1986), *Libra* (London: Penguin, 1988), *Mao II* (London: Jonathan Cape, 1991), *Underworld* (London: Picador, 1998), *Great Jones Street* (London: Picador, 1992).

2. Don DeLillo, quoted by Thomas LeClair (1982), *Anything can Happen: Interviews with Contemporary American Novelists*, Urbana: University of Illinois Press, p. 81.

3. Don DeLillo, quoted by Anthony DeCurtis (1990), 'An outsider in this society', *South Atlantic Quarterly*, 89 (2), Spring, p. 290.

4. Fredric Jameson, (1993), *Postmodernism, or, The Cultural Logic of Late Capitalism*, London: Verso.

5. For a useful discussion of the immaterial zones of information technology see Scott Bukatman, (1993), *Terminal Identity*, Durham: Duke University Press, especially pp. 1–22, 157–182.

6. See also George Stade (1976), '*Ratner's Star*', *New York Times Book Review*, June 20.

7. DeLillo in LeClair, p. 80.

8. Ibid., p. 89.

9. Jean Baudrillard (1988), *America*, London: Verso, p. 50.

10. For a surprisingly positive view of Postmodern consumerism, see Michael J. Ferraro (1991), 'Whole families shopping at night', in Frank Lentricchia (ed.), *New Essays on White Noise*, New York: Cambridge University Press, pp. 22–4.

11. John Frow (1990), 'The last things before the last', *South Atlantic Quarterly*, 89 (2), Spring, p. 423.

12. DeLillo in DeCurtis, p. 287.

13. William Kowinski, quoted in Bukatman, p. 232.

14. John A. McClure (1990), 'Postmodern romance: Don DeLillo and the age of conspiracy', *South Atlantic Quarterly*, 89 (2), Spring, p. 342.

15. Jean Baudrillard (1990), *Cool Memories*, London: Verso, p. 36.

16. DeLillo in DeCurtis, p. 286.

17. Ibid., p. 294.

18. Ibid.

19. Ibid.

20. Jameson, p. 355.

21. Cf. Jean Baudrillard's assertion that 'the medium has all to do with repetition and nothing with representation'. Quoted by Mike Gane (1991), *Baudrillard's Bestiary*, London: Routledge, p. 102.

22. DeLillo (1998), 'The moment the Cold War began', *The Observer*, 4 January.

23. George Steiner (1972), *Extra Territorial*, London: Faber, p. 63.

24. DeLillo, *The Observer*.

25. Ibid.

26. For example Michael Herr's comment that 'if a book like that can be written in a culture like this, it's terrific for all of us'.

27. DeLillo, *The Observer*.

28. Ibid.

29. Ibid.

30. Ibid.

31. For a short time in the early '60s, DeLillo worked as a sportscaster for a local radio company. Sportscasting is also central to *End Zone* (1972).

32. Long before the events of 11 September, the World Trade Centre occupied an ominous role in DeLillo's fiction. A terrorist plot to bomb the building fails to occur in *Players* (1977), while the photographer, Brita, is haunted by a vision of the twin towers in *Mao II* (1991).

33. DeLillo, *The Observer*.

34. Ibid.

BIOGRAPHY

Don DeLillo was born on 20 November 1936, and raised in the Fordham area of the Bronx, a mainly Italian-American neighbourhood. He has described his childhood as revolving around sports, family and church. Brought up as a Catholic, a concern with ritual, incantation and transcendence permeates his fiction. Otherwise, DeLillo's early life was shooting pool, playing cards, and 'every conceivable form of baseball'. DeLillo attended Cardinal Hayes High School and then Fordham College, 'where the Jesuits taught me to be a failed ascetic'. He majored in 'Communication Arts', but took his inspiration from the vibrant arts scene of New York, in particular 'the paintings in the Museum of Modern Art, the music at the jazz gallery and the Village Vanguard, the movies of Fellini and Godard and Howard Hawks'. He lists his greatest literary influences as Joyce, Faulkner, Stein, Pound, and *Moby Dick*, but admits that 'probably the movies of Jean-Luc Godard had a more immediate effect on my early work than anything I'd ever read' (his first novel, *Americana* (1971), is, in part, a Godardian deconstruction of a road movie).

After graduation he took a job in advertising and worked as a copywriter until 1964. After a number of short stories, he began work on *Americana* in

1966, an astonishingly undisciplined mixture of autobiography, office-satire, road-trip and extended language games. 'I finished it in a spirit of getting a difficult, unwieldy thing out of the way,' he later noted, 'in a spirit of having proved certain things to myself.' Thereafter, his output as a writer was prolific (his ostensible 'subjects' including American football, nuclear war, rock music, hypothetical maths, international banking and espionage), and he supported himself solely through the writing of fiction.

In 1975 he married Barbara Bennett, her banking job taking the couple first to Canada, then to Greece, the setting for one of his most difficult and explicitly political works, *The Names* (1982), which analyses the clash between Western bureaucracy and Islamic fundamentalism. Resolutely a 'writer's writer', DeLillo's audience at this point seemed split between the academic structuralists who analysed his works in terms of systems and codes, and, in DeLillo's words, 'crazy people, conspiracy theorists, underground drop-outs, mail-fraudsters and the like'. DeLillo himself shunned the public gaze, his response to inquiring journalists or academics being an embossed card emblazoned 'I don't want to talk about it'. He returned to the United States in 1982 and published his best-known novel, *White Noise*, in 1984, a book often cited as the epitome of the Postmodern concern with the hyper-real and the simulacrum. The book which brought him wider recognition was, however, *Libra* (1988), which grew out of an article written on Lee Harvey Oswald and the Kennedy assassination for *Rolling Stone*. Despite an infamous review in the *Washington Post* branding DeLillo a 'bad citizen' for suggesting governmental involvement, *Libra* won the National Book Award and demonstrated how closely DeLillo's over-riding themes (technology, conspiracy, secret codes and cabals) tallied with historical reality. DeLillo's next novel, *Mao II* (1991) a satirical appraisal of the role of the winter in contemporary society, earned a rare commendation from Thomas Pynchon ('a vision as bold and a voice as eloquent and morally focused as any in American writing') as well as the PEN/Faulkner award, and, ironically for a novel about a reclusive writer, marked DeLillo's entry into the world of promotional tours, book-readings and the like. His biggest (in every sense of the word) novel, *Underworld*, appeared in 1997, taking the Cold War, and the connection between technology and superstition (a recurrent motif in DeLillo's *oeuvre*) as its central themes. With the publication of *The Body Artist* (2001) DeLillo is now routinely described as the most influential writer working in America.

DeLILLO ON DeLILLO

What writing means to me is trying to make interesting, clear, beautiful language. Working at sentences and rhythms is probably the most satisfying thing I do as a writer. I think after a while a writer can begin to know himself through his language. He sees someone or something reflected back at him from these constructions. Over the years it is possible for a writer to shape himself as a human being through the language he uses. I think written language, fiction, goes that deep. He not only sees himself but begins to make himself or remake himself. Of course, this is mysterious and subjective territory.

I do wonder if there is something we haven't come across. Is there another, clearer language? Will we speak it and hear it when we die? Did we know it before we were born? If there are life forms in other galaxies, how do they communicate? What do they sound like? The 'untellable' points to the limitations of language. Is there something we haven't discovered about speech? Is there more? Maybe this is why there's so much babbling in my books. Babbling can be frustrated speech, or it can be a purer form, an alternate speech.

Movies in general may be the not-so-hidden influence on a lot of modern writing, although the attraction has waned, I think. The strong image, the short ambiguous scene, the dream sense of some movies, the artificiality, the arbitrary choices of some directors, the cutting and editing. The power of images.

So much modern fiction is located precisely nowhere. This is Beckett and Kafka insinuating themselves onto the page. Their work is so woven into the material of modern life that it's not surprising so many writers choose to live there, or choose to have their characters live there. Fiction without a sense of place is automatically a fiction of estrangement, and of course this is the point. As theory it has its attractions, but I can't write that way myself. I'm too interested in what real places look like and what names they have. Place is color and texture. It's tied up with memory and roots and pigments and rough surfaces and language, too . . . it has to be responsive to the real world, one way or another, in order to keep its vitality and to cleanse itself of effeteness and self-absorption.

Fiction does not obey reality even in the most spare and semi-documentary work. Realistic dialogue is what we have agreed to call certain arrays of spoken exchange that in fact have little or no connection with the way people speak . . . Fiction is true to a thousand things but rarely to clinical lived experience. Ultimately it obeys the mysterious mandates of the self (the writer's) and of all the people and things that have surrounded him, and all the styles he has tried out, and all the other fiction (of other writers) he has read and not read. At its root level, fiction is a kind of religious fanaticism, with elements of obsession, superstition and awe. Such qualities will sooner or later state their adversarial relationship with history.

Let language shape the world. Let it break the faith of conventional re-creation. Language lives in everything it touches and can be an agent of redemption, the thing that delivers us, paradoxically, from history's flat, thin, tight and relentless designs, its arrangement of stark pages, and that allows us to find an unconstraining otherness, a free veer from time and place and fate.

The sweeping range of American landscape and experience can be a goad, a challenge, an affliction and an inspiration, pretty much in one package.

LINKS TO OTHER AUTHORS

Paul Auster: Auster shares with DeLillo a concern with language and what may lie outside it, the realm of the unworded. An ascetic notion of paring down reality in search of the essential, stripping away excess discourse to reveal some mysterious elemental truth, underpins *The New York Trilogy*, *Moon Palace*, and much of DeLillo's early work, especially *End Zone* and *Great Jones Street*.

Cormac McCarthy: Rejecting the notion that his work is 'cold and pitiless', DeLillo notes 'I don't know how work that contains so much evident love of language can be called pitiless, more or less regardless of what happens to the characters. I mean, you can read Cormac McCarthy and find pitiless-ness, as in *Blood Meridian*, but isn't it redeemed by language, balanced by language?'

Rolando Hinojosa: Like Hinojosa, DeLillo believes in the democratic basis of the novel. He has described fiction as 'a kind of syncopated reality in which diverse human voices ultimately come into conflict with a single uninflected voice, the monotone of the state, the corporate entity, the product, the assembly line', an idea obviously relevant to the scope and form of Hinojosa's *Klail City Death Trip*.

Bret Easton Ellis: Both writers are concerned the hyper-real, simulated nature of contemporary reality, the Postmodern logic of endless reproduction; what DeLillo calls 'the wider cultural drama of white-hot consumption and instant waste'. However, whilst *Underworld* seeks to resist the tenor of the times, Ellis's work seems self-destructively to embody it.

Douglas Coupland: Many of the characters in DeLillo's early novels see language as a kind of grammatical conscription, a way of forcing everyone to talk and think alike. Logos College in *End Zone* acts as a kind of sanatorium for linguistic ailments, a way of unlearning the words which other people have put inside your head. This notion of semantic asceticism thus has obvious links with the desert landscape of *Generation X*. DeLillo's hero also believes that 'what we must know must be learned from blanked-out pages. To begin to reword the overflowing world. To subtract and disjoin. To recreate the alphabet. To make elemental lists. To call something by its name and no other sound.' It doesn't work in either book, alas.

Thomas Pynchon: DeLillo shares with Pynchon a serio-comic obsession with conspiracies, 'plots' (in at least two senses of the word), linguistic games, puns and mimicry, and endless play with various types of language and modes of address. *Ratner's Star*, with its bizarre cast of endless mutating scientists, and dizzying mixture of erudite mathematical research and flat-out nonsense, is probably the most 'Pynchon-like' of DeLillo's work. In 1982, DeLillo wrote that Pynchon had, more than any other writer, set the standard for contemporary fiction.

READING EARLY DeLILLO

DeLillo's free-wheeling and undisciplined debut, *Americana* (1971), starts as a strange satire on bureaucracy, shifts to a self-parodic take on the 'coming of age' novel, switches gears to become the fictional equivalent of the '70s road-movie (think *Two Lane Blacktop* (1971) by way of Godards's *Pierrot le Fou* (1965)), and then deconstructs itself in a number of odd language games which unmakes what has come before. *End Zone* (1972) is a more sustained and comic exploration of the gap between jargon and reality, in which the rules of American football become intermingled with simulated nuclear warfare. *Great Jones Street* (1973) concerns rock star Bucky Wunderlick's attempt to evade the reach of the dominant culture by taking a drug which robs the user of speech; significantly DeLillo draws no distinction between the counter cultural underground or the shadowy intelligence agencies, both of which are trying to destroy conventional language. *Ratner's Star* (1976) concludes DeLillo's quartet of novels searching for a space outside of language, this time exploring theoretical mathematics. The question of whether a mysterious message emanates from outer space or whether it originates as an internal glitch in the programming system, interrogates whether language creates meaning internally or through its relation to the outside world. *Players* (1977) and *Running Dog* (1978) are both parodic espionage thrillers: the first deliberately played too slowly (appointments are missed, plots result in odd dead-ends, events never happen); the second too fast, the scenario jumping from spy movies to westerns to kung-fu mysticism, in one vast, unspooling reel. *The Names* (1982) is possibly DeLillo's most difficult novel, and concerns the murderous activities of a strange linguistic cult, attempting to put words and objects back together by way of violence. In all of DeLillo's work, the attempt to get back to the primal or the real is ultimately revealed to be regressive, even fascistic; Gladney's obsession with Hitler in *White Noise* (1984), is another example of this.

BIBLIOGRAPHY

Primary Works

Americana (1971), Boston: Houghton Mifflin.
End Zone (1972), Boston: Houghton Mifflin.
Great Jones Street (1973), Boston: Houghton Mifflin.
Ratner's Star (1976), New York: Knopf.
Players (1977), New York: Knopf.
Running Dog (1978), New York: Knopf.
Amazons (1980), New York: Holt, Rinehart & Wilson (as Cleo Birdwell).
The Names (1982), New York: Knopf.
White Noise (1984), New York: Viking.
Libra (1988), New York: Viking.
The Day Room (1989), New York: Penguin (play).
Mao II (1991), New York: Viking.
Underworld (1997), New York: Scribner.
Valparaiso (2000), New York: Scribner (play).
The Body Artist (2001), New York: Scribner.

Critical Sources

Aaron, Daniel (1990), 'How to read Don LeLillo', *South Atlantic Quarterly*, 89 (2), Spring, pp. 305–20.
Allen, Glenn Scott (1994), 'Raids on the conscious: Pynchon's legacy of paranoia and the terrorism of uncertainty in Don DeLillo's *Ratner's Star*, *Postmodern Culture* 4 (2).
Baker, Stephen (2000), *The Fiction of Postmodernity*; Edinburgh: Edinburgh University Press.
Barrett, Laura (1999), but also there: subjectivity and postmodern space in *Mao II*', *Modern Fiction Studies*, 45 (3), pp. 788–810.
Bell, Pearl (1992), 'DeLillo's world', *Partisan Review*, 59 (1), pp. 138–46.

Bigsby, Christopher (1997), 'The country where history is more inventive than fiction', *Daily Telegraph*, 27 December.

Brooker, Peter (1996), *New York Fictions*, London: Longman.

Brown, Mick (1998), 'They're all out to get him', *Daily Telegraph*, 11 January.

Bryant, Paula (1987), 'Discussing the untellable: Don DeLillo's *The Names*', *Critique*, 29 (1), Fall, pp. 16–29.

Bryson, Norman (1980), 'City of Dis: the fiction of Don DeLillo', *Granta* 2, pp. 145–57.

Bukatman, Scott (1993), *Terminal Identity*, Durham: Duke University Press.

Bull, Jeffrey (1999), 'What about a problem that doesn't have a solution?: Stone's *A Flag for Sunrise*, DeLillo's *Mao II*, and the politics of political fiction', *Critique* 40 (3), Spring, pp. 215–29.

Carmichael, Thomas (1993), 'Lee Harvey Oswald and the Postmodern subject: history and intertextuality in Don DeLillo's *Libra, The Names* and *Mao II*, *Contemporary Literature*, 34 (2), Summer, pp. 204–18.

Civello, Paul (1994), *American Naturalism and its Twentieth Century Transformation*, Athens, GA: University of Georgia Press.

Crowther, Hal (1990), 'Clinging to the rock: the novelist in an age of mediocrity', *South Atlantic Quarterly*, 89 (2), Spring, pp. 321–36.

Conroy, Mark (1994), 'From Tombstone to tabloid: authority figured in *White Noise*', *Critique* 35 (2), Winter, pp. 97–110.

DeCurtis, Anthony (1990), 'An outsider in this society: an interview with Don DeLillo', *South Atlantic Quarterly*, 89 (2), Spring, pp. 281–304.

— (1990), 'The product: Bucky Wunderlick, rock and roll, and Don DeLillo's *Great Jones Street*', *South Atlantic Quarterly*, 89 (2), Spring, pp. 369–80.

DeLillo, Don (1998), 'The moment the Cold War began', *The Observer*, 4 January.

Dewey, Joseph (1990), *In a Dark Time: The Apocalyptic Temper in the American Novel of the Nuclear Age*; Lafayette: Perdue University Press.

Duvall, John (1994), 'The (super)market of images as unmediated mediation in DeLillo's *White Noise*', *Arizona Quarterly*, 50 (3), Autumn, pp. 127–53.

Engles, Tim (1999), 'Who are you, literally?: fantasies of the self in *White Noise*', *Modern Fiction Studies* 45 (3), pp. 755–87.

Foster, Dennis (1990), 'Alphabetic pleasures: *The Names*', *South Atlantic Quarterly*, 89 (2), Spring, pp. 395–412.

Frow, John (1990), 'The last things before the last', *South Atlantic Quarterly*, 89 (2), Spring, pp. 413–30.

Goodheart, Eugene (1990), 'Some speculations on DeLillo and the cinematic real', *South Atlantic Quarterly*, 89 (2), Spring, pp. 355–68.

Green, Jeremy (1999), 'Disaster footage: spectacles of violence in Don DeLillo', *Modern Fiction Studies*, 45 (3), pp. 571–99.

Hantke, Stefan (1994), *Conspiracy and Paranoia in Contemporary American Fiction*, Frankfurt: Peter Lang.

Harris, Robert (1982),'A talk with Don DeLillo', *New York Times Book Review*, 10 October.

Heyler, Ruth (1999), 'Refuse heaped many stories high: DeLillo, dirt and Disorder', *Modern Fiction Studies* 45 (4), pp. 987–1006.

Hutchinson, Stuart (2000),'What happened to normal? Where is normal?: DeLillo's *Americana* and *Running Dog, Cambridge Quarterly*, 29 (2), Summer, pp. 117–32.

Johnson, Stuart (1985),'Extra-philosophical investigations in Don DeLillo's *Running Dog*', *Contemporary Literature*, 26 (1), Spring, pp. 74–90.

Johnston, John (1989), 'Generic difficulties in the novels of Don DeLillo', *Critique*, 30 (4), Summer, pp. 261–75.

— (1998), *Information Multiplicity: American Fiction in an Age of Media Saturation*, Baltimore: John Hopkins University Press.

Karnicky, Jeffrey (2001),'Wallpaper Mao: Don DeLillo, Andy Warhol, and seriality', *Critique* 42 (4), Summer, pp. 339–56.

Keesey, Douglas (1993), *Don DeLillo*, New York: Twayne.

Knight, Peter (2000), *Conspiracy Culture: From the Kennedy Assassination to The X-Files*; London: Routledge.

Kucich, John (1998),'Postmodern politics: Don DeLillo and the plight of the white male writer', *Michigan Quarterly Review*, 27 (2), Spring, pp. 328–41.

LeClair, Thomas (1988), *In the Loop: Don DeLillo and the Systems Novel*, Urbana: University of Illinois Press.

LeClair, Thomas & McCaffery, Larry (1982), *Anything can Happen: Interviews with Contemporary American Novelists*, Urbana: University of Illinois Press.

Lentricchia, Frank (ed.), *Introducing Don DeLillo*, Durham: Duke University Press.

— (1991), *New Essays on White Noise*, New York: Cambridge University Press.

— (1990), '*Libra* as Postmodern critique', *South Atlantic Quarterly*, 89 (2), Spring, pp. 431–53.

Maltby, Paul (1996),'The romantic metaphysics of Don DeLillo', *Contemporary Literature*, 37 (2), Summer, pp. 251–77.

McCaffery, Larry (1986), *Postmodern Fiction: A Bio-bibliographical Guide*, West-Point: Greenwood Press.

McClure, John A. (1990), 'Postmodern romance: Don DeLillo and the age of conspiracy', *South Atlantic Quarterly*, 89 (2), Spring, pp. 337–54.

Melley, Timothy (2000), *Empire of Conspiracy: The Culture of Paranoia in Postwar American Literature*, Ithaca: Cornell University Press.

Millard, Kenneth (2000), *Contemporary American Fiction*, Oxford: Oxford University Press.

Molesworth, Charles (1990), 'Don DeLillo's perfect starry night', *South Atlantic Quarterly*, 89 (2), Spring, pp. 381–94.

Moran, Joe (2000), *Star Authors: Literary Celebrity in America*, London: Pluto.

Morris, Matthew (1990), 'Murdering words: language in action in Don DeLillo's *The Names*', *South Atlantic Quarterly*, 89 (2), Spring, pp. 113–27.

Muirhead, Marion (2001), 'The occult geometry of time in *White Noise*', *Critique* 42 (4), Summer, pp. 402–15.

Nadeau, Robert (1981), *Readings from the New Book on Nature: Physics and Metaphysics in the American Novel*, Amherst: University of Massachusetts Press.

O'Donnell, Patrick (2000), *Latent Destinies; Cultural Paranoia in Contemporary US Narrative*, Durham: Duke University Press.

Oriard, Michael (1978), 'Don DeLillo's search for Walden Pond', *Critique*, 20 (1), Spring, pp. 5–24.

Osteen, Mark (2000), *American Magic and Dread: Don DeLillo's Dialogue with Culture*, Philadelphia, University of Pennsylvania Press.

— (1996), 'Children of Godard and Coca-Cola: cinema and consumerism in Don DeLillo's early fiction', *Contemporary Literature*, 37 (3), Fall, pp. 439–70.

Parrish, Timothy (1999), 'From Hoover's FBI to Eisenstein's unterwelt: DeLillo directs the Postmodern novel', *Modern Fiction Studies* 45 (3), pp. 696–723.

Ruppersburg, Hugh & Engles, Tim (2000), *Critical Essays on Don DeLillo*, New York: G. K. Hall.

Saltzman, Arthur (1990), *Designs of Darkness in Contemporary American Fiction*, Philadelphia: University of Pennsylvania Press.

— (1994), 'The figure in the static: *White Noise*', *Modern Fiction Studies* 40 (1), pp. 807–26.

— (2000), *This Mad 'Instead': Governing Metaphors in Contemporary American Fiction*, Columbia: South Carolina University Press.

Sante, Luc (1997), 'Between hell and history', *New York Times Book Review*, November 6.

Shaub, Thomas (1989), 'What is now natural', *Contemporary Literature*, 30 (1), pp. 128–32.

Simmons, Philip (1997), *Deep Surfaces: Mass Culture & History in Contemporary American Fiction*, Athens: University of Georgia Press.

Stade, George (1976), 'Ratner's Star', *New York Times Book Review*, 20 June.

Tabbi, Joseph (1995), *Postmodern Sublime: Technology and American Writing from Mailer to Cyberpunk*, Ithaca: Cornell University Press.

Tanner, Tony (2000), *The American Mystery*, Cambridge: Cambridge University Press.

Updike, John (1978), 'Layers of ambiguity', *The New Yorker*, 27 March.

Weinstein, Arnold (1993), *Nobody's Home: Speech, Self and Place in American*

Fiction from Hawthorne to DeLillo, New York: Oxford University Press.

Wilcox, Leonard (1991), 'Baudrillard, Don DeLillo's *White Noise*, and the end of heroic narrative', *Contemporary Literature*, 32 (3), Fall, pp. 346–65.

Williams, Richard (1998), 'Everything under the bomb', *The Guardian*, 10 January.

Wood, James (1999), *The Broken Estate*, London: Jonathan Cape.

Wood, Michael (1982), 'Americans on the prowl', *New York Times Book Review*, 10 October.

Useful Websites

http.//www.ksu.edu/english/nelp/delillo/biblio/litcrit.html
http.//www.perival.com/delillo/ddlitcrit.html

PAUL AUSTER[1]

'There is no out-of-doors in the world where language is the land.'
William H. Gass[2]

Auster's best-known work, *The New York Trilogy* (1987) opens with one of the most disorientating scenes in contemporary American fiction. Quinn, a lonely and melancholic detective writer, is woken by a phone call in the middle of night. When he answers it, a voice asks for Paul Auster, of the Auster detective agency. Quinn denies all knowledge and puts the phone back down. However, when the same stranger rings a few nights later, Quinn acts very differently. Fascinated by the idea of becoming somebody else, he affirms that he is indeed Auster and takes the case. In an instance Quinn steps out of his own life and into somebody else's; from this point on there will be no going back, the novel argues, the line between his true self and a second, fictional self hopelessly erased.

But what is it that makes this scene (and the trilogy as a whole) so mysteriously disturbing? The immediate response is to point to Auster's own name as a fundamental disruption of the fictional apparatus of the work. What on earth is the author doing embroiling himself in his own plot, wandering onto the stage (still dressed in his work-clothes) in the middle of the action? If Auster is a character in the novel, then who is the third-person narrator? What is the relation between Auster the character and Auster the author? And by extension of course, what is the relation (if any) between the work of fiction and the real world in which the real Auster is typing these words in the first place? In an instance the illusion of a self-contained fictional world is dispelled, and this in turn unsettles the reader's own sense of security; after all, if the boundary between the fictional and the real is so unstable then the reader's own safety is compromised too. How solid is our own sense of the real?

At this point a second source of existential uncertainty sets in. At the start of the trilogy, Quinn decides, quite arbitrarily, to become someone else; what if we too could walk out of our lives, shed our skin, assume a different, invented identity? And what if this might be easier than we would think? What if, for example, rather than getting up and going to work as always, we decided to travel somewhere else entirely? What if we chose to assume a different role, don a new personality, never went home again? How much of what we call 'reality' is simply a matter of routine, of going through the same mundane motions? If we chose to turn left rather than right; if instead of keeping an appointment we randomly disembarked at some unknown stop, then who knows what we might discover – maybe some kind of trap-door (an image dear to André Breton and the Surrealists) releasing us from the realm of the everyday; an 'everyday' which might not prove as insoluble as society assumes. Of course, this is a concept as disturbing as it is liberating. If the solid appearance of the world is down to our own reliance upon habit and routine – if a simple wrong turn (or wrong number) is sufficient to reveal the flimsiness of its foundations (grounded in repetition, convention and conformity) – then our existence suddenly seems very fragile indeed. Any door could open onto the unknown, any accident suddenly (and irrevocably) exile us from the comforts of the familiar. After all, trap-doors only work one way. If we disguise ourselves as somebody else, then there is the danger that nobody will ever recognise us again. More disturbingly still, there might not be any essential 'us' left to recognise.

This chapter explores the existential anxieties which underpin Auster's textual manoeuvres. In doing so, I hope to argue that his consideration of key theoretical concerns – language, authorship, signification – have little to do with any kind of intellectual game-playing but rather point toward the most fundamental of metaphysical doubts, obsessions and anxieties; 'the question of who is who and whether or not we are who we think we are', as Auster puts it (*Red Notebook*, 109).

'To enquire into the sources of language by using language is a circular process, a juggling with mirrors.'

George Steiner[3].

It is easy to see why *The New York Trilogy* (1987) – and in particular, its opening section, *City of Glass* – has been seen as the quintessence of Postmodern introversion, a kind of Post-Structuralist game or textual booby-trap, a labyrinth of mirrors reflecting only its own vanishing point. In this reading, Auster has artfully constructed his text in such a manner that it refers only to itself, a network of scenes which possess no content, only pattern, an elaborate glass-structure, which for all its abstract ingenuity, proves utterly empty, a mirrored hall with no way out. What is the book about? Only its own lack of meaning, less self-sufficient than self-devouring, a gigantic textual snake gorging itself on its own tail (or tale).

This kind of appraisal – which can be either positive or negative depend on how zealous about Structuralism you are – derives from the novel's status as a kind of anti-detective novel, consciously setting up a series of generic expectations only to deconstruct and subvert them. As Quinn helpfully spells out at the start of the book, 'classic' detective stories construct mysteries in order to solve them, proffering a sense of comforting closure whereby the case (and its clues) finally makes sense. 'In the good mystery there is nothing wasted, no sentence, no word that is not significant. And even if it is not significant, it has the potential to be so – which amounts to the same thing' (*New York*, 8) he notes. There are no arbitrary scenes in such books; everything is present for a reason. Each new location opens up new lines of enquiry and provides further clues. New characters are always implicated in events and perform a specific function in the unfolding plot. Nothing is extraneous, unmotivated or pointless. There may be red herrings, but even these are in some way related to the twists and turns of the investigation. The aleatory has been expunged; nobody ever wanders into the story for no good reason.

The intricate plot of the novel is therefore fully worked out by the author, and the reader re-traces this pattern alongside the detective. This participation is active in that the reader (like the crime-busting protagonist) must be able to sift through passages of dialogue or description in order to sniff out clues, but passive in that the structure of the book is utterly unbending: everything coheres around a single point (the initial crime) and all roads lead toward its eventual unmasking. This solution, even for the most casual of readers, certainly feels empowering; one has 'mastered' the text, plumbed its mysteries, exhausted its possibilities. One feels in the same omnipotent position as the author himself: everything makes sense, all secrets are revealed, all reasons laid bare. But this sense of dominating the text can also be seen as an illusion. After all, the reader has simply followed the preordained trail laid out by the author. If one wishes to receive the reward of ultimate comprehension, then this path cannot be digressed from.

Needless to say, this assertion of authorial order – a world which makes transparent sense, in which transgressions are punished, a world where all things possess an assignable role and purpose – is inimical to the profound sense of doubt and uncertainty which underpins Postmodern thought. In *Ghosts*, the second in Auster's trilogy, the old master-detective, Gold, becomes obsessed with solving the seemingly unmotivated murder of an anonymous child (*New York*, 142). There are no clues, no motives, not even any suspects; but how can such a thing happen, Gold demands? The death of a child represents the overturning of any kind of moral order or meaning, an indictment of the very way of things, a crime against nature, against chronology itself. How can such a thing go unpunished and unexplained? The death-mask of the boy's face haunts the entire story, refuting any easy answer. In *City of Glass* the collapse of the case is more gradual, but equally unsettling. Quinn is hired to protect a strange young man, Peter Stillman, from the (supposedly) evil machinations of his father, who has just been released from prison. Quinn is handed a photograph of the elder Stillman and informed, by the boy's mother, that he will be arriving at Grand Central Station at a specific time; however, when he positions himself to wait, he is horrified to be confronted by two individuals who both resemble Stillman's photograph – one prosperous, the other down-at-heel (*New York*, 56). His resolution to follow the more destitute Stillman is wholly arbitrary, a split-second decision, and thereafter Quinn is haunted by the randomness of his choice, the fear that he may be tailing and watching the wrong man entirely; for the reader, of course, the uncanny appearance of Stillman's double further weakens the novel's verisimilitude, its own sense of fictional coherence. What kind of novel are we reading after all?

Throughout the text, Quinn is tormented by his own inadequacies as a detective – a reversal of the classic, Holmesian superiority. What if he is missing some vital clue? What if his attempts at surveillance – keeping watch outside the shabby Stillman's rundown apartment – prove insufficient? After all, he too has to eat, sleep, rest, thereby running the risk of letting Stillman slip through his fingers – assuming

that this is the 'right' Stillman, in the first place. What if he misinter-
preted the entire scene at the station? How trustworthy are his senses,
his logical deductions, his understanding of the case? Moreover, the
novel subverts the very notion of apprehensible 'clues' which provide
the back-bone of any investigation. In the most famous section of the
novel, Quinn follows Stillman on a torturous tour of New York, his
strange itinerary seemingly aimless and unmotivated. However, by
transcribing Stillman's roundabout route onto a city map, he discovers
that Stillman seems to be spelling out a series of letters, the pattern
of his footsteps forming eerie, invisible hieroglyphics. Quinn dutifully
inscribes each of these alphabetical perambulations, and eventually
realises that Stillman is engraving the words 'The Tower of Babel'
(*New York*, 72) upon the city streets – the subject of Stillman's published thesis. Surely this must be significant, but in what way? Stillman
might be insane, but that in turn robs his activities of any rational
meaning. More worryingly, Stillman may be aware of Quinn's dogged
pursuit and acting deliberately to confound him, mapping out an
astonishingly elaborate red herring. But a third interpretation is the
most disturbing of all; what if it is Quinn who is insane, seeing shapes
where none exist, making paranoic connections like some kind of
madman glimpsing faces in the clouds? The very action by which the
detective determines meaning – making connections, finding patterns,
uncovering significance – here borders on a kind of pathological
obsession. Are such patterns real or projected? Does the detective unveil
a hidden order or arbitrarily impose it? After all, Quinn missed the first
part of the sentence, and takes action before Stillman has a chance to
map out the 'el' – which, as the narrator points out, is Hebrew for
'God' (*New York*, 72) – divine order being absent from Auster's world.

The trick of *The New York Trilogy* is to introduce an unreliable
narrator into a genre which requires, as a fundamental first principle,
that we trust the protagonist's point of view. If the very act of looking
for meaning is called into doubt, configured as the fanciful projections
of a madman, then the notion that there is some stable truth out there
also begins to diminish. If things make sense, the novel seems to be
suggesting, then it is because we have artificially arranged it so.

Hence, the more the case unravels, the more desperate becomes
Quinn's need to provide a sense of structure and coherence. At the
start of the book, he writes down Marco Polo's adage ('We will set

things down as seen, things heard as heard, so that our book may be an accurate record, free from any sort of fabrication' (*New York*, 8)) as his own guiding principle – the irony being, of course, that Polo's travelogues are themselves notoriously unreliable. Quinn, ever the detective-writer, purchases a 'red note-book' (a recurrent motif in Auster's work) and conscientiously documents the bare facts of the case – the verifiable certainties of which he can be sure (he writes in the nude as a sign of his commitment to the naked truth). Alas, this faith in language once again proves to be misplaced. How accurate are his descriptions? How honest his account of his own actions? He experiences the same nagging doubts as Blue undergoes in *Ghosts*: 'It's as though his words, instead of drawing out the facts and making them sit palpably in the world, have induced them to disappear,' (*New York*, 147). His words do not match the actual reality, and into this fissure – a gap between word and object, language and matter – all his linguistic certainties begin to slip. The reader too, begins to distrust any kind of textual claims to veracity. At the end of the novel, after Quinn has vanished from its pages, an unnamed narrator (and one-time friend of Auster!) abruptly steps out of the shadows to claim that (s)he has put together the preceding text from the decipherable fragments of Quinn's note-book. This sudden shift from third to first person narrator effectively pulls the carpet out from under the reader's feet once more, and also (as John Zilcosky points out) logically makes no sense.[4] After all, Quinn doesn't start the notebook until a third of the way into the novel; nor are his entries in any way synonymous with the ostensible 'plot' of the story we have just finished reading. This unnamed editor may claim that he or she has 'done their best with it and . . . refrained from any interpretations' (*New York*, 132), but we can hardly believe such a claim. Whose story is this anyway? We now not only know nothing of what has gone on but also are left in the dark as to the identity of the author (the novel ends with the narrator berating Paul Auster, who has 'behaved badly throughout' (*New York*, 132)).

There is still, however, one more twist to come. In the process of writing the text, the narrator has in a sense 'become' Quinn, just as Quinn 'becomes' the detective Paul Auster. 'He will be with me always' states the narrator (*New York*, 132), an ambiguous conclusion which mirrors Quinn's bizarre disappearance in the text. To write is to disappear, it seems. To be an author is to be a ghost, haunting one's own disembodied words. But what does any of this mean? Auster's detached, toneless prose seems to slip through our fingers, cancelling itself out at every turn. How can one even begin to approach such a book?

'Neither absolute terror nor mild anxiety, the uncanny seemed easier to describe in terms of what it was not, than in any essential sense of its own.'

Anthony Vidler[5]

The text seems to warns us against such acts of interpretation on its very first page: 'The question is the story itself, and whether or not it means something is not for the story to tell' (*New York*, 3) it avers. However, this supposed privileging of plot above exposition is itself a kind of a false lead; the 'plot' constantly twists, rewinds and crosses itself out, until by the time of Chapter ten, its hero has simply no more lines of inquiry to go on – the novel no longer functioning as a generic text.

On the other hand, one might interpret the novel's *raison d'être* in terms of a preference for mystery above resolution, the uncanny over explanation, the unknown rather than the known. Such a notion escapes the inherent narrative redundancy of the genre; the fact that once the mystery has been solved, the traditional detective text becomes fundamentally exhausted. Only the enigmatic, the unresolved, one might argue, can continue to lay claim to our attention and our fascination. Moreover, this idea contradicts facile assumptions that the world is wholly explicable, transparently amenable to logic, reason and sense. Instead, Auster is interested in 'the presence of the unpredictable, the utterly bewildering nature of human experience' (*Red Notebook*, 117). 'We brush up against these mysteries all the time,' he argues. 'The result can be truly terrifying – but it can also be comical' (*Red Notebook*, 118). Hence his interest in chance, luck, and the inexplicable – in philosophical terms he is interested in contingency rather than causality; the existence of the inexplicable as an unescapable constituent of everyday life. 'What I am after,' he asserts, 'is to write fiction as strange as the world I live in' (*Red Notebook*, 117). Auster still sees himself as a realist therefore; it is simply that this sense of reality is ultimately unknowable.

But even given this stress on mystery and non-resolution, *City of Glass* remains a very strange – even at times impenetrable – text. Auster's conception of reality links him to other contemporary American Surrealists – I am thinking here primarily of poets such as Charles

Simic and Mark Strand – who aver that there is some kind of reality out there, but that it's stranger than anyone can possibly imagine. However, Structuralist critics of Auster – for example, Steven Alford or William Little – take their linguistic solipsism much further.[6] It is a mistake, they argue, to assume that books are written about the world. Rather, words only refer to other words. Meaning is inherent in the way these words are put together rather than in terms of any kind of correspondence with an assumed, lived, reality. Over and over again in the trilogy, Auster's characters profess a longing for some kind of transparent language, a straightforward union between the thing described and the words used to do so. In *Ghosts*, Blue wants to believe that words are 'great windows that stand between him and the world' and admits that 'until now they have never impeded his view, have never even seemed to be there' (*New York*, 146). At the start of the story, Blue lives in a state of pre-Structuralist ignorance, naïvely believing that 'words fit snugly around the things they stand for' (*New York*, 148); by its conclusion, however, he comes to see words not as windows but mirrors (the two meanings of *City of Glass*), signs reflecting other signs, an optical illusion of reality which actually has nothing in common with any such thing. In terms of Structuralism, meaning resides in the relationship between signs rather than in terms of any actual referent; which is to say, meaning is all about structure – how the signs fit together – and nothing about content. Meaning is language talking about language. The world itself doesn't mean anything.

Hence, a Post-Structuralist reading of *City of Glass* stresses its status as a wholly textual artifact which only makes sense in relation to other textual sources. At the start of the book, Quinn admits that what he liked about detective novels was 'not their relation to the world but their relation to other stories' (*New York*, 8); Auster has fashioned a book which deconstructs its own generic conventions and thereby demonstrates their (and its) essential, dizzying, emptiness. It is about nothing but itself and therefore literally about nothing. As such it aims to achieve the impossible state of the red note-book which concludes the last volume in the trilogy:

> All the words were familiar to me, and yet they seemed to have been put together strangely, as though their final purpose was to cancel each other out. I can think of no other way to express it.

Each sentence erased the sentence before it, each paragraph made the next paragraph impossible.' (*New York*, 314)

As such, the reader may well concur with the narrator who states, 'And yet, underneath this confusion, I felt there was something too willed, something too perfect, as though in the end the only thing he had really wanted was to fail – even to the point of failing himself' (*New York*, 314). This is a structure which is all scaffolding and no floors: in short, a city of glass.

But does such an intellectual reading of the book explain the reason why the book is so profoundly unsettling? Certainly, Auster employs a kind of metafictional sleight-of-hand which constantly undermines our usual reading practice, thereby making us oddly conscious of it. By this I mean that he continually draws our attention to the fact that we are actively reading a book, only to use this self-awareness further to disorientate and disarm us. The telephone call which instigates the case, for example, can be interpreted as a kind of communiqué from a fictional character to its author, an idea which undermines any sense of dramatic illusion:

> 'I need your help,' said the voice. 'There is great danger. They say
>   you are the best one to do these things.'
> 'It depends on what you mean.'
> 'I mean death. I mean death and murder.'
> 'That's not my line,' said Quinn. 'I don't go around killing people.'
> 'No,' said the voice petulantly. 'I mean exactly the reverse.' (*New
>   York*, 11)

Fictional characters come to life only when they are inscribed on the page; once they leave the text again they vanish. Likewise, characters exist only when the book is being read, making theirs a very vulnerable state indeed, dependent upon the twin acts of reading and writing. The voice petitions Quinn (as author) in order to come into being, but Quinn's position of authorial supremacy soon collapses. The writer suddenly finds himself a character in someone else's book, exposed to the vagaries of plot and expediency, his existence placed under the aegis of a second shadowy narrator. Quinn undergoes an eerie loss of control ('I seem to be going out,' he said to himself. 'But if I am going out, where exactly am I going?' (*New York*, 12); is unable to 'see' in scenes where the text fails to provide any description (most notably when he enters Virginia Stillman's apartment); and perhaps most disconcertingly, is prone to sudden shifts in time and space (Peter Stillman's speech somehow takes a whole day), dependent upon the will of the author. Quinn is no longer 'the writer' but merely another character, and the novel generates a sense of existential unease through his own growing awareness of this fact. He is at the mercy of someone else's text, trapped in a book not of his making. For faithful Post-Structuralists, of course, all this is simply common-sense. Of course Quinn is made of ink and paper not flesh and blood, of course his existence is purely textual – he is a fictional character after all. But for the reader expecting verisimilitude, this transformation from author to subject, writer to written, is genuinely terrifying, with unsettling implications for our own sense of existential security.

Indeed, I would argue that *City of Glass* is no cerebral, detached literary exercise, but rather is motivated by an instantly apprehensible concern with loneliness, loss and isolation. At the start of the book, Quinn has lost his wife and son in a car crash. He has no other living relatives, few friends, only the most tentative of moorings to the everyday world. So what then does he do? He sits in his apartment and writes – detective novels, under the pseudonym of William Wilson – a solitary, cloistered existence which possesses little connection to the outside world. He has, in a sense, taken up residence in his own head, engineered an introspective withdrawal from the social world, from other people, from any kind of contact. Entombed in his own prose, Quinn flickers between self-sufficiency and unbearable loneliness; the words on the page are more real to him, more alive, than his own sequestered existence. In one sense, his fictional protagonist, Max Work, embodies all the vital attributes which Quinn lacks: 'Whereas Quinn tended to feel out of place in his own skin, Work was aggressive, quick tongued, at home in whatever spot he happened to find himself' (*New York*, 9). But the more Work is fleshed-out as a character, the more pale and insignificant Quinn becomes. Eventually Quinn cannot recognise himself either in the resilient and independent Work or in the hardboiled prose which William Wilson writes. Rather than self-expression, writing appears as a kind of self annulment, a strange literary vanishing trick. All Quinn does now is write – but he is even absent from his own writings.

'Je est un autre.'

Rimbaud.

This peculiar act of self-abrogation has been noted by many other writers. Borges' infamous essay, 'Borges and Me', for example, comments on the strange alienation a writer may feel toward their own prose: 'He (Borges) is not the same as me . . . I recognise myself less in his books than in many others or in the laborious strumming of a guitar.'[7] Borges freely grants that he may share certain similarities and tastes with the author of his books, but also admits that he feels a strange sense of repugnance; the Borges who writes in the prose 'shows my preferences, but in a vain way that turns them into the attributes of an actor'.[8] He cannot see himself reflected back from his own creation; rather he sees a double, ('William Wilson' being the title of Poe's famous story of a sinister *doppelgänger*) who is at the same time a stranger.

Likewise, Auster has also spoken of his phenomenon in *The Red Notebook* (1995):

> You see Leo Tolstoy's name on the cover of *War and Peace*, but once you open the book, Leo Tolstoy disappears. It's as though no one has really written the words you're reading. I find this 'no-one' terribly fascinating – for there's finally a profound truth to it. On the one hand, it's an illusion: on the other hand, it has everything to do with how stories are written. For the author of a novel can never be sure where any of it comes from. The self that exists in the world – the self whose name appears on the covers of books – is finally not the same self who writes the book. (*Red Notebook*, 137)

The sources of artistic inspiration are profoundly mysterious, Auster avers; the voice in which you write (and it may be very difficult ever to modulate this voice) is ultimately not your own. Thus, to return to Quinn, you may expect his hermetic retreat inside his own skull to act as the agency of some kind of self-revelation, to foster some kind of deeper understanding of who he is. After all, what would it mean to cut yourself off from all the things which furnish you with a social sense of identity – your friends, family, work, possessions, the entirety of your commitments to the outside world? If, for example, you turned your back on how other people perceive you – the roles you have to play as employee, spouse, acquaintance – would you find yourself;

some essential you, unencumbered by the weight of others' assumptions – or would you lose yourself, find in solitude only a blank, a disintegration of all the sources of stable selfhood? This profound existential question is played out again and again in Auster's fiction (most obviously in *Moon Palace* (1989)), and appears to be of special pertinence to the experience of the writer.

For Auster, the solitary activity of writing is a kind of shadowy internal exile, a turning away from the world and its incessant demands, an activity which is private, anti-social, and secretive. There's something more than a little unhealthy about all of this; something infantile even, an immersion in make-believe which is the antithesis of adult responsibility. Reality is kept at bay but the cost is very great: loneliness, passivity, even a sense of autistic separation from the world. His fiction stresses the idea of writer as hermit and outcast, marooned inside his own room, a claustrophobic privacy which can be either *sanctum sanctorum* or solitary confinement. Quinn can still see the world, but he is separated from it, as if by a sheet of glass; a glass which grows ever more opaque.

After all, what does it mean to create a fictional character – to pretend to be somebody else; to free oneself from the prison of one's personality; to sever the ties of servitude and liability. Thus when Quinn takes on the guise of Paul Auster, private investigator, and acts out this role for real: 'he felt though he had been taken out of himself, as if he no longer had to walk around with the burden of his own consciousness. By a simple trick of the intelligence, a deft little twist of naming, he felt incomparably lighter and freer' (*New York*, 50). This sense of lightness – of liberation – recalls his earlier sorties across the streets of New York, another source of escape from oneself:

> New York was an inexhaustible space, a labyrinth of endless steps, and no matter how far he walked, no matter how well he came to know its neighbourhoods and streets, it always left him with the feeling of being lost. Lost, not only in the city, but within himself as well. Each time he took a walk, he felt as though he were leaving himself behind, and by giving himself up to the movement of the streets, by reducing himself to a seeing eye, he was able to escape the obligation to think, and this, more than anything else, brought him a measure of peace, a salutary emptiness within. (*New York*, 4)

To lose oneself in the labyrinth of the city, and to lose oneself in the labyrinth of words on a page; Auster constantly draws parallels between the two (Stillman's code, for example), fiction a kind of typographical travel taking place within the quietude of an empty room. Certainly, Quinn's vision of the city – an endless maze or sea of signs, routes, patterns, shapes – recalls Roland Barthes' famous description of the linguistic sphere:

> Writing is the destruction of every voice, of every point of origin . . . Writing is that neutral, composite, oblique space where our subject slips away, the negative where all identity is lost, starting with the very identity of the body writing.[9]

Hence, the central dilemma facing Auster's heroes: does one find or lose oneself in language? Is writing a necessary means of self-articulation or just the opposite; namely the process by which the writer cuts him or herself off from the world and then vanishes within the text. Indeed, one might conclude from *The New York Trilogy* that writing – and in particular the writing of fiction – is an inherently harmful activity. It isolates, separates, traps – like the wall Nashe builds in *The Music of Chance* (1990) or the explorer trapped beneath the ice in *The Locked Room*, each breath adding to the solidity of his prison (*New York*, 255).

Quinn elects to take on the role of Paul Auster in order to act out his fantasies, to erase the border between his fictional creation (Max Work) and his 'real' life; but in doing so, he cancels out his own (admittedly rather dismal) existence, lets go of his last few remaining ties to the world of real things – possessions, money, his home. The scene where Quinn returns home to find a stranger living in his apartment (*New York*, 123) is as terrifying a sequence as one can find in modern fiction; it is his very sense of self which has disappeared. He looks in a shop window but can no longer recognise himself; he thinks thoughts which do not seem to be his own. He is rendered homeless in the most profound sense – absent from his abode, his life, his body, even his mind. So where is he?

'The homelessness of ideas is . . . one of the most menacing features of thought.'

Charles Baxter[10]

In *The Invention of Solitude* (1982) Auster reflects at length on Freud's definition of 'the uncanny' as unheimlich, or literally 'not at home' (*Solitude*, 148). Freud argues that we experience intimations of the uncanny (interestingly citing the idea of meeting one's double as an example) as something profoundly alien, something out of the ordinary, something 'other'. But this sense of supernatural otherness is an illusion, Freud argues; rather the unfamiliar is the familiar which we have forgotten and then forgotten that we've forgotten. Hence the importance of the 'double' motif; apparently 'supernatural' occurrences are in actual fact dimly remembered vestiges of earlier modes of thinking, prior states of being. Otherness is actually an aspect of the self buried deep within the unconscious; it returns us to an earlier, more primitive state of consciousness.

When babies are born, Freud argues, they possess no sense of self. Rather it is as if they are the whole world and everything within it. They have no idea where their bodies end and other material objects begin; they cannot differentiate themselves from the world around them. Hence the profound psychic shock registered when they feel cold and hungry and existence fails to provide nourishment, or when their soft, fleshy skin comes into contact with something sharp or hard or painful. The first contours of consciousness are outlined by frustration and want; the child is not omnipotent, and there is a limit to the degree of control it can exert over its surroundings. In essence, it is no longer king of the world.

The second stage in the development of identity is 'the mirror stage', exhaustively discussed by Jacques Lacan. Partly as a result of visual data (gazing at its own reflection), and partly as a result of trial and error, the baby begins to gain a sense of its dimensions, its body, mass and extensions, and hence its property of forming a discrete and limited being. But the first and most important mirror is the mother's face. The child copies its expressions, gazes upon its visage, and at some point suddenly realises that it is being seen. As Auster explains in *The Red Notebook*:

> The infant feeding at the mother's breast looks up into the mother's eyes and sees her looking at him, and from that experience of being seen, the baby begins to learn that he is separate from his mother, that he is a person in his own right. We literally acquire a self from this process. (*Red Notebook*, 143).

The child has learnt that there are things which do not belong to it; now it learns that there other beings who are separate from it. Its earlier sense of an undifferentiated, oceanic world where all is one is already starting to fade; the discovery of language will finally obliterate it. The child, gazing at the mirror, realises that its reflection is not actually it but merely an image or a sign of it. The world is separated still further into things and representations of things – and eventually into objects and words. Language permits the articulation of a sense of selfhood, but it also cuts one off from this lost Eden of pure being. Learning to speak, like catching one's reflection in another's eyes, is a realisation of selfhood attained through the agency of others – if someone is looking at me then I must exist. But this existence is, in turn, determined by another.

In Auster's work, characters start to disappear when they turn aside from the world. So much of our lives is determined by what others think of us, the roles which the world assigns us; Auster's idealists divest themselves of all these extraneous guises, pare down their lives (there are obvious parallels with DeLillo here) to the bare essentials, but this act of withdrawal carries with it enormous risks. Our sense of self, Auster argues, is dependent on the views of others – friends, lovers, family, workmates – and solitude runs the danger of obliterating all the things that make us who we are. The more his characters retreat into themselves, the more they become aware of enigmatic symbols, inexplicable events, eerie connections – in short, Freud's sphere of 'the uncanny'. Their retreat into the womblike environ of their individual garrets suggests a return to infantile ways of thinking; the border between themselves and the world starts to blur and dissolve, returning them to the most primitive sense of being in the world - a dissolution into the world around them. Quinn in *City of Glass*, or Fogg in *Moon Palace* suddenly perceive strange connections in the ether around them – omens, auguries, strange symbols which suggest some kind of hidden pattern or supernatural order – all revolving around the obsessional concerns of Auster's protagonists. In essence, the outline of their character bleeds into external reality. Where they end and the world begins once again becomes blurred and uncertain.

The spectre of a lost Eden, a state of grace characterised by feelings of belonging and wholeness, a sense of being in the world, is explicitly raised in *City of Glass* through the strange figure of Peter Stillman Snr, whose search for a 'pure' language underpins the central narrative. In a disturbing experiment (which has a number of historical precedents), Stillman is revealed to have brought up his child in a state of darkness, isolated from any kind of human contact and cut off from any vestige of human speech and language. Stillman's plan is to discover if his child will spontaneously begin to speak some 'natural' tongue, a divine patois which will, in some mystical sense, restore a sense of unity and completeness to the world. Our language is corrupt, abstract, broken, he believes; it no longer refers to real things, only to itself. Only this strange speaking in tongues – lost since the collapse of the Tower of Babel – can save us from linguistic exile, return us to the world as it really is.

As Auster makes clear in the novel, this idea is an ancient one. One can trace its origins through Jewish Cabbalism (the notion of hieroglyphics embedded in the world), Plato (the myth of Cratylus, the naïve etymologist 'who thinks that language is meant to *name* things'), the Bible, and onwards through Rousseau (dreaming of a tongue untainted by corrupt civilisation) to Thoreau (a key source for Auster): an ideal which stands as the profound antithesis of Post-Structuralism, whose central tenet is that textual meaning is wholly artificial and inwards-tending.[11] All these scribes dreamt of a language which perfectly responded to reality; a form of christening which would reveal the true name of every living thing. 'You see, the world is in fragments, sir,' states Stillman. 'And it is my job to put it back together again' (*New York*, 77).

Auster is less concerned with any kind of political critique – the idea that words hide ideological imperatives under the guise of a naturalistic 'way things are' – than with an apprehension of the fundamental shortcomings of the notion of naming itself. Take, for example, the idea of a tree, a simple living thing. We assign to this thing either an abstract type (the word 'tree') or else an only slightly more specific appellation (oak, yew, sycamore, whatever). But no tree is wholly like any other tree. Even if one summoned up all one's powers of description, employed all of one's sense of imaginative perception, one could never begin to put any tree into words; rather, reality exceeds transcription. The delicate microstructure of each individual leaf; the intricate tracery of the bark: these things are beyond words. Nor does the tree stay frozen in the one state – it both grows and dies, ever-changing. And then if one considers the changing play of light, the different possible perspectives, its gradations of movement in the wind – how could one describe such a thing? Words are abstract, general, universal; but we inhabit a world of specific, unique, unreproducible things.

And, if this wasn't problematic enough: 'everything is subject to metamorphosis . . . change always occurs unexpectedly, with lightning swiftness' (*Red Notebook*, 54). Auster's universe in *The New York Trilogy* – and even more extremely in *In the Country of Last Things* (1987) – is in a state of constant decay: organic matter warping, rotting, melting, eroding, dissolving. Auster's New York is a broken city, where the flotsam and jetsam of the streets has reached such a point of decomposition, their original names no longer seem to apply. Stillman notes:

> When you rip the cloth off the umbrella, is the umbrella still an umbrella? You open the spokes, put them over your head, walk out into the rain, and you get drenched. Is it possible to go on calling this object an umbrella? . . . Unless we begin to embody the notion of change in the words we use, we will continue to be lost. (*New York*, 77–8)

One way of conceiving of *The New York Trilogy* is to compare it to the Cubist paintings of Picasso or Braque: mangled bottles, tables, junk, randomly compacted and combined until they begin to lose any identifiable characteristics. Cubism argued that the certainties of classical realism were an illusion, that the world required a new means of seeing which took into account both the multi-dimensional and the mutable nature of matter. The peeling textures, washed-out colour, and flattened space of early Cubism captures something of the sense of dereliction which informs Auster's work; and one might also mention Kurt Schwitters (1897–1947) whose random montages of discarded items – envelopes, packaging, bus tickets – also suggests the dilapidated fabric of the trilogy, with language portrayed as the most broken tool of all.

The word 'tree' then has nothing in common with the unnamable specificity of an actual tree. It is an arbitrary sign – there is nothing tree-like about the letters 'tree'. Reality is infinitely richer, infinitely more complex, infinitely more dense than the realm of words. The two things possess no implicit connection – one belongs to the realm of abstract knowledge (epistemology), the other to the sphere of physical being (ontology). Stillman dreams of a perfect diction which might bridge this gap, a language of real things which might heal this fissure at the very heart of representation. In a sense, his alphabetic wanderings across New York are in themselves a crude form of concrete typography, his physical footsteps translated into literal hieroglyphics. But a name which perfectly described its subject? Such a thing is literally unimaginable – it is impossible to use words to conceive of such a thing.

'What lies outside language ought not to be spoken of, cannot be spoken of without gross falsification, but it is by no means negated.'

Wittgenstein[12]

Nevertheless, Auster's *City of Glass* concludes with just such a paradox. After losing track of Stillman and having run out of leads, Quinn resorts to hiding outside Virginia Stillman's apartment, constructing for himself a makeshift shelter in a foetid rubbish bin, where he both forages for food and evacuates his bowels (*New York*, 116). Inexplicably, this crude mode of surveillance goes on for months. The motif of 'homelessness' which can be traced throughout the novel appears here in its most literal form; irrevocably separated from his previous life, Quinn is now one of the discarded, the destitute, the profoundly dispossessed. He still refuses to abandon the case, however. Dutifully, doggedly, he records his observations in his ever-more replete red note-book. These records become more precise, responsive, specific. He notes the passage of clouds, the motes of dirt in the air, gradations of light as the sun begins to set: colours, textures, scents, tastes. He opens himself up to the overwhelming physicality of things, 'brief visions of the immediate' (*New York*, 115), transcribing the tiniest details of his diminished world: his shoes, his hands, the garbage, the alley. However, the more exact his descriptions become, the less substantial he appears. Impossibly nobody ever seems to notice him, or question his activities: 'It was though he had melted into the walls of the city' (*New York*, 116). Like some kind of modern stylite, he experiences this separation from the bustle of the city streets as a state of grace. He is finally at peace. Quinn begins to merge with the physical world, to become at one with it. Mysteriously, his writings seem to pierce that membrane which divides the textual from the material. What he writes in his note-book are no longer words.

His final disappearance from the text takes place in circumstances which deliberately complete the linguistic experiments of Peter Stillman at the start of the book. Alone, in darkness, concealed in a mysterious apartment, he records the final few entries in the red note-book. Even the thoughts in his head can no longer be described as words; he is thinking in things, not abstract signs but unimaginable monads of the universe.'He felt that his words had been severed from him, that they were now part of the world at large, as real and specific as a stone, or a lake, or a flower' (*New York*, 130). He is no longer Quinn because he cannot continue to formulate any sense of linguistic identity in his head. The words are gone. Significantly, one of his last coherent thoughts is a memory of 'the moment of his birth and how he had been pulled gently from his mother's womb' (*New York*, 130). He has at last returned to that undifferentiated infantile state dreamt of by Freud. Nothing separates him from the world around him – or rather language no longer separates him from the world outside. Ultimately, Quinn vanishes from the book because he has transcended language entirely; he has made the leap from the textual to the material and the novel can follow him no further. Where is he? All we can say for sure is that he is no longer there on the page.

'The deconstructive quest is motivated by the absence of Truth. Deconstruction is driven by nostalgia for a lost angelic world.'

Robert Scholes[13]

How one chooses to interpret such a bizarre conclusion (beautiful? terrifying? incomprehensible?) in a sense depends upon how one feels about Stillman's idea of a perfect language (*Ur-Sprache*) in the first place. In terms of Structuralist practice, any notion of a 'transparent' language, where words always directly refer to things, where only one meaning is possible, smacks of a kind of authoritarian positivism.[14] There becomes only one way to perceive or 'read' the world, only one tongue with which to speak, and this in turn is confined to the very narrow field of naming material things. Dissent is no longer possible. Rather, we become trapped in the realm of the way things are. Even on poetic rather than political grounds, the discovery of some kind of literal translation may not be entirely desirable. After all, if one came up with a perfect description of a tree, wouldn't one just have another tree? Isn't there a difference between creation and labelling – indeed, doesn't our very notion of the aesthetic reside in the space between the world and our representations of it? Reality is all around us; who needs more? What use is an exact copy, anyway? In this sense, the ideal of perfect reproduction is just as threatening to art as the idea that the real is totally inaccessible. Even if one could speak a perfect *lingua franca* of things – is that all there is?

Hence, Nicholas Dawson argues that Stillman's semantic machinations represent a tyrannical attempt to impose authority, to usher in a world which possesses a single meaning, a single tongue and a single lexicon – an inherently autocratic notion.[15] Chris Tysh connects this notion with Auster's obsessional concern with the 'criminal father', whereby the Logos, the word of the father, threatens the existence of the son – dominating, controlling, and ultimately destroying.[16] In this sense, Stillman's abusive treatment of his son is parallelled by Auster's sadistic treatment of Quinn – whose first name is Daniel, the same as Auster's own son. For Chris Pace the very idea of authorship appears as a dictatorial construct, limiting meaning, controlling the free-reading of the text, tormenting and abusing the fictional constructs – little wonder then that book concludes with the suggestion that Auster 'has behaved badly throughout' (*New York*, 132).[17] He imprisons Quinn for the same nefarious reasons that Stillman tortures his own offspring – to impose his own twisted dominion upon the text. Rather problematically, however, Pace also posits the existence of a 'good' Auster working to subvert his own illusory omnipotence, unravelling the plot and resisting closure through his use of the inexplicable.[18] One might well object that this 'good' Auster is every bit as 'guilty' of the sin of dominating and controlling the text as any traditional novelist – perhaps even more so, given the mental gymnastics which the unwary reader is put through. But Post-Structuralism prefers dissolution above unification, subversion above certainty, dubiety above proclamations of Truth.

Despite these arguments, however, I cannot help but feel that *The New York Trilogy* is much more ambivalent regarding its relation to the real. Both *City of Glass* and its immediate sequel, *Ghosts*, are composed of a number of encounters staged between the textual and the physical, the realm of language and the realm of matter. This bifurcation may be comic – at the start of the novel's metafictional shenanigans, Quinn is caught 'in the act of expelling a turd' (*New York*, 9) – or else strangely moving – Quinn escapes from the 'crypt'-like library where he researches Stillman's mad lexical dreams to breathe in the air of a 'bright May morning' (*New York*, 41), sensual reality configured as the antithesis of the textual. This binary opposition in a sense structures the whole text. Either pole, in extremis, appears as a mortal threat to one's sense of self. The notion of Quinn losing himself amongst the physical bustle of the New York streets ('flooding himself with externals . . . drowning himself out' (*New York*, 61)) is twinned with the idea of Quinn losing himself in his prose, taking on a second (but unrecognisable) persona at the expense of the first. On the one side, we find what Robert Scholes calls 'the radical otherness of the world', the world 'undescribed' (and undescribable), 'the world of things in themselves'.[19] On the other, we see an endless labyrinth of mirrors, the textual as a kind of infinite regression, never revealing anything outside of its own reflection. Whether submerged in base matter or endless text, Quinn's sense of existence appears precariously balanced between the two.

There are, of course, a number of serious philosophical objections one might level against such a model. Richard Rorty, for example, has satirised any kind of nostalgia for some elemental language in explicitly Edenic terms: 'When asked by Eve why he named a certain animal 'elephant', Adam replied, 'Well, it just *looked* like an elephant.'[20]

The whole idea of some perfect correspondence of name and subject is patently absurd, Rorty argues. The word 'snake' may suggest a sibilant hissing, the letter 's' suggest a curved body, the sharp 'k' suggest a sudden bite, but, as the *Zaumnik* movement demonstrated, this way madness lies.[21] These properties belong to the word 'snaky' rather than to the actual slithering thing. Meaning is wholly linguistic. Which is not to say that real snakes don't exist or that they don't slither – only that the meaning of the words 'slither' or 'snake' is a wholly linguistic matter, separate from the actual living thing. In a version of the famous Zen koan, Rorty affirms that snakes would exist even if there were no humans to use the word snake, but nevertheless, we would not think a snake snaky unless we had the word in our vocabulary.[22]

Such linguistic arguments, however, need not necessarily detain us. After all, we are concerned with the imaginative ideas which inform Auster's fictional universe, rather than with their philosophical viability. It is enough for us that such ideas are of central importance to the trilogy. The difference between the words on the page and the thing described, the distinction between the writer typing at his desk and the world outside, the question of whether a life lived in fiction is equal to a life lived in fact – this is the very stuff of a writer's everyday life. Rather than being a mere intellectual folly, *City of Glass* introduces the central concern of *The New York Trilogy* and indeed Auster's own literary practice – namely, what is the border between the work of fiction and one's own life, and is it possible to use the act of writing somehow to cross or transcend this?

'My life has been the poem I would have writ / But I could not both live and utter it.'

Thoreau[23]

Each section of *The New York Trilogy* contains within itself one key scene which seems both to encapsulate its central theme and illuminate its most profound source of anxiety. In *City of Glass*, this is Quinn's traumatic discovery that his apartment is now occupied by a stranger and that every last trace of his previous life is now gone. In *Ghosts*, it is Blue's realisation that the subject on whom he has been spying is also gazing back at him across the street. His own reports lie piled on this strangers's desk, and these typed reports could refer equally to Blue or his quarry: a man sits gazing out of his window, occasionally writing, occasionally reading. Blue's window onto the world suddenly appears as a mirror, his actions an eerie pantomime of his quarry. What on earth is going on? Either Blue's target has also been hired to spy on him – or else the other man (Black) is really Blue's employer, White, and has hired Blue to watch over him for reasons undeclared. Either solution however, renders the whole operation meaningless.'They have trapped Blue into doing nothing, into being so inactive as to reduce his life to almost no life at all' (*New York*, 169). There is nothing to see. And the man doing nothing is himself.

In a sense, this set-up parallels the essential dilemma of Postmodern, Post-Structuralist, Post-Realist writing: words about words, books about books, a self-reflexive textual dead-end. There is no outside to Blue's apartment – between the typed pages of each man's little cell lies a void, a black hole which language cannot penetrate. *Ghosts* is haunted by a sense of absence. The name of his quarry, Black, denotes not a colour, but the absence of light. The falling snow and gathering shadows suggest textual emptiness, an endless blank page. And in this sense, the discovery that Black may or may not be White appears as a kind of solipsistic bad joke, indicative of the impossibility of finally knowing anything.

Like the homeless Quinn in *City of Glass*, Blue becomes another disembodied author figure, 'only half alive at best, seeing the world only through words, living only through the lives of others' (*New York*,

169). At the start of the narrative, he is cast as the generic hero of the piece, a stereotypical man of action, masculine, potent, alive. But as his surveillance drags on, as the case becomes more and more sedentary and each day is filled only with the written reports of his note-book entry, he feels himself slowly start to slip away. His assiduous observation of Black leaves no room for his own life. He neglects 'the future Mrs-Blue' (*New York*, 145), he limits his material needs to the bare minimum, he spends as little time away from the window as possible. His vigil – and his written record – is all that's left. As Black tells him, late in the narrative, 'Writing is a solitary business. It takes over your life. In some sense, a writer has no life of his own. Even when he's there, he's not really there' (*New York*, 175). *The New York Trilogy* is set in the busiest, noisiest, most energetic and hyper-kinetic city on earth – but none of this penetrates the writer's monastic cell. The city in *Ghosts* is eerily silent, muffled, unimaginably distant. The writer's passive solitude entails an absolute separation from the real. Worse still, Blue's subject, Black, refuses to do anything beyond read or take notes. He is 'no more than a shadow' (*New York*, 141), a hole in the story-line, an empty 'plot'. Bored with his reports, Blue begins to make up stories, to become more introspective, to project his own life onto the blank screen opposite (a parallel text here could be Alfred Hitchcock's *Rear Window* (1954)), literary invention posited as an attempt to deny the void. But for all this, the more Blue writes, the more he disappears. Only a response from his client (White) proves that he is still alive, that he has a role and a job and a reason. Thus, even threats are gratefully received ('No Funny Business' (*New York*, 167)); someone else knows of his existence and hence he must still exist. Otherwise, his life would be as vacant as his target's.

But what is Black doing? He spends his waking hours reading *Walden* (1854) by Henry David Thoreau, a strange sister-text to Blue's own narrative. Like the trilogy, *Walden* is concerned with the notion of ascetic withdrawal and retreat, a renunciation of the social world in favour of a more introspective and simpler life, lived closer to the nature and the changing seasons of one's self. Only in solitude will nature reveal its true face. Similarly, only when surrounded by the natural (rather than the artificial) can one define a sense of self. However, as critics of Transcendentalism have exhaustively pointed out, Thoreau's idea of an idyllic pastoral hermitage is questioned throughout *Walden*, which indeed exhibits many of the same doubts and anxieties as Auster's work. Thoreau too, wants to penetrate the real, to see things as they really are, but as with Auster, language proves a problematic tool: too blunt, too abstract, too infected with man's own artificial assumptions. Moreover, as Mark Ford has argued, in Thoreau's reflective meditations on the nature of selfhood, he discovers no one sovereign soul, a kernel of selfhood, but 'multiple, metamorphic selves', Thoreau's writing less an act of self-expression than a splintering and dissolution of any kind of identity.[24] *Walden* thus reinforces Auster's own thematic concerns, but its significance to the text is much more disturbing than mere intellectual uncertainty. Rather Auster now shifts his concerns from the notion of writing to the notion of reading – with, of course, unsettling consequences for his audience.

Blue reads – or tries to read – *Walden* in order to get inside the mind of Black, to ferret out clues regarding his future plans or motivation, to gain some sense of just who the shadowy Black really is (a mere shadow of Blue himself?). As he checks on the exact page which Black is reading and peruses the book himself, a strange idea suddenly occurs to him. He is reading exactly the same words as Black. The same thought – the same voice – is echoing inside both their heads, a voice which ultimately belongs to neither reader; rather it is the voice of a man over a century dead, yet another disembodied ghost in the text.

In his essay, 'Criticism and the experience of interiority', Georges Poulet sought to show just how uncanny the idea of reading really is. When utterly absorbed in a book, the 'I' who reads vanishes, replaced by the thoughts of another; or, as Poulet phrases it 'Whenever I read, I mentally pronounce an 'I', and yet the 'I' which I pronounce is not myself'.[25] After reading intensely for a while, one's own thoughts take on the accent of the book, and this continues for a while, even after one puts the book down. To read is thus to think using someone else's thoughts, to be possessed by another's consciousness. 'I am on loan to another, and this other thinks, feels, suffers and acts within me,' writes Poulet.[26] One recognises the 'I' of the author, experiences it as if it were one's own 'I', but ultimately it is not oneself – this 'I' is another. The very act of reading thus parallels the central themes of the book – the homelessness of thoughts, the amorphous nature of consciousness, the spectral existence of the author – only now the reader too is implicated in this bewildering phenomenon. When we read our own sense of self is temporarily evicted, the border between ourselves and another suspended and erased – and the brilliance of *The New York Trilogy* lies in its ability to make us experience this sensation as both a threat and a possibility.

At the end of *Ghosts* we learn – or intuit, as this may or may not be the true conclusion to the story – that Black has hired Blue to record his every movement to prove that he is still alive, to rescue him from his solitude and thereby deliver him from the vanishing which overtook Quinn. 'He needs me . . . he needs my eyes looking at him,' notes Blue (*New York*, 181), and once again we are back at Lacan's 'mirror-stage', where the awareness of another's gaze is the inception of our sense of self. We can also read this conclusion in terms of the novel's metafictional form. Black, as a fictional character, requires a reader in order to exist, to come to life; he will only flicker into being for as long as we scan the page. But the implications of all of this for Auster's own art are extremely far-reaching. When we read, we trespass beyond the boundaries of who we are; other's thoughts make themselves at home in us. The same is true of writing; the voice we hears in our prose is unrecognisable as our own. What would it mean for such ideas to spill over from our literary activities into our 'real' life? Is it possible to use these to break down the distinction between living and writing, art and existence? At the end of *Walden*, Thoreau writes:

> There is always a poem not printed on paper . . . It is *what he has become through his work*. Not how is the idea expressed in stone, or on canvass or paper, is the question, but how far it has obtained form and expression in the life of the artist.[27]

It is to this radical reworking of the autobiographical that we now turn.

'The author in his work ought to be like God in the universe, present everywhere, and visible nowhere.'

Flaubert[28]

In one sense, *The Locked Room* offers a kind of 'solution' to the ineffable mysteries of its predecessors. The 'author' of *City of Glass* and *Ghosts* turns out to be the unnamed narrator of the final section, their convoluted plots, rough drafts of the 'real' story of the narrator and Fanshawe. 'These three stories are finally the same story, but each one represents a different stage in my awareness of what it is about,' the narrator notes (*New York*, 294) and echoes of the previous works (a detective called Quinn, ideas of watching and being watched, the question of whether a writer's real life is lived in reality or on the page) sound throughout the piece, now located in a more or less realistic, or at least recognisable, universe. But, perhaps unsurprisingly, this resolution is rather less complete than it at first appears. Peter Stillman, Henry Dark and Daniel Quinn all rematerialise, but their presence unsettles the surface realism of the prose, intimating that this appearance of reality is yet another staged back-drop, less abstract but no more solid than the generic settings of the previous works. The Chinese-box structure of the trilogy – plots within plots, authors within authors, an incestuous web of self-reference – counteracts any sense that we have finally arrived at what really happened, some kind of bed-rock reality from which all other narratives derive.

After the first two parts, we are now on our guard, suspicious of anything that gives even the appearance of solid ground. After all, who is this final narrator anyway? Is this the real Paul Auster? But Auster bestows key autobiographical characteristics upon the missing Fanshawe, whose appearance at the novel's end disrupts any kind of verisimilitude. The temptation then is to take a further step back and search for coherence outside the text, to explain its mysteries by recourse to Auster's own life. Can we say then that this is the book's true subject and resolution; Auster the missing figure whose discovery will solve the case? The text may prove dangerously rickety and unstable, but in biography we finally reach real events, stable facts, specific references. Surely this level of reflection won't prove to be yet another trap-door too?

In both interviews and straight non-fiction essays (most particularly *Hand to Mouth* (1997)), Auster has spoken at length of the circumstances surrounding the writing of the trilogy and the idea of approaching it as 'subterranean autobiography' (*Red Notebook*, 108), 'the story of my obsessions . . . the saga of the things that haunt me' (*Red Notebook*, 123). Indeed, the origin of *City of Glass* is disarmingly literal:

> The opening scene in the book is something that actually happened to me. I was living alone at the time, and one night the telephone rang and the person on the other end asked for the Pinkerton Detective Agency. I told him that he had the wrong number, of course, but the same person called back the next night with the same question. When I hung up the phone the second time, I asked myself what would have happened if I had said 'Yes'. That was the genesis of the book, and I went on from there. (*Red Notebook*, 108)

More importantly, perhaps, the central themes of the book – loneliness, isolation, the sense of being cut off from life – are rooted in very specific, personal circumstances. Auster broke up with his first wife in 1979, and thereafter, for a year and a half, he 'lived in a kind of limbo' (*Red Notebook*, 141), first in a dismal apartment in Manhattan, then in an equally solitary cell in Brooklyn. Separated from his son, desperately poor, and unable to write, Auster's sense of terrible isolation – of coming untethered from everyday life – forms the basis of his first work, *The Invention of Solitude* (1982) and provides the despairing tone for the later, and more distanced, *The New York Trilogy*. Salvation took the form of Auster's second wife, Siri Hustvedt, and Auster later commented that he had 'tried to imagine what would have happened to me if I hadn't met her, and what I came up with was Quinn' (*Red Notebook*, 142). Significantly, Auster had written a hack-detective novel, *Squeeze-Play* 1978, under the pseudonym Paul Benjamin, and, as he muses, 'perhaps my life would have been something like his' (*Red Notebook*, 142) – the artist buried alive in his garret, the writer drowning in his own text, windows that reflect only inwards – in a sense, the abstractions of Auster's prose can be seen as translated memories rather than textual games, informed by an immediately apprehensible sense of loss and desertion.

Indeed, the eerie continuity between Auster's fiction and non-fiction is one of the defining features of his *oeuvre*. His investigations into his family-tree in *Portrait of an Invisible Man* (the first part of *The Invention of Solitude*) turn unexpectedly into a murder-mystery, revolving around the murder of Auster's grandfather by his grandmother. The eccentric antics of the real novelist H. L. Humes segue into the bizarre figure of Thomas Effing in *Moon Palace* and then Willy Christmas in *Timbuktu* (1999) whilst Auster's friendship with the high-wire artiste Phillipe Petit forms the genesis of *Mr Vertigo* (1994). More importantly, the fact that his late father's inheritance provided the means for Auster to go on writing informs the narratives of several of his key works (most explicitly *Moon Palace* and *The Music of Chance*), and helps to explain the obsessive sense of guilt and responsibility (writing is always at the expense of somebody's life) central to Auster's art. Indeed, the more one reads of Auster's own life, the more tempting it is to regard it as a literal extension of the central themes of his writing. *Hand to Mouth*, for example, Auster's autobiographical account of his early struggles as a writer, appears virtually indistinguishable from his novelistic creations, replete with strange coincidences, bewildering apparitions, and eccentric philosophic enterprises. The line between writing and living, invention and memory, appears virtually indetectable at such times; when Auster reports that in 1992 a stranger phoned his apartment in the middle of the night asking for a Mister Quinn (*Red Notebook*, 38), we feel a sudden frisson of uncertainty – the uncanny seems to have stepped out from the textual and infiltrated Auster's real life – which is the central theme of *The New York Trilogy* after all.

Is the trilogy then a particularly bizarre self-portrait, Auster the 'body' around which the mystery is chalked? Whilst it may be tempting to think so, *The Locked Room* can also be read as an explicit warning against such assumptions. At first, one recognises elements of Auster's life in both the unnamed narrator – whose writings closely resemble the various commissions, from movie rewrites to book reviews, which Auster was forced to undertake in order to stay afloat in the late '70s and early '80s – and his closest friend Fanshawe, whose strange hermetic poems and enigmatic prose work clearly parallel Auster's 'serious' art, including, of course, the trilogy itself. Even a cursory knowledge of Auster's life reveals a series of direct links between Fanshawe's existence and that of the author – an ailing sister, his time as a crewman aboard a tanker in the Gulf, a lengthy sojourn in France, and so on. Fanshawe's refusal to publish his work and disdain for any literary activity beyond the pure act of creation itself (his name derives from the title of Nathaniel Hawthorne's first novel, which Hawthorne first published himself but then disowned and managed to suppress until after his death) appears in stark distinction to the narrator's pleasure in seeing his work in print, even though he admits that 'it amounted to a mere fraction of nothing . . . the slightest wind would blow it away' (*New York*, 207). Both men are 'doubles' of Auster (in *Hand to Mouth* he speaks of art both as a holy calling and as 'doing everything in my power to prostitute myself' (*Hand to Mouth*, 121)) and Siamese images of each other – Fanshawe remote and inaccessible, the narrator more human but painfully aware of his own failings as a writer.

In a sense, one can interpret their relationship as a specifically literary reflection upon the nature and origin of inspiration. In a key scene from their shared childhood (the third of those defining scenes which punctuate and thereby structure the trilogy) Fanshawe informs the narrator of his 'magic box', the 'private place' where he goes to dream; the narrator, however, is forever proscribed entry, for 'if another person ever entered his box, then its magic would be lost for good' (*New York*, 220). This most intimate part of Fanshawe is utterly sealed off, wholly unapproachable and remote, linked in the narrator's mind to a separate scene wherein Fanshawe lies in a freshly dug grave so as to imagine better his father's death (*New York*, 221). Fanshawe's thoughts here are utterly unknowable, wholly other (the box metaphor unavoidably carries connotations of Freud's configuration of the unconscious, as well as being suggestive of the title of the piece itself) and it is significant that Auster speaks of his own late father in *The Invention of Solitude* in strikingly similar terms: sealed off, distant, utterly inscrutable, an unfathomable mystery in every sense.

The questions which derive from this are, of course, utterly fundamental. Can one really know what is going on inside another's head? Can one even begin to imagine a consciousness other than one's own? But if one sees the narrator and Fanshawe as complementary images of Auster, this question becomes even more disturbing. Can one ever truly know oneself? As we have already seen, the private self may be very different from the public face. Here Fanshawe acts as a trope of everything that is unknowable and incommunicable – including what for Auster is the terrible knowledge that we all face death alone. The sources of art are for Auster profoundly private. What then does it mean to communicate them?

The longing to penetrate this private space underpins the narrator's actions in the text. When Fanshawe disappears, the narrator takes over his life: he moves in with Fanshawe's wife, raises their child, edits his work, and acts as curator of his literary estate. In essence, he usurps the author's role in every sense; he basks in the literary attention generated by Fanshawe's genius, and finds personal and literary fulfilment by stepping into the shoes of the man he has always longed to be. But even this isn't enough. Although he now possesses the outward trappings of his double's life, he still cannot access Fanshawe's 'mysterious centre of hiddenness' (*New York*, 210), his ineffable otherness. In a sense, his relationship with Fanshawe is a distorted version of the dialectic between reader and author. The author is assumed to occupy a privileged position as creator and source; for the reader, she is the point around which the whole text (no matter how mysterious) coheres, the origin of the book's meaning. Thus the narrator's search for Fanshawe parallels our own search for Auster – the author represents the idealised centre of the work from whose perspective all things make sense. But this is ultimately an illusion, Auster implies; a work of art can remain ineffable even for its creator. In interviews, he has spoken of fiction as 'passageways into our unconscious' (*Red Notebook*, 112), whereby his 'novels emerge from those inaccessible parts of ourselves' (*Red Notebook*, 123), as foreign to their creator as they are to the wider audience at large.

This idea is, of course, directly linked to both ancient and contemporary debates regarding 'authorship'. On the one hand, we retain a romantic, individualist view of the great writer: the original, inimitable genius, art as self-expression, personal creation, the deepest, most rounded expression of the writer's sense of self. But against this individualist tradition, one can posit a contrary notion of the writer as impersonal vessel, a mere mouthpiece for some vast supra-personal force – whether the Divine, the forces of nature, artistic tradition, the unconscious, or more prosaically, the forces of ideology, politics and culture. In the first model, the author appears as producer and source. In the second, 'authorship' is merely a mirage, the author produced by the language he uses, a language which both precedes and supersedes any individual voice. Ghosts of the American Renaissance – Thoreau, Hawthorne, Whitman, Poe and Emerson – haunt *The New York Trilogy*, at times possessing Auster's text and determining its direction. The voice of the text is not simply Auster's own – other writers speak through it; similarly, the self-portrait or 'I' which emerges from the work is by no means a straightforward reproduction of Auster himself.

The narrator's search for the 'real' Fanshawe in *The Locked Room* is a contradictory exercise from the very start. He not only wants to find and understand the author, but also to erase and take his place. Hence the great problems of any kind of objective biographical search. How much can one learn about the life of another and how much does one invent? How can one impose some kind of literary form and continuity upon a life and not falsify its meandering or contradictory nature? If one assumes many different guises for any number of different circumstances, how can these be unified into a single, coherent portrait? How does time and the capricious workings of memory disqualify any kind of objective record or account? And most importantly of course, the central enigma touched upon earlier: can one truly know the inside of another human being?

The most disturbing sequence in *The Locked Room* comes in the form of the narrator's brutal sexual encounter with Fanshawe's mother, a perversely literal example of his search for Fanshawe's origins: after all, this is where he came from (*New York*, 264), his actual point of entry to the world. Earlier, when the narrator sleeps with a prostitute who has in turn slept with Fanshawe, he is fascinated by the idea that he is entering the very space where his friend has just been (*New York*, 216). His tryst with Jane Fanshawe is the logical extension of this idea; he finally occupies Fanshawe's space, but at the same time begins to disintegrate, for his friend appears as an absence rather than a presence, a vanishing point rather than centre of thematic density. In a sense, Fanshawe is a blank space which he has tried to fill with his own fantasies, longings and inflated sense of self; but when he finally assumes this role, like Auster's earlier protagonists, he falls into an infinite black hole, a trap-door in language itself. He finally 'becomes' Fanshawe only to discover that he has no idea who Fanshawe actually is. Hence, this vertiginous fall precipitates the narrator's complete mental collapse; to become the author is to become a ghost, the man who isn't there. Or, to put it another way; he is like a reader who becomes so immersed in a book that he begins to think, speak and imagine using another's voice – to the extent that when he puts the book down he no longer recognises his own life, but rather only exists within the pages of his novel. Unlike Auster's other protagonists however, the narrator is permitted deliverance from this fate. Whilst Fanshawe (as author) is condemned to a strange kind of textual purgatory (hidden behind the locked door, he is both there and not there, parallelling the idea of expressing one's self through language), the narrator (as reader) finally abandons his notion of transcendence and is permitted to return to the realm of the real, as denoted by his adopted family. Once again we are faced with a stark dualism between writing and living, words and the real; but if this is the case then we might legitimately ask why Auster writes at all? If writing is a trap, a disappearance, then why write?

'The true purpose of art was not to create beautiful objects, he discovered. It was a method of understanding, a way of penetrating the world and finding one's place in it.'

(*Moon Palace*, 170)

Peter Stillman's mad dream of a perfect language resonates throughout Auster's fiction, providing a corollary to his deepest concerns and themes: language and matter, words and objects, writing and living. In

The Locked Room, Fanshawe's prose begins to attain a transcendent state through his immersion in nature:

> By now Fanshawe's eye had become incredibly sharp, and one senses a new availability of words inside him, as though the distance between seeing and writing has been narrowed, the two acts now almost identical, part of a single unbroken gesture. (*New York*, 277)

Similarly, in *Moon Palace*, the painter Julian Barber produces his masterpiece on the walls of a cave in the middle of Utah, a work which 'internalizes' the endless desert space outside, breaking down any distinction between the thing represented and the act of representation itself. The search for this point of transcendence motivates both texts, but in each case, the moment of final revelation is withdrawn: Barber's cave has been flooded and proves utterly inaccessible, whilst Fanshawe's novel is unreadably obscure. Nevertheless, one key scene recurs again and again in Auster's fiction. For various reasons, the hero of each work is led to describe his physical surroundings in as exhaustive a detail as possible; to describe the shape, texture and essence of the material world, its specifics, peculiarities, and individual forms. As we have seen earlier, this attempt is doomed to failure; language is too blunt a tool to winkle out all the individual characteristics of the world. Nevertheless, this struggle – the attempt to reconcile the inner and outer, the objective and the subjective – is conceived of as a profoundly spiritual enterprise. Through this engagement with apparently neutral matter, a voice emerges, and it is this voice, rather than any notion of perfect correspondence, which lies at the centre of Auster's idea of art. In a sense, the artist is always doomed to failure, as the world will always evade his grasp, but by this struggle – this engagement with the real – artists both make themselves at home in their surroundings (*heimlich*) and give voice to something beyond themselves, something *unheimlich*.

There is a mystical side to all of this, of course, as there was with Thoreau. Both believe that immersion in the real will act as some kind of spiritual purgative; that to describe or represent nature serves a moral purpose, revealing something essential. The distinction here is that while for Thoreau poetry is a matter of bestowing nature with a voice, for Auster the voice is human rather than divine, albeit no less foreign or other.

Near to the conclusion of *The Invention of Solitude*, apparently Auster's most nakedly confessional piece of prose, he makes a startling remark regarding any kind of autobiographical writing. It is impossible for any writer – for any person – to be wholly honest about himself, he admits. One hides, distorts, exaggerates, censors or imposes some kind of pattern or narrative which revises and reworks one's actual experiences. His shift from first to third person narration in the book is thus an attempt to gain some sense of objectivity and critical distance, to sneak up himself, as it were; to treat 'Paul Auster' as a fictional character. 'He speaks of himself as another in order to tell the story of himself,' he avers; 'He must make himself absent in order to find himself there' (*Solitude*, 154). His fictional treatment of this idea in *The New York Trilogy* and *Moon Palace* represents the logical culmination of this line of reasoning. The struggle to describe the world requires all one's skill, imagination, perception and artistry; but at the same time, the realm of real things is made up of a material profoundly separate from one's cognate being, and its description requires a kind of surrender of consciousness, an absorption or forgetting of oneself. 'This was the tiny hole between self and not-self, and for the first time I saw this nowhere as the exact centre of the world' (*New York*, 232), Auster writes; from this 'nowhere' comes a voice which both is and is not his own.

It's hard to think of any other contemporary writer who sees so much at stake in the very act of writing. 'I had slipped through a hole in the world . . . I was falling into a place I had never seen before' states the narrator of *The Locked Room* (*New York*, 203). This conception of art as a profound risk, as a kind of high-wire act (to use one of Auster's favourite analogies) performed in the face of a dizzying loss of self, has thus little to do with Postmodern characteristics of kitsch, parody or apathetic stabs at irony. Nor, despite appearances, does it have much in common with the lexical doctrines of Post-Structuralism and critical theory; indeed, one rather gets the feeling that he would agree with Goethe's famous aphorism, 'theory is grey, but the world is green'. Auster's concerns – with authorship, reading, language and reality – may overlap with the shibboleths of Barthes or DeMan, but his notion of what constitutes literature – what counts as the act of creation – is ultimately very different. Auster's seriousness of moral purpose, his metaphysical (rather than ideological) bent, and stress upon art as an all-or-nothing proposition, links him to the ideals of High Modernism, in particular Kafka (the terrifying loss of the self),

Beckett (nothingness and matter), and Mallarmé (the search for some divine poetic tongue). As Charles Baxter has noted, Auster 'combines an American obsession with gaining an identity with the European ability to ask how, and under what circumstances, identity is stolen or lost.'[29] In the European tradition, the loss of selfhood is experienced as a terrible fall, 'seasickness on dry land'(to borrow Kafka's phrase), a vertiginous loss of moorings. America, however, is founded upon the idea of a new beginning, abandoning one's own skin (with all its markings of class, place and caste) and becoming someone else; these two possibilities map out the existential boundaries of Auster's terrain, which are brought together through his concentration upon the act of writing.

I would like to end this discussion with one more disquieting example drawn from Auster's 'real' life. By his own account, 1978 was a particularly bleak year. His marriage was disintegrating, his money situation desperately tight, and Auster found himself virtually unable to write, the sources of his poetry drying up whilst he felt increasingly dissatisfied with his experiments in prose:

> Then, in December of 1978, I happened to go to an open rehearsal of a dance piece choreographed by the friend of a friend, and something happened to me. A revelation, an epiphany – I don't know what to call it . . . The simple fact of watching men and women moving through space filled me with something close to euphoria. The very next day, I sat down and started writing *White Spaces* . . . which was an attempt on my part to translate the experience of that dance performance into words. It was a liberation for me, a tremendous letting go . . . everything was going to be different now. A whole new period of my life was about to begin. (*Red Notebook*, 132)

By trying to write about physical things – the movement of bodies in space, and nothing more – Auster seemed to break free from the crippling introspection which had dogged his relentlessly personal, private prose. By taking himself out of the frame – by immersing himself in concrete, sensory appreciation – he discovered a new form of literary lightness and freedom, an airy release from the 'clenched fist' of his buttoned-down intellectualism. He completed the piece and then realised that he had written it using a voice he had never heard before, the source of this inspiration an utter mystery. This 'was the piece that convinced me I still had it in me to be a writer' he notes (*Red Notebook*, 132), and he completed the strange prose-poem in a state of near-delirium. The very next day, however, he was awoken by a call from his uncle. His father had died during the night, an event which, by way of an unexpected inheritance, would allow Auster to continue to write. 'It's a terrible equation,' admits Auster. 'To think that my father's death saved my life' (*Red Notebook*, 132).

But coincidence and synchronicity run even deeper than this. Why did Auster feel 'haunted' by another's voice? Why the strange out-of-body experience produced by writings about bodies in space? Why the literal conception of art as a matter of life or death? There are, of course, intimations of the numinous and the supernatural here, as if somehow Auster's 'new' life is at the expense of his father's, his literary leap into the dark possessing mortal consequences; but what I want to underline here is just how far we have moved from Structuralist ideas of language; how much closer we seem to old-fashioned ideas of transcendence and the sublime. For the nineteenth-century Transcendentalists, Nature (with a capital 'N') was central to the mysteries of artistic inspiration. By struggling to represent it, to capture its form in words, one engaged with fundamental things, with the gap between the objective world and one's subjective perception, defining oneself through what one was not. Freud's model of infantile consciousness concurs with this; the child learns of its true shape through its encounter with external forces, determines its outline through otherness. But in both cases, the longing for transcendence remains. Thoreau believed that if he immersed himself in the elemental, if he finally succeeded in erasing himself from the picture, then Nature itself would speak, and he would act as oracle or messenger. Auster shifts this idea to language, but the terms remain the same – the struggle to describe the world (a struggle which takes precedence over Stillman's idea of perfect success), and also intimations of 'an impossible totality' (*Red Notebook*, 54), a haunted inner landscape in which the writer loses any sense of self. Through writing one can both define oneself and disappear. Self-expression and self-transcendence are linked.

One of the great ideals of Modern Art was to break down the distinction between art and life, to make one's life a living poem. In turn-of-the-century Paris and Prague this took the form of Poeticism, and its ideals underpin both Dada and Surrealism. How to make one's very existence a work of art, to carry over the revolutionary energies of artistic invention into one's actual day to day experiences? Whilst Auster frequently positions 'living' and 'writing' as mutually exclusive categories, this idealistic notion survives intact in his work. Literature carries within itself the capability both to make and unmake our relation with the world and our deepest understanding of self. Language in his works becomes the medium by which we can both find and lose ourselves, a fluid medium, whereby the thinking 'I' is subject to a bewildering series of transformations. Reading and writing are ways of becoming someone else – an idea which is both liberating and terrifying.

Perhaps the greatest achievement of Auster's art, then, is to make us feel the importance and possibility of literature. Both when we read and when we write, our cognate 'I' becomes untethered, our sense of self dissipates. Although this eerie dispossession may be temporary, dependent on our continuing to turn the pages of our book, its implications carry over into our 'real' life. Whilst Structuralism avows the absolute separation between the linguistic and the real, Auster's art is founded upon its profound interconnection, the way in which fiction spills out into the real world, and the ways in which the self can be rewritten. For Auster the act of writing is all or nothing, a state of constant transformation which carries with it terrible risks – to one's sanity, one's solidity, to one's very sense of self. And this in turn matters because he simultaneously extends this sense of risk to the reader. As he wrote of the poet Pierre Reverdy, 'the result is at once beautiful and disquieting – as if [the poet] . . . had emptied the space of the poem in order to let the reader inhabit it' (*Red Notebook*, 54).

NOTES

1. Abbreviations and page references refer to the following editions of Auster's work: *Solitude* (*The Invention of Solitude*, London: Faber (1988), *New York* (*The New York Trilogy*, London: Faber (1988), *Moon Palace* (*Moon Palace* London: Faber 1990), *Red Notebook* (*The Red Notebook*, London: Faber, 1996), *Hand to Mouth* (*Hand to Mouth*, London: Faber, 1998).
2. William H. Gass, quoted by Arthur Saltzman, *The Fiction of William H. Gass: The Consolation of Language* (1986), Carbondale and Edwardsville: Southern Illinois University Press, p. 46.

3. George Steiner (1972), *Extra-territorial*, London: Faber, p. 65.
4. John Zilcosky (1998), 'The revenge of the author: Paul Auster's challenge to theory', *Critique*, Spring, 39 (3), p. 199.
5. Anthony Vidler (1992), *The Architectural Uncanny*, London: M.I.T. Press, p. 3.
6. See Steven E. Alford (1996), 'Mirrors of madness: Paul Auster's *The New York Trilogy*', *Critique* 37 (1), Spring, pp. 16–32, and William G. Little (1997), 'Nothing to go on: Paul Auster's *City of Glass*, *Contemporary Literature*, 38 (1), Spring, pp. 133–63.
7. Jorge Luis Borges, quoted by Sean Burke (1995), *Authorship: From Plato to the Postmodern*, Edinburgh: University of Edinburgh Press, p. 339.
8. Ibid.
9. Roland Barthes, ibid., p. 125.
10. Charles Baxter (1994), 'The bureau of missing persons: notes on Paul Auster's fiction', *Review of Contemporary Fiction*, 14 (1), Spring, p. 40.
11. See Steven Cassedy (1990), *Flight from Eden*, Los Angeles: University of California Press, p. 22.
12. Ludwig Wittgenstein, quoted in Steiner, p. 79.
13. Robert Scholes (1993), 'Tiön and Truth', in George Levine (ed.), *Realism and Representation*, Madison: University of Wisconsin Press, p. 182.
14. Pascale-Anne Brault (1998), 'Translating the impossible debt: Paul Auster's *City of Glass*', *Critique*, 39 (3), Spring, p. 230.
15. Nicholas Dawson, 'An examination of author and character and their relationship within the narrative structure of Paul Auster's *New York Trilogy*', http.//bluecricket.com/auster/articles/dawson.html, p. 3.
16. Chris Tysh (1994), 'From one mirror to another: the rhetoric of disaffiliation in *City of Glass*', *Review of Contemporary Fiction*, 14 (1), Spring, p. 50.
17. Chris Pace, 'Escaping from *The Locked Room*: overthrowing the tyranny of artifice in Paul Auster's *New York Trilogy*', htp.//www.bluecricket.com/auster/articles/thesis.html, p. 3.
18. Ibid., p. 21.
19. See Robert Scholes in Levine, pp. 171–86.
20. Richard Rorty, ibid., p. 189.
21. The *Zaumnik* movement was founded in the Soviet Union by Khlebnikov and Shklovsky in 1913, and intended to create a new language possessing no gap between the sound used and the thing described. The result was a strange kind of speaking in tongues where the sound 'k' suggested violence and death, 'v' meant to take away, 's' to move and so on. Needless to say, the cacophonous results (which involved much hawking and snarling) didn't really catch on.
22. Rorty in Levine, p. 189.

23. Henry David Thoreau, quoted by Mark Ford (1999), 'Inventions of soli-
    tude: Thoreau and Auster', *Journal of American Studies*, 33 (2), p. 218.
24. Ford, ibid., p. 205.
25. Georges Poulet, quoted by Burke, p. 104.
26. Ibid., p. 105.
27. Thoreau, quoted by Ford, p. 218.
28. Gustave Flaubert, quoted by Burke, p. xxiii.
29. Baxter, p. 48.

BIOGRAPHY

Auster was born on 3 February 1947 to Jewish, middle-class parents (his father a landlord) in Newark, New Jersey. His early home-life was difficult: his parents' marriage was deeply unhappy, his father emotionally distant and his younger sister prone to debilitating mental attacks. Auster's parents divorced as he graduated from high-school, and thereafter he attended Columbia University, whilst also travelling for extended periods in Europe, in particular Paris. After his university graduation in 1969, Auster began early drafts of what would eventually become *In the Country of Last Things* (1987) and *Moon Palace* (1989), as well as writing essays and poetry. He supported himself as best he could with various occupations, the most demanding being a stint aboard the *Esso Florence*, a tanker sailing around the Gulf of Mexico.

In 1971, Auster settled again in Paris and eked out a precarious existence, primarily as a translator; transposing the North Vietnamese Constitution into French proved to be one of the more bizarre commissions. In 1974 he married Lydia Davis (also a writer) and desperately short on funds, they settled back in the USA, ultimately in New York. He published two poetry collections in 1975 (their titles, *Wall Writings* and *Disappearances* prescient of his later work), as well as contributing reviews to the *New York Review of Books*, *Commentary* and elsewhere. Despite a number of grants and awards, money remained tight, and the birth of Auster's son coincided with the low-point of his financial situation.

After a disastrous performance of his 1977 play *Laurel and Hardy Go to Heaven* (elements of which are recycled in *The Music of Chance*) Auster found himself unable to write and turned to increasingly desperate schemes to make money. The dismal failure of his Baseball cardgame is related in his memoir, *Hand to Mouth*, and although he recovered from his bout of writer's block to complete an unremarkable crime-novel, *Squeeze-Play* in 1978, his marriage was disintegrating.

Auster seemed to resolve his crisis of confidence with the writing of *White*

Spaces, an elliptical essay on art, which he wrote in 1979. The day after completing it, he learnt that his father had died, bequeathing him a small inheritance which was instrumental in allowing him to continue to write. By the spring of 1979 Auster had moved out to a bleak one-room apartment at 6 Varick Street, Manhattan, a location (and dismal existence) which recurs throughout his work. Here he worked on translations of Mallarmé and Beckett, and completed *The Invention of Solitude* (1982), an autobiographical meditation on the nature of solitide and the death of his father.

In 1980 he met Siri Hustvedt, who would become his second wife. *City of Glass*, the first part of what would become *The New York Trilogy* (1987) is in part a homage to Hustvedt, an examination of Auster's possible fate if he had failed to meet her. Although an 'anti-detective' novel, it was perversely nominated for an Edgar award by the Mystery Writers of America in 1985. The completed trilogy was rejected by seventeen publishers before coming out of a small firm, Sun & Moon Press, in Los Angeles. After this, Auster abandoned poetry and devoted himself to prose. Excellent reviews saw the trilogy reprinted as a single-volume and the acquisition of a contract with Viking.

Although he lectured at Princeton from 1987 to 90, Auster was now able to support himself wholly by writing. In the mid-'90s, however, he increasingly turned to film-work, writing and co-directing (with Wayne Wang) *Smoke* (1995) an adaptation of perhaps his most famous short-story, *Auggie Wren's Christmas Story*, which had been published in the *New York Times* Op-Ed page on Christmas Day, 1990. With the film completed under schedule, Wang and Auster also shot *Blue in the Face* (1995), an improvised companion-piece set in the same Brooklyn cigar shop as the previous film. His first film as solo director – *Lulu on the Bridge* (1998) – reunited Auster with Harvey Keitel, but failed to procure a distributor in the UK. His return to fiction was marked by *Timbuktu* (1999). Most recently he has edited a collection of 180 short narratives submitted to the National Story Project as *I Thought my Father was God*, published in Britain as *True Tales of American Life* (2001).

AUSTER ON AUSTER

The astonishing thing, I think, is that at the moment when you are most truly alone, when you truly enter a state of solitide, that is the moment when you are not alone anymore, when you start to feel your connection with others. I believe I even quote Rimbaud . . .'Je est un autre' – I is another – and I take that sentence quite literally. In the process of writing or thinking about yourself, you actually become someone else.

(On coincidence and blind chance) As a writer of novels, I feel morally obliged to incorporate such events into my books, to write about the world as I experience it – not as someone else tells me it's supposed to be. The unknown is rushing in on top of us at every moment. As I see it, my job is to keep myself open to these collisions, to watch out for all these mysterious goings-on in the world.

No one can say where a book comes from, least of all the person who writes it. Books are born out of ignorance, and if they go on living after they are written, it's only to the degree that they cannot be understood.

LINKS TO OTHER AUTHORS

Don DeLillo: Stillman's search for a purer form of language, rooted in physical things, finds any number of echoes in DeLillo's work – most especially *Americana*, *End Zone* and *The Names*. Auster's *Leviathan* (1992) is dedicated to DeLillo, and its examination of the political role of the writer provides an interesting parallel-text to *Mao II*, written around the same period.

Cormac McCarthy: Marco Fogg's journey west in *Moon Palace* is concerned with the struggle to represent the emptiness of the desert, as is McCarthy's *Blood Meridian* (1985). McCarthy's exploration of entropy and the decay of matter can be compared to Auster's treatment of the same theme in *In the Country of Last Things*.

Rolando Hinojosa: Both authors explore identity in terms of borders, frontiers, and linguistic space.

E. Annie Proulx: Both Auster and Proulx see themselves as realists, but do so in a manner which questions our very understanding of the term.

Bret Easton Ellis: Manacing father-figures – and the return of some kind of patriarchal law or revenge – recur in both writers' work.

Douglas Coupland: *The New York Trilogy* and *Moon Palace* are concerned with the stripping away of public identity in search of the essential, a theme central to Coupland. Both writers employ the American archetype of the wilderness to this end.

Thomas Pynchon: The question of whether there are secret patterns, shapes and maps hidden in the world – or whether this is all a paranoid delusion – connects *The New York Trilogy* to the world of Pynchon, especially his 'detective' novel, *The Crying of Lot 49* (1966).

BIBLIOGRAPHY

The Invention of Solitude (1982), Los Angeles: Sun & Moon Press.
Squeeze-Play (1982), London: Alpha-Omega, (as Paul Benjamin).
The New York Trilogy (1987), London: Faber.
In the Country of Last Things (1987), New York: Viking Penguin.
Moon Palace (1989), New York: Viking Penguin.
Groundwork (1990), London: Faber, (essays and poetry).
The Music of Chance (1990), New York: Viking Penguin.
Leviathan (1992), New York: Viking.
The Art of Hunger (1992), Los Angeles: Sun & Moon Press (essays).
Mr Vertigo (1994), New York: Viking.
The Red Notebook (1995), London: Faber (essays and interviews).
Smoke/Blue in the Face (1995), Los Angeles: Talk Miramax Books (screenplays).
Hand to Mouth (1997), New York: Henry Holt (memoir).
Lulu on the Bridge (1998), New York: Owl Books (screenplay).
Timbuktu (1999), New York: Henry Holt.
I Thought my Father was God (2001), New York: Henry Holt (editor, published in the UK as *True Tales of American Life* (2001), London: Faber).

Critical Sources
Alford, Steven (1995), 'Spaced-out: signification and space in Paul Auster's *The New York Trilogy*', *Contemporary Literature*, 36 (4), Winter, pp. 613–31.
—(1995) 'Mirrors of madness: Paul Auster's *The New York Trilogy*', *Critique*, 37 (1), pp. 16–32.
Alsen, Eberhard (1997), *Romantic Postmodernism in American Fiction*, New York: Rodopi.
Barone, Denis (ed.) (1995), *Beyond the Red Notebook: Essays on Paul Auster*, Philadelphia: University of Pennsylvania Press.
Baxter, Charles (1994), 'The bureau of missing persons: notes on Paul Auster's fiction', *Review of Contemporary Fiction*, 14 (1), Spring, pp. 40–3.
Birkets, Sven (1992), *American Energies: Essays on Fiction*, New York: William Morrow.
— (1994), 'Reality, fiction and *In the Country of Last Things*', *Review of Contemporary Fiction*, 14 (1), Spring, pp. 66–9.
Brault, Pascale-Anne (1998), 'Translating the impossible debt: Paul Auster's *City of Glass*', *Critique*, 39 (3), Spring, pp. 228–38.

Bray, Paul (1994), The currents of fate and *The Music of Chance'*, *Review of Contemporary Fiction*, 14 (1), Spring, pp. 83–6.

Brooker, Peter (1996), *New York Fictions*, London: Longman.

Dawson, Nicholas, 'An examination of author and character and their relationship within the narrative structure of Paul Auster's *New York Trilogy'*. http.//bluecricket.com/auster/articles/dawson.html

Dotan, E. (2000), 'The game of late capitalism: gambling and ideology in *The Music of Chance'*, *Mosaic* 33 (1), March, pp. 161–76.

Dow, William (1998), 'Paul Auster's *The Invention of Solitude*: glimmers in a reach to authenticity', *Critique*, 39 (3), Spring, pp. 272–81.

Drentell, William (1994), *Paul Auster: A Comprehensive Bibliographic Checklist of Published Works 1968–1994*, New York: William Drentell.

Fleck, Linda (1998), 'From metonymy to metaphor: Paul Auster's *Leviathan'*, *Critique*, 39 (3), Spring, pp. 258–70.

Ford, Mark (1999), 'Inventions of solitude: Thoreau and Auster', *Journal of American Studies*, 33 (2), pp. 201–19.

Henriksen, M. F. (1999), 'An art of desire: reading Paul Auster', *American Studies in Scandinavia* 31 (2), pp. 80–2.

Irwin, Mark (1994), 'Inventing *The Music of Chance'*, *Review of Contemporary Fiction*, 14 (1), Spring, pp. 80–2.

—(1994), 'Memory escape: inventing *The Music of Chance* – a conversation with Paul Auster', *Denver Quarterly*, 28 (3), pp. 111–22.

Jarvis, Brian (1998), *Postmodern Cartographies*, London: Pluto.

Lavender, William (1993), 'The novel of critical engagement: Paul Auster's *City of Glass'*, *Contemporary Literature*, 34 (2), Summer, pp. 219–39.

Lewis, Barry (1994), 'The strange case of Paul Auster', *Review of Contemporary Fiction*, 14 (1), Spring, pp. 53–61.

Little, William (1997), 'Nothing to go on: Paul Auster's *City of Glass'*, *Contemporary Literature*, 38 (1), Spring, pp. 133–63.

Mackenzie, Suzie (1999), 'The searcher', *The Guardian*, 29 May.

Millard, Kenneth (2000), *Contemporary American Fiction*, Oxford: Oxford Oxford University Press.

Nealon, Jeffrey (1996), 'Work of the detective, work of the writer: Paul Auster's *City of Glass'*, *Modern Fiction Studies*, 42 (1), Spring, pp. 91–110.

Nikolic, Dragana, 'Paul Auster's Postmodernist fiction: deconstructing Aristotle's 'Poetics', http.//www.bluecricket.com/auster/articles/aristotle.html

Osteen, Mark (1994), 'Phantoms of liberty: the secret lives of *Leviathan'*, *Review of Contemporary Fiction*, 14 (1), Spring, pp. 87–91.

Pace, Chris. 'Escaping from *The Locked Room*: overthrowing the tyranny of artifice in Paul Auster's *New York Trilogy'*, http.//www.bluecricket.com/auster/articles/aristotle.html

Rowen, Norma (1991), 'The detective in search of the lost tongue of Adam: Auster's *City of Glass*', *Critique*, 34 (2), Summer, pp. 224–34.

Russell, Alison (1990), 'Deconstructing *The New York Trilogy*: Paul Auster's anti-detective fiction', *Critique*, 31 (3), Winter, pp. 71–84.

Saltzman, Arthur (1990), *Designs of Darkness in Contemporary American Fiction*, Philadelphia: University of Pennsylvania Press.

Segal, Alex (1998), 'Secrecy and the gift: Paul Auster's *The Locked Room*', *Critique* , 39 (3), Spring, pp. 239–57.

Springer, Carsten (2001), *A Paul Auster Sourcebook*, Frankfurt: Peter Lang.

Swope, Richard (1998), 'Approaching the threshold(s) in Postmodern detective fiction: Hawthorne's 'Wakefield' and other missing persons', *Critique*, 39 (3), Spring, pp. 207–27.

Tysh, Chris (1994), 'From one mirror to another: the rhetoric of dissaffiliation in *City of Glass*', *Review of Contemporary Fiction*, 14 (1), Spring, pp. 46–51.

Washburn, Katherine (1994), 'A book at the end of the world', *Review of Fiction*, 14 (1), Spring, pp. 62–9.

Wesselling, Elizabeth (1991), '*In the Country of Last Things*: Paul Auster's parable of the Apocalypse', *Neophilologus*, 75 (4), October, pp. 496–504.

Weisenburger, Steven (1994), 'Inside *Moon Palace*', *Review of Contemporary Fiction*, 14 (1), Spring, pp. 70–9.

Zeta, Alfa, 'Paul Auster's urban nothingness', http.//www.bluecricket.com/auster/articles/aristotle.html

Zilcosky, John (1998), 'The revenge of the author: Paul Auster's challenge to theory', *Critique*, 39 (3), Spring, pp. 195–205.

Useful Websites
http.//www.paulauster.co.uk/body.html
http.//www.bluecricket.com/auster/auster.html
http.//www.ils.unc.edu/~gards/pathfinder.html

CORMAC McCARTHY[1]

What is America? Land, scale, *space*. When America's most famous landscape painter, Thomas Cole, set up his easel high above the Hudson river in the Catskill Mountains in the 1820s, he committed to canvas one of the great iconic images of the American Sublime: a terrible, limitless sky somehow combining fire and air, the ferocious savagery of the awesome Kaaterskill Falls, the vast, untouched (and untouchable) forest-wilderness, boundless, limitless, as wild and infinite as the heavens above.[2] And hidden amongst it, a lone Mohican, the very embodiment of the land, composed of the same savage matter as the earth around him. Cole's painterly genius is at its greatest here. Somehow the figure is in a state of perpetual vanishing, reabsorbed into the divine brushwork, until only the shadow of his shadow is left behind. In retrospect however, the Indian wasn't the only thing to have been studiously removed from the picture. By 1820 the Catskills was already a busy tourist destination, particularly popular with wealthy vacationers from New York. On closer inspection, Cole had also eliminated the central viewing platform, the hand-rails, the steps, and the crowds. This specific view of the Kaaterskill Falls was already famous before Cole's painting but afterwards it became immortalised as the sight to see, the spectacle one had to consume. And if nature couldn't live up to its copy then imagination provided the rest; many sight-seers swore that they had glimpsed Cole's timeless Indian, his ghostlike trace a kind of tourist attraction in itself.

The notion of mythic America as a wilderness continent, uncontaminated by history, is of course a paradoxical one. This untouched virgin land was occupied by around eight million inhabitants with complex social, religious and economic practices when Europeans first started to inscribe this 'blank page' of unvarnished nature. Moreover, the act of subduing the land carried with it unforeseen circumstances. If American heroism and moral fibre was a direct result of this engagement with

wild and savage forces (allowing no space for moral laxity, self-centredness or indulgence) then what would come to pass when the battle
was done? After all, the American hero needed a sense of Otherness
to define himself in opposition to; without this space civilisation might
fall into the same patterns of corruption and licence as back in Europe.
The tragedy of the American Adam is that he kills the very thing he
loves. He tames the barbaric country, breaks in the wild stallion, drives
fences and boundaries into the free earth. Ultimately, the Western
genre is elegiac because its creation exhausts its own materials; the
very act of representation disqualifies any notion of an untouched
land, like boot-prints in the snow.

In Cole's painting, the Native embodiment of the land is already
fading: now you see him, now you don't. By the time of his successor,
Fredrick Edwin Church, painting only a matter of some thirty years
later, the entire landscape seemed to exist in the past tense. Hence
the iconic title 'Twilight in the Wilderness' (1860); his portentous
landscapes are heavy with a sense of their own passing, the 'real' land
turning into a kind of elemental afterlife, always at the point of its own
demise. Once we have arrived at the slick draughtsmanship of Albert
Bierstadt, the West seems already a copy of itself, his much sought-
after canvases adorning the walls of railroad barons and logging firms,
the very agencies disfiguring the land forever. What then remains?

Modern Artists were forced to construct their own wildernesses,
whether in terms of Arthur Dove's abstract landscape of the soul or
Jackson Pollock's paint-spattered relief maps. In terms of Postmodernism, contemporary America's soul seems to reside in the parking lot
and gift-shop rather than in the sublime prototype of nature. Indeed,
in many ways, this is one of the central tenets of our times. We live,
argue the Postmodernists, in a world which is absolutely artificial. The
passage of the seasons has been displaced by the symbols of the TV
weathercast. Chemically-enhanced gardening is the closest one gets
to toiling with the land. Space is a matter of freeways and service-
stations, the scene outside our windscreen oddly weightless and
detached. And when we arrive at the tourist site? We want the 'sight'
to be the one we've already seen in the brochure, the real to conform
to the image. No wonder we feel so disappointed. The new 'sublime'
is the vision of the screen or terminal and brute matter simply cannot
compete. What isn't commercialised, mediated, dirty with our fingerprints? Our reality is air-brushed, air-conditioned, packaged and labelled

for our convenience; the fad for 'cowboy' ranching holidays or dangerous sports merely makes the absence of the real even more apparent.

All of this is, of course, extremely problematic for the myth of the American wilderness. For Thomas Cole, the terrain was the literal fingerprint of God, imbued with what de Tocqueville called 'a kind of religious terror'; the romantic sublime was what was utterly beyond us, untouched by man, unfashioned by his (sic) hands. It called for a response of exalted awe, a humble acknowledgement of forces beyond anything which man could hope to copy. But for Postmodernism, the copy is better than the original – better facilities, better merchandise, better on-site parking. Everything is manmade; nature has been institutionalised into National Parks, great museums of the sublime, labelled, preserved, tended. Who still believes in a Nature with a capital 'N'? The history of the landscape is a story of ownership, exploitation and domination – and Cole's pious tourism plays its part in this. After all, doesn't Cole's elision of the human element suggest there never was such a thing as unmediated space? And don't we want our reality to be better than the real anyway?

What then are we to make of a writer like Cormac McCarthy, a contemporary writer whose central subject is 'the wildness about him, the wildness within' (Horses, 60), who struggles with the great themes of Nature, Man and God, and who employs the most American archetypes – the frontier, here transmogrified into the border – in order to do so? One response would be to label his work as pastiche, no matter what McCarthy himself might intend. After all, how can one write an 'innocent' Western free of cultural preconceptions, assumptions and clichés? According to this argument, no matter how meticulously detailed or physically redolent are McCarthy's descriptions of the US–Mexico border, the reader will always substitute stock footage of Monument Valley, generic images of the Wild West, and stock cowboy 'types' summoned up from central casting. The title of Michael Coyne's recent study of the Western – The Crowded Prairie (1998) – in a sense sums up the problem. Far from being a virgin environment, it is hard to think of a more exhausted setting than the Wild West, parodied (in Ishmael Reed's Yellow Back Radio Broke-Down (1969)), subverted (in Thomas Berger's Little Big Man (1970), deconstructed (in E. L. Doctorow's Welcome to Hard Times (1960), and mourned in its passing by any number of cultural elegists from Larry McMurtry to Thomas

McGuane. Politically too, the Western paradigm now seems as reactionary as John Wayne's conservatism.

The notion of Manifest Destiny – America's sacred duty to subdue the savage wilderness, to bring civilisation to the primitive, so as to confirm the destiny of the human race – is seen by revisionist historians as aggressive imperialist expansion, accompanied by genocide and exploitation on a vast scale. And this critique in turn undoes the whole paradigm of the frontier, predicated as it is on a series of traditional oppositions: man/nature, civilisation/savagery, farm/wilderness and so on. The frontier requires a sense of otherness, and in terms of the traditional Western, this is a specifically racial otherness, whether in positive terms (the Native American's mystical union with the land) or a negative demonising. Instead, contemporary cultural critics, as we shall see in the chapter on Rolando Hinojosa, explore border regions in terms of heterogeneity, an impure mixing of historical and cultural traditions.

McCarthy's border, however, always looks out onto the unknown, his heroes defined by their encounters with implacable and utterly alien forces, wholly outside of them. In a sense, McCarthy takes us back to the grandiose metaphysics of Thomas Cole's canvases, whereby the topography of the land appears as the very inscription of God; in McCarthy we may have the suspicion that we are trapped in Hell instead, but the metaphysical grounding remains the same. We are dealing with what is beyond us, what is implacably inhuman; an awful (in every sense of the word) notion of the sublime.

So how does a contemporary novelist approach this idea of an awful, numinous Nature? The first stumbling block seems to be the problem of authenticity. Even in 1823, Cole had to paint out carefully any intrusive traces of rubbernecking tourists; for McCarthy, the wilderness must either be placed in a specific historic context (the 1840s in *Blood Meridian* (1985)) or else signified by its passing (or at least shifting south of the border) as is the case within the Border trilogy. Moreover, many of Cole's most famous paintings are imaginative transpositions of specifically literary scenes – most especially from the work of James Fenimore Cooper. McCarthy is working in such a well-worn American groove, that critics have been given free rein to attribute any number of literary sources, from Faulkner's rolling, free-range sentences to Hemingway's terse, matter-of-fact practicality to

Melville's cosmic preachifying. Is McCarthy thus once again trapped by the Postmodern curse of the already said, the inescapable repetition of used-up formulas and conventions? McCarthy's occasionally archaic diction and unfashionable religiosity runs the risk of plagiarising an earlier literary canon. Can we discriminate between a copy of the Great American Novel and the real thing?

A second problem can be approached through issues of representation. If McCarthy wishes to express a sense of the unutterably foreign, the sense of 'another world entire' (*Crossing*, 4) then how does he go about defamiliarising the desert's well-worn scenery and props? Visitors to the actual locations of the American West can be forgiven a sense of déja-vu. Who hasn't been here before, albeit vicariously via the films of John Ford or the novels of Zane Grey? And how can one capture a sense of the utterly foreign, extraterritorial nature of the landscape in words? In order to be communicated, the numinous landscape has to be cut down to size, reduced to sentences and descriptive phrases, consumed by the reader. How then to restore any kind of innocence of perception? How to defamiliarise the landscape?

And yet McCarthy's sense of place *is* strange and disconcerting, even when his plotting is at its most conventional. His most easily-read work, *All the Pretty Horses* (1992), the first volume of the Border trilogy, is set in a 'West' (actually the US–Mexican border) which confounds our topographical and even perceptual expectations.

As suggested earlier, the Old West in the novel is initially signposted by its absence, the modern setting (1949) inimical to any kind of acting out of the traditional cowboy yarn. In this sense, the death of John Grady Cole's grandfather and the sale of the family ranch signposts the demise of the ways of the Old West. The meek have now inherited the world – lawyers, accountants, pen-pushing corporations – and what is stressed over and over again in the opening sections of the novel is a loss of masculine potency. Grady's father is ineffectual, defeated, dying of cancer and unwilling to contest the stock-clearing of an older, more 'grounded' way of life. Instead, the deeds to the farm reside with Grady's mother, and femininity unavoidably suggests here modern consumerism and the breakdown of traditional roles and ways of life. Grady's mother is an actress, denoting to the puritan mind falsity, artifice and frivolity. Her son attends her play in the belief 'that there would be something in the story itself to tell him about the way the world was or was becoming but there was not. There was nothing in it at all' (*Horses*, 21). The stage is inauthentic, unreal – and questions of authenticity are central to McCarthy's prose. The reader may well be sympathetic to the mother's desperate need to escape the farmstead in search of 'a little more social life' (*Horses*, 17), but womanhood is portrayed through Cole's eyes as something essentially capricious and untrustworthy. Even Grady's girlfriend abandons him, depressed by his refusal to drive a car and uninterested in his stubborn allegiance to an older masculine code of behaviour. When they part, John Grady Cole turns his back on the girl's reflection in the Federal Building's glass façade and 'stepped out of the glass forever' (*Horses*, 29) saddling up in search of 'the real'; her image is false, duplicitous, a symbol of meretricious modernity, and the first of a number of false reflections which will determine the course of the trilogy.

But what does Grady actually mean by the real? In a sense, his vaguely articulated sense of the Old West is as ersatz as anything else. As Grady and his buddy Rawlins head toward the Mexican border there is an inescapable sense of role-playing, an acting out of an adolescent fantasy of irresponsibility and freedom. Their jokes and banter suggest the kind of ironic self-awareness which threatens to turn their self-conscious 'adventure' into a kind of self-parody. When they encounter a third boy on the way, they ham it up as bank-robbers lighting out for Mexico ('I always wanted to be a badman' admits Rawlins later, purchasing a pair of iconic black boots (*Horses*, 121) and the boy's response is profoundly ambivalent: 'You all just funnin', said the boy (*Horses*, 41)). When the kid, Blevins, starts to eulogise about the good old days of the Wild West, Cody's put-down in a sense applies to the whole gang, not one of whom is older than sixteen; 'What in the putrified dogshit would you know about the old days?' (*Horses*, 57). So far, so Postmodern (or 'ten pounds of shit in a five pound sack' as Rawlins puts it (*Horses*, 49)).

Throughout the early part of the novel generic expectations are subverted so as to stress their comic misplacement. It is as if the boys have turned up on the wrong set, their Stetsons the wrong size, their costumes too big. They know that they are playing to an imagined audience ('What do you reckon they're saying at home about now?' (*Horses*, 51), but the modern staging keeps getting in the way. They warily stay clear of state highways, are constantly confronted by electric fences and barbed wire, feed their mounts oatmeal from discarded hubcaps: 'How the hell do they expect a man to ride a horse in this country? said Rawlins. They dont, said John Grady' (*Horses*, 31).

The detritus of civilisation smothers everything, the desert here less wilderness than trackless dump. The reader may thus be led into characterising the book as a kind of anti-Western, stressing how inappropriate the form appears when juxtaposed with the reality of modern America. But the closer the band get to Mexico, the less parodic the tone becomes. Another myth is being set up here: Mexico as inherently atavistic, a kind of historical regression to the lawlessness (but also freedom) of the Old West, a land, primitive, violent, elementally present. At times McCarthy punctures this myth too; as Peter Messant has pointed out, the first person the group encounters in Mexico is a girl reading an American comic-book, and the text is full of Mexicans dreaming of America.[3] But more frequently, McCarthy's mythical border appears disconcertingly literal. The boys cross the river into Mexico naked and are thereby baptised into the sphere of the real, the corporeal or bodily: they have crossed the line from the realm of images to the realm of matter.

It is in his description of the natural world that McCarthy feels most Modernist and if one were looking for painterly comparisons, then Cézanne might be a better choice than Thomas Cole. McCarthy's concentration is upon 'the earth and the eye beholding it' (*Horses*, 225), stressing perception as an active rather than a passive process, the landscape never something to be taken in (or consumed) in a single gaze, but rather struggled with, fought over, engaged. Rather than intoxicatingly beautiful, McCarthy's descriptions are linguistically thorny, typographically difficult and occasionally utterly intractable. He constantly shifts his focus from the microscopic to the cosmic, defamiliarises specifics through unfamiliar diction, and leans heavily upon similes which seem at first to yoke together wholly separate qualities, forcing us to follow the winding sentences like half-hidden tracks across the page:

> He rode on, the two horses following, riding doves up out of the pools of standing water and the sun descending out of the dark discolored overcast to the west where its redness ran down the narrow band of sky above the mountains like blood falling through water and the desert fresh from the rain turning gold in

the evening light and then deepening to dark, a slow inkening over of the bajada and the rising hills and the stark stone length of the cordilleras darkening far to the south in Mexico. (*Horses*, 286)

Such passages are not read, but traversed. We are left with a sense of a writer actively at work, wrestling with notions of depiction, refusing to accept the notion of a 'view' as a given. McCarthy's is not the passive tourist's gaze – rather we are presented a jagged assemblage of shadows, rocks, tracks and muddied holes which must be endlessly, even laboriously, navigated. Indeed, for all the apocalyptic sunsets which imbue McCarthy's novels, the main constituents of his landscape are mud, dust and bone, an ashen, etiolated formlessness. Everything seems preternaturally weathered, faded, bleached, shrouded in spectral dust or lumped together from unpigmented earth. This is the base material of matter, huge daubs of darkness and soil, less mimetic (drawing attention to an immediately apprehensible outside world) than almost abstractly physical; to continue our painterly analogy, one senses the weight and tactile mass of McCarthy's brushstrokes, is left with an impression of base materials and unfashioned clay. The prose thus plays with notions of presence and absence; McCarthy stresses again and again the 'formless emptiness' (*Horses*, 256) of the landscape, its utter barrenness, its strange property of tangible 'nothingness' (*Horses*, 57). The infinite darkness above shades into the endless greyness below. Everything, from the pale, spectral riders to the looming patterns of shale and scree, seems composed from dust mixed with rain, perpetually destroyed and recombined in strange, distorted shapes.

As with DeLillo's prose, there is a constant tension between geographic specifics (San Angelo and San Antonio, Langtry and Pumpville, Coahuila and Zacatecas) and a sense of timeless abstraction, McCarthy's prose obsessively reiterating that from dust man came, and to dust he will return. 'It's just dark and dark and then more of it,' writes McCarthy in *The Crossing* (1994) (249), and this sense of non-existence and nullity suggests a cosmology very different to Thomas Cole's interpretation of the physical hieroglyphics of God. Frequently the only signs which disturb or imprint the empty plains are the bones and ruins of the dead, and it is this connection between mortality and landscape which can be used to illuminate McCarthy's awful representations of the real.

The wilderness as ossuary: the bone-yard of the West in *Blood Meridian* (1985)

When critics argue over who might be the ideal film-maker to shoot McCarthy's vision, the tendency is to plump for Sam Peckinpah, director of perhaps that most McCarthyite of films, *The Wild Bunch* (1969). Mark Winchell has even gone so far as to describe *Blood Meridian* and the Border trilogy as 'a novelization of Peckinpah's West', complete with slow-motion atrocities, fatalistic nostalgia, and a view of Mexican, peasant life which is one part cruelty to two parts pastoral innocence).[4,5] But if one wanted to be a little more provocative, then how about the Keystone Cops creator, Mack Sennett? Such an idea isn't idle silliness. After all, if one views the novel from a sufficiently detached perspective, isn't there something a little absurd about the tiny stick-figures endlessly slaughtering each other on a vast and empty plain, *Blood Meridian* a kind of cannibalistic flea-circus, with the minute specks endlessly rubbing each other out? The butchery of the novel is so relentless that we are left with an abiding sense of hunks of meat ceaselessly cutting and chopping, badly animated cadavers acting out a kind of meaningless, violent, slapstick routine, a kind of death hilarious, as McCarthy puts it (*Blood Meridian*, 53) or some terrifyingly violent St Vitus Dance. Caked in dust or mud (more slapstick) its protagonists are less characters than stick-figures, mud effigies (*Blood Meridian*, 13), grotesque scarecrows or voodoo dolls (*Blood Meridian*, 8), the plot a kind of gratuitous cartoon; maybe one ought to think of particularly cruel animators such as Chuck Jones (those endless routs in an endless desert) or Jan Švankmajer (skeletal forms repeatedly devouring each other) to catch the true flavour of the work. Mud, clay, excrement, meat: from a cosmic perspective, this is just brute matter changing form, a kind of internecine conflict within the realm of things.

Several critics – most persuasively Barcley Owens – have argued that *Blood Meridian* is an exhilarating, even arousing work, which implicates the reader in its inexhaustible appetite for violence.[6] But I have to admit that I just can't see this. Like all of McCarthy's later work, the key structural device of *Blood Meridian* is repetition, and by the midway point of the book (if not sooner) the massacres have become indistinguishably numb, indifferent and absurd, no matter how many infants are torn apart or corpses violated. In many ways it is the sheer scale of the landscape which drains the blood-letting of significance. The figures are so tiny, so mindless (little more than a collection of conditioned responses, as Denis Donaghue argues), so inconsequential in comparison with the overwhelming *terra damnata* (*Blood Meridian*, 61), that the crude lumps of flesh quickly become meaningless.[7] As Jacob Boeme's quote which prefaces the novel states, there will be 'no sorrowing' just 'death and darkness'. Or as the judge puts it later, 'the mystery is that there is no mystery' (*Blood Meridian*, 252) just the mute, senseless decay of matter.

The deserts in *Blood Meridian* form the most extreme landscape in McCarthy's fiction, composed, it would seem, of varying degrees of nothingness. The sky is a hole in the heavens, the ground a 'void' or 'caesura' (*Blood Meridian*, 66), the physical manifestation of the emptiness above. Perspective is annihilated here, as is any notion of depth or scale. Figures are just chalk-marks on a board, the stick-figures ultimately erased by the omnipresent darkness. They too are ghostlike, spectral, indistinguishable from their surroundings. McCarthy repeatedly stresses that they are not alien to this land, but composed of the same material as it: ultimately, dust and bone, their pleasant fleshy incarnation just some temporary state, a kind of pestilent disease, before they revert to their skeletal essence.

Indeed, when describing one of the many ruined encampments which mark the landscape, McCarthy notes that 'death seemed the most prevalent feature of the landscape' (*Blood Meridian*, 48). The only signs in this 'namelessness' (*Blood Meridian*, 46) are bodies, bones, the tracks of the departed. Only blood stains the empty wasteland; mortal remains form the only hieroglyphics. From the tree of pierced infants (*Blood Meridian*, 57) to the caves of prehistoric relics and mummified remains, the only signposts are corpses, the only map the markers of the dead. It is as if only in death can anything be registered; everything else vanishes in 'the changeling land' (*Blood Meridian*, 47). Indeed, in many ways this is McCarthy's most striking formal feature. Thomas Cole's idea of the Book of Nature becomes in McCarthy the Book of the Dead. The landscape is not a garden but an ossuary, the 'real' not nature but death.

By far the most troubling and haunting figure in the novel is the judge. As featureless as the lunar plains, the monstrous bulk of Judge Holden suggests a corollary with the barren environment of the book, almost an incarnation of the dreadful void without. He carries a weighty tome in which he records the flora, fauna, tools and shards he comes across, turning each artifact into a terrible kind of *memento mori*; after his drawings are complete he silently destroys the artifact and sometimes even the sketch, tossing both into the fire (*Blood Meridian*, 141) before riding on. Other times the entry imprisons the original, the found object pressed within the pages of his seemingly inexhaustible ledger, entombed within its binding. The judge explains:

> Whatever in creation exists without my knowledge exists without my consent . . . Only nature can enslave man and only when the existence of each last entity is routed out and made to stand naked before him will he be properly suzerain of the earth. (*Blood Meridian*, 198)

Holden's book thus suggests multiple interpretations. As the judge's title suggests, the encyclopaedia immediately signifies the biblical Book of the Dead, wherein is recorded a list of man's transgressions to be judged at the end of the world. Small wonder then that one of the gang, Webster, refuses to have his portrait sketched by the judge (*Blood Meridian*, 141), for the subject is immediately dispatched as soon as its likeness is recorded. The displacement of the real by its copy also suggests all those paintings by Albert Bierstadt and Washington Allston adorning the libraries of railroad kings and mining chiefs like trophies of a depleted land. When the earth is exhausted, idealised images are created to take its place. Such an idea, of course, suggests Baudrillard's notion of simulacra, one of the central planks of Postmodernism discussed in the introduction: the simulation supplants the original, the sign erases the object, the copy is enthroned and legitimised as the real. Such a notion also acquires a political dimension here. As Neil Campbell, David Holloway and others have pointed out, imperialist conquest writes its own history, and 'recorded history is a process of selection and control'.[8] This gathering of data, this obsessive documentation, is itself a display of dominance and power, a kind of epistemological conquest of the indigenous land. The conquerors determine the facts, define the truth, write the historical record; the judge stamps his claim on the land by transcribing it within his ledger. The original must then be destroyed so as to admit no dissent.

Throughout his fiction, McCarthy stresses the importance of witness, and draws attention to the distinction between the deed and its record. But witness is not truth, for as the judge himself notes, 'books lie' (*Blood Meridian*, 116) and 'a false book is no book at all' (*Blood Meridian*, 141). David Holloway writes that 'A capacity for representation . . . gives political power over the material world. In whatever semiotic form – speech, ledger, story, parable – it is Holden's ownership of language and meaning, his control over the act of representation, which underpins his agency and guarantees suzerainty.'[9] In *Blood Meridian*, the only representations are representations of the dead; entombment within Holden's ledger entails erasure on the plains. The judge argues that 'God speaks in . . . the bones of things' (*Blood Meridian*, 116), and McCarthy configures a new kind of morbid sublime here: the judge's book does represent the real, but this reality is not life but extinction.

Before writing the novel, McCarthy visited the sites designated in the book, and retraced the bloody trails of Glanton's gang across the Mexican border. Indeed, it is sobering to note how McCarthy's phantasmagoric displays of unrestrained violence are actually grounded in historical research, the central characters in the novel based upon actual individuals, the most terrible scenes rooted in actual events.[10] A careful reading of McCarthy's sources challenges my reading of the text as an abstract inferno, 'a hell without purpose' as Eileen Battersby wrote in the *Irish Times*; this hell was nevertheless rooted in grubby economics, in the payment of dollars for scalps in order to stem Comanche raids on the northern Mexican state of Chihuahua.[11, 12] But for all this, I would still argue that McCarthy's aims in the novel remain metaphysical rather than revisionist. Certainly one can read the book as an extremely stark critique of the binary opposite of civilisation and savagery which is so central to notions of the frontier. After all, each party here is so irredeemably violent that such distinctions are rendered absurd; Turner's Frontier thesis, the notion of Manifest Destiny, the myth of 'redemption through violence', are all subverted by the novel's unrelenting stress on armed gangs slaughtering each other for money.

But there is something even more deathly about the novel than the charnel house of history. Let us turn back to the image of McCarthy doggedly tracking the furrows of his departed killers across the Old West, digging up the relics, the vestiges, the textual remains. There is of course something of the judge in this, and I am very much taken with Richard Godden's description of him as a kind of demonic tour-guide, indicating points of interest, narrating the history, displaying his trophies of the dead.[13] This tour is of course very different from Hollywood's theme-park West and leads us back to Thomas Cole's pilgrimage into the awful real; only in this case, the metaphysical bedrock of McCarthy's *oeuvre,* its absolute reality, is Death. Just as Nature once stood as an existential given beyond man's creation, mortality indicates an ultimate state of being with which there is no reckoning. This idea transforms the pastoral into the terminal and thereby alters the very nature of the Western myth. For all its morbidity it also rescues the notion of a reality beyond false signifiers, and turns representation into a kind of sepulture. As with DeLillo's notion of electronic space, McCarthy also seeks to rescue representation through (paradoxically) the absence of the thing being signified. Signs do represent something beyond their own textual nature in McCarthy's work; they are the gravestones of the real.

But, one might argue, does any of this actually do us any good? If there is 'no mystery' as the judge suggests, then aren't we just left with a plain of decaying bodies? I have a great deal of sympathy with those who simply can't get through the book. As Peter Joseph writes, 'One gluts upon a baroque of thieving, raping, shooting, slashing, hanging, scalping, burning, bashing, hacking, stabbing . . .'; if man is simply a vehicle for destruction, history merely an endless cycle of meaningless butchery, evil the norm rather than an aberration, then what is the point?[14] The novel, exhausts, dispirits, numbs; one is left with the apathetic wisdom that such is the lot of man, irrespective of our civilised objections. Of course, those who argue for the political significance of the work have a get-out clause for such accusations of nihilism. The novel demythologises the notion of America's sacred past and thereby destroys its blind illusion of virtue. One can find any number of parallels between *Blood Meridian* and America's imperialist excursions (most strikingly in terms of the burning, raping and pillaging of Vietnam), and the novel can thus be seen as an attack upon patriotic self-righteousness, a critique of America's sacred mission to civilise the world and the terrible consequences which ensue.[15]

But in formal terms, the novel's most significant achievement is to instate McCarthy as an important (albeit heretical) religious novelist. Admittedly, we are given Hell rather than Heaven, Death rather than Nature, but the very fact that he can take such absolutes seriously suggests a way through the kitsch over-familiarity of the genre, allowing the frontier to function as a valid aesthetic possibility once again.

The sublime is reinstated in terms of the awful mystery of the grave. But didn't the judge state that there was no mystery? As the defrocked priest says, 'As if he were no mystery himself, the bloody old hood-winker' (*Blood Meridian*, 252). The last words before the epilogue read ' He says that he will never die' (*Blood Meridian*, 335).

Don't fence me in: issues of authenticity in *All the Pretty Horses*

Issues of authenticity are present from the very first, extremely cine-matic, line of the novel; 'The candleflame and the image of the candle-flame caught in the pierglass twisted and righted when he entered the hall and again when he shut the door' (*Horses*, 3). Images, reflections, mirrors, distortion; in contrast to the open frankness of the conven-tional Western setting, the Border trilogy is obsessed with notions of illusion and veracity. At the opening of the novel, John Grady Cole approaches the body of his grandfather and immediately sees through the hollow euphemisms used by those around him. 'That was not sleeping,' he states twice (*Horses*, 3), for as in *Blood Meridian*, death remains the touchstone of the real.

However, it is not the only marker of reality employed in the novel. The equine is used as a synonym for the authentic throughout the book, horses a direct link to that physical, elemental property of being which is the opposite of modern fakery. 'What he loved in horses was what he loved in men,' writes McCarthy, 'the blood and the heat of the blood that run them' (*Horses*, 6). Horses are 'ardenthearted' (*Horses*, 6), share 'a common soul' (*Horses*, 111), are at one with their world and thereby incapable of falsity or deceitful separation from the real; ultimately they represent the state of grace which Grady aspires to. Rather like Hemingway's bullfighters and aficionados, those who truly understand horses wear a badge of masculine candour and veracity to which all honest folk respond. Cole's saddle becomes a token of male camaraderie, his instinctive understanding of the colts on Don Héctor's ranch a mark of his moral straightness and validity.

In short, we're back to the romantic equation of Nature with Truth. But just how tenable is such a notion? At times, McCarthy seems to be indulging in the hoariest of clichés, from the spectral parade of slain Comanches ('a dream of the past . . . riders of a lost nation') (*Horses*, 6) to Grady's dream of equine union, a kind of metaphysical *Horse Whispering*:

He was among the horses running and in the dream he could himself run with the horses and they coursed the young mares and fillies over the plain where their rich bay and their rich chestnut colors shone in the sun and the young colts ran with their dams and trampled down the flowers in a haze of pollen that hung in the sun like powdered gold . . . and they moved all of them in a resonance that was like a music among them and they were none of them afraid horse nor colt nor mare and they ran in that resonance which is the world itself and which cannot be spoken only praised. (Horses, 161–2)

Given the candid brutality of McCarthy's earlier work, such soft-focus sentimentality rings false here. Even worse is the link between the equine and the romantic in terms of Grady's love affair with the ranch-owner's daughter Alejandra; her appearance on horseback ('she sat the horse more than well' notes Grady (Horses, 109)), and later erotic assignation (Grady's stallion 'lathered and dripping and half-crazed . . . the veins pulsing under the wet hide' (Horses, 129)) teeters perilously close to self-parody and suggests the worst kind of purple prose. Little wonder this scene in the film version elicits loud sniggers; it suggests the reduction of McCarthy's writing to a kind of camp, romantic trash. So does McCarthy intend us to take such scenes straight, stripped of irony? It was 'a real horse, real rider, real land and sky and yet a dream withal' he writes (Horses, 132). Thus, I would argue, we are back to his concern with the authentic and the illusory.

The title of the novel is suggested by a key scene at its beginning where the young Grady asks his grandfather about the oil painting which hangs in the family dining room. The painting shows half a dozen horses 'breaking through a pole corral . . . their manes were long and blowing and their eyes wild. They'd been copied from a book' (Horses, 15). Prefiguring his later adventure, the young John Grady Cole is fascinated, his grandfather less so; 'those are picture-book horses' he notes 'and went on eating' (Horses, 16). For Grady, these horses aren't just real, they are better than real; he guesses that they must possess some of the blood of the mystical stud Steeldust in their veins. The scene is then echoed later in the novel, when Grady has taken up his position at Don Héctor's ranch. Cole's appraisal of the stock is unerringly accurate and true. 'I aint forgotten what they're supposed to look like' he tells Rawlins (Horses, 99), and his almost preternatural status at the ranch is down to his instinctive sense of a horses's worth, which in a more metaphysical sense, lies in its capacity as a symbol of truth. But why then his fascination with 'picture-book horses'?

Time and time again, McCarthy makes the link between Cole's horse sense and masculine authenticity. He wins respect from his peers because he can perceive the actual value of the stock, irrespective of appearance. The hands on the ranch, 'like most men skilled at their work ... were scornful of any least suggestion of knowing anything not learned at first hand' (*Horses*, 96). Hence the relentless attention to detail of McCarthy's prose, its proof of utility and practical know-how, the repeated descriptions of how to loop a rope, set a trap, fix a saddle, break in a colt. All this suggests a sense of pragmatic knowledge which is free from the duplicity attached to paperwork and the modern in the novel. But there is a paradox at work here; after all, McCarthy also stresses the ruthless violence and mastery necessitated by horse breaking, the will to dominate and control. In one of the harshest passages in the book, McCarthy describes how Cole systematically and remorselessly breaks the will of the colts, separating them from each other, severing their union with the collective group and imprisoning them within an unfamiliar and alien environment. By the end of the day, 'they looked like animals trussed up by children for fun' (*Horses*, 105), their communion with the wilderness broken. They are now property.

This transformation of the elemental ('their fluid and collective selves' (*Horses*, 105)) into commodities, a turning of Grady's horsemanship into dollars, questions the apparently Edenic setting of the ranch. We are dealing less with the real than with issues of power, domination and profit; the very factors which doom Cole's affair with Alejandra. After all, put bluntly, Grady is of the wrong class and thereby of the wrong mating stock; Mexico is not an unwritten, lawless land, but rather possesses a complex history and class structure which McCarthy's naïve hero is unable to comprehend. Like the horses in the family painting he seeks to escape into a sense of the physically real – but legislative authority and economics will pursue him everywhere.

Earlier in the novel, immediately after crossing into Mexico, the kid, Blevins, proves his outlaw status by shooting a hole straight through Grady's thrown pocketbook (*Horses*, 48). His skill, as ever with McCarthy, suggests some degree of honesty; he really is a sharpshooter rather than just talking the talk, and for John Grady Cole this further validates his cowboy ideals. In essence, they are who they are pretending to be. Moreover, the shooting of the pocketbook, containing Grady's money and papers, suggests an escape from the world of exchange into the realm of matter and the real; in Mexico he can escape the stenographed accountancy which has swallowed his family ranch. However, although violent and hostile, Mexico is not simply a blank space; the textual law still operates there, albeit in a foreign and frequently incomprehensible manner. (Indeed, McCarthy's use of Spanish reinforces this; the purely English-speaker is punished for his or her ignorance by a worrying sense of missing exactly what is going on or what each speaker means.)

Grady and Rawlins' imprisonment in Saltillo prison parallels the earlier horse breaking and taming of the individual will. More terrifying than the brute, atavistic violence displayed within the prison, is the complete sovereignty of those who set the rules, who decide issues of identity, punishment and freedom, who determine the textual reality of the place itself. As the Captain explains on the way:

> Papers is lost. Papers cannot be found. Some people come here to look for some man but he is no here. No one can find these papers. Something like that. You see. No one wants these troubles. Who can say that some body was here? We dont have this body. Some crazy person, he can say that God is here. But everybody know that God is no here. (*Horses*, 180)

God – or truth, or reality – doesn't enter into things here. Falsified papers – or more especially, money – determine who is who and what is what; a direct link to the judge's jurisdiction in *Blood Meridian*. And indeed, it is only money – rather than a daring escape – which enables the pair to be freed.

It is this loss of volition – rather than McCarthy's stress on the anachronistic nature of the boy's adventure – which most profoundly breaks with the generic Western formula. Arguably it is the Western which most succinctly expresses the quintessential myth of America: the escape from a determinist past (or history), an individualistic assertion of free will and limitless possibility, grounded in the wide open spaces of an untouched land. Grady, however, becomes enmeshed in issues of class, money and history over which he has no control, and indeed scarcely understands. In this sense, his affair with Alejandra is inevitably doomed because of external forces which exercise an invisible dominion over the novel, an influence which exists irrespective of any course of action he might himself pursue: Alejandra's relationship with her parents, Dueña Alfonso's influence over the girl's destiny, the legacy of the Mexican revolution, the tangled mass of personal and political history which casts a long shadow over the affair. As Patrick W. Shaw has pointed out, Alejandra's actions in the novel have less to do with Grady than with her own family and in this sense their fling can be seen as an attempt to punish her absent mother and rebel against her domineering great aunt.[16] Although her true motivations are never made wholly clear to us, her ultimate abandonment of Grady only makes sense if we assume that she chooses the love of her father over the attractions of her lover; otherwise her character appears fickle and flighty, another example of capricious womanhood and another betrayal of the masculine hero. Indeed, the text makes a number of implicit connections between Alejandra and John Grady Cole's mother, for ultimately both leave their cowboy lover for an ambiguous sense of modern emancipation. Dueña Alfonsa will not allow Alejandra to be tied to the ranch by the patriarchal codes of Mexican society and in this sense her 'freeing' of Alejandra will be her final revolutionary act. The lament of the father at the start of the book could thus be the son's at the conclusion: 'She liked horses. I thought that was enough' (*Horses*, 24).

The reader's sympathy may not wholly be with the wronged male, however. Certainly, John Grady Cole is guilty of a fatal ignorance, if nothing else. As he admits at the close of the novel, he never truly understands Mexico but passes through as a quasi-heroic tourist, its historical sources forever murky and intractable to him. McCarthy is deliberately reticent with his research here. Without prior knowledge, we, like Grady, can only understand the revolution in terms of failed idealism rather than ideology, brute determinism as opposed to subtle political shadings. The revolution in *All the Pretty Horses* is plucked from its political and economic moorings to become another example of the inevitably (and repetitively) blood-thirsty nature of man: 'What is constant in history is greed and foolishness and a love of blood and this is a thing that even God – who knows all that can be known – seems powerless to change' (*Horses*, 239).

For Grady, the only lesson of history is the inevitability of defeat, a pacifying determinism. Instead of free-will and individual volition, history entangles the individual in an infinitely regressive puppet show; as the hero 'traces the strings upward he finds they terminate in the hands of yet other puppets, themselves with their own strings, and so on' (*Horses*, 231). In short, history is the opposite of freedom, a process of entanglement with invisible (but nevertheless actual) forces.

Grady, however, fulfils the criterion for the Western hero in that he refuses to accept this. His quixotic mission to retrieve the horses and restore them to their rightful place (north of the border, back in America) is in this sense an only vaguely understood attempt to reimpose a sense of agency and control, even to oppose the determining forces of history by rewinding time, reversing the events which have led to Grady's sense of loss and disillusionment. Even if invisible and intangible forces are ranged against him, Grady still has space to act – an independence which was stripped from him when he fell under the aegis of Mexican law in Saltillo prison and within the clutches of Dueña Alfonso. John Grady Cole will retrieve his property ('It was my horse and my saddle and my gun' (*Horses*, 158)) and thereby counter this fear of passivity. Hence the importance of the shift from Mexican jurisdiction to the American judge who grants him legal (and moral) absolution at the story's end (*Horses*, 290).

The kindly judge of *All the Pretty Horses* appears, very self-consciously, as the absolute antithesis of the demonic Judge Holden in *Blood Meridian*. Indeed, in overtly didactic fashion, he appears so as to restore a sense of moral (indeed, explicitly Christian) order at the conclusion of the tale; he approves of Grady's actions, justifies his necessary violence (all acts of self-defence) and reimposes a sense of right and wrong crucially missing from the unknowable machinations of a foreign country. Grady once again submits to a higher textual authority, but it is one which is comprehensible and reasonable ('There's nothing wrong with you son. I think you'll get it sorted out' (*Horses*, 293)). In short, we understand the language once again. Grady has proved his ability (rescued his property), acted out of his own free-will (and thereby escaped being reduced to just another puppet), and returned home to justify his actions in accordance with an accepted rule of law. So why then, is the ending of the novel – only a few short pages after the scene with the judge – so bleak?

Firstly, and most obviously, McCarthy quickly acts to deny us this neat sense of closure. The issue of the ownership of the horses (remembering that horses act as emblems of truth) is never resolved, Blevins' identity is never satisfactorily resolved and Grady's encounter with the 'real' Jimmy Blevins – a radio evangelist – is strange enough to question the Christian certainties proffered by the judge. Moreover, the novel's return to a rapidly industrialising and bureaucratic America literally leaves its hero with nowhere to go. We are back under the dominion of American law, but that in turn signals the end of the central Western narrative.

The novel's closing paragraph wrests defeat from the jaws of victory. The last border which John Grady Cole passes over – at least until the final novel of the trilogy – seems to be that frontier with which McCarthy is most concerned: the border between the living and the dead:

> He rode with the sun coppering his face and the red wind blowing out of the west across the evening land and the small desert birds flew chittering among the dry bracken and horse and rider and horse passed on and their long shadows passed in tandem like the shadow of a single being. Passed and paled into the darkening land, the world to come. (*Horses*, 302)

This is *Shane* passing out of history and into mythology, Thomas Cole's Indian (Grady's face coppered by the sun) vanishing from the canvas, reabsorbed within the undifferentiated wholeness of nature; but it is also extinction, the realisation of Grady's quest through a kind of death and disappearing.

I have always had great problems with the character of John Grady Cole. Ostensibly sixteen at the time of the novel's narrative, there is little of the gauche teenager about him. All these awkward characteristics are embodied in the doomed punk, Blevins, whilst Grady remains oddly out of focus for a novel's central character, somehow otherworldly and unreal; a picturebook hero to go with those picturebook horses. For this reason, I find it difficult to accept the received wisdom that the novel is a *Bildungsroman*, a coming-of age tale or initiation rite whereby the crossing of the border marks a movement from innocence to experience; Grady already seems so old, so timeless, that the struggles between relativism and absolutism, determinism and free-will, seem to be more the author's than the character's.[17] Indeed, John Grady Cole seems separated from the other characters in the book, almost as if he is already dead – or at the very least, only passing through this world. At times he seems supernaturally at one with nature ('He put his hands on the ground at either side of him and pressed them against the earth and in that coldly burning canopy of black he slowly turned dead centre to the world, all of it taut and trembling and moving enormous and alive under his hands' (*Horses*, 119)), but in the second half of the book at least, is more at one with death ('He felt something cold and soulless enter him like another being and he imagined that it smiled malignly and he had no reason to believe that it would ever leave' (*Horses*, 254)). For all his lost love, the pain he feels at his inability to save Blevins, the bond of friendship between himself and Rawlins, there is an emptiness and absence about him which seem to link him to the themes explored in *Blood Meridian*.

So what then *is* real in the novel? Riding out with his son one last time at the start of the story, John Grady Cole's father looks out at the landscape '[a]s if he might never see it right again. Or worse did see it right at last. See it as it had always been, would forever be' (*Horses*, 23), which is to say, mortal, perishable, a moribund landscape which reflects back to him both his wartime experiences and his slow cancerous demise. Later, Dueña Alfonso makes an even more explicit proclamation of the deathly, sanguine notion of the real; 'Nothing can be proven except that it be made to bleed. Virgins, bulls, men. Ultimately God himself' (*Horses*, 230). We are a long way from Grady's pastoral vision of the equine here. Luis, the lame *mozo* who lives in the mountains tells Grady that 'horses also love war . . . His own father said that no man who has not gone to war on horseback can ever truly understand the horse and he said that he supposed he wished that this were not so but that it was so' (*Horses*, 111). Such sentiments parallel *Blood Meridian*'s assertion that war is the true aim of man and its chief religion. Such a religion is not the pantheism of Grady's horse sense but the eschatology of McCarthy's earlier works. After all, Grady's dream of the horses on the plain is not the only vision he receives whilst imprisoned:

> He slept and when he woke he'd dreamt of the dead standing about in their bones and the dark sockets of their eyes that were indeed without speculation bottomed in the void wherein lay a terrible intelligence common to all but of which none would speak. When he awoke he knew that men had died in that room. (*Horses*, 205)

All the Pretty Horses acts as the first novel of a trilogy not because its narrative-arc remains unfinished, but because it raises a whole series of questions, tensions and aesthetic problems which McCarthy seeks to resolve in the final two works. There is the conflict between a pantheistic faith in life and nature and a morbid concentration upon death as the final reality or substratum of existence; there is a tension between McCarthy's Christian morality and his nihilism; and, most importantly, there are the formal problems of the authentic and the sublime.

In the final analysis, how can we square a concern with the authentic with the novel's generic form? John Grady Cole wants to escape the mendacity of the modern by embracing the Western mythus of the freedom of the plains; is this authentic (an escape into the real) or inauthentic (enacting a banal B-movie script?)? Do the generic staples of the novel allow McCarthy to reference and revisit notions of nature and the sublime, or do they doom the work to self-parody and pastiche? I would argue that the novel's ending is astonishingly moving (unlike Grady's loss of Alejandra, which is simply banal) precisely because he can draw upon the mythic resonance of the Western (the hero reabsorbed into the landscape) alongside the notion of the awful sublime advanced by *Blood Meridian*: the border less that between man and nature than man and death. But even here there is internal conflict within McCarthy's prose. The 'flat sort of pop' (*Horses*, 178) of the gunshot which kills Blevins is the most terrifying sound in the novel, for it strips death of any sense of metaphysical mystery; of the sublime or mythical resonance which McCarthy attributes to it elsewhere. It is simply the sound of a boy being killed, his corpse collapsing into the mud rather than passing to some shadowy, preternatural realm. Moreover, such tensions – between the generic and the metaphysical, the authentic and the parodic, the religious and the corporeal – becomes even more explicit in the following two works.

'The husk is not the thing': Representational strategies in *The Crossing* (1994)

The Crossing is an infinitely more demanding work than *All the Pretty Horses*, more explicit in its use of generic Western staples as a kind of philosophical shorthand for McCarthy's deeper concerns. Indeed, one might argue that the novel shifts genre entirely, dispensing with the expected Western narrative for the less familiar form of the Mexican

Corrido: remorselessly tragic, romantically-pitched, classical in its sense of inexorable destiny.

Here, the central conceit of *All the Pretty Horses* – that the existential border which McCarthy's heroes must ultimately cross is the line between life and death, an intense awareness of mortality – is married to the remorseless repetition of *Blood Meridian*: the novel s protagonist, Billy Parham, crosses over into Mexico three times, losing along the way the wolf he tries to save, his parents and his brother; each significant crossing marked by loss, pain and abandonment, the constituent elements of McCarthy's fiction. It is this relentless repetition which makes *The Crossing* such a gruelling read, its cast-iron structure utterly pitiless and unforgiving. 'Lo que debemos entender as que ultamante todi es plovo' (*Crossing*, 292), Billy is repeatedly informed – what we must understand is that ultimately all is dust. Such is the melancholy wisdom of the Mexican folk-tales and songs which supplant the Western narrative of triumphant expansionism; there are fewer picture book horses (or heroes) on display here. One might also argue that McCarthy's central concerns move from questions of authenticity (whether a thing is true or false, authentic or fake) to questioning categories of knowledge: a more complex, relativistic world view than a simple pursuit of 'the real'.

As before, one can investigate these ideas through McCarthy's engagement with the natural world, and *The Crossing* offers us a number of animalistic metaphors with which to explore man's relationship with his surroundings: the bovine, a passive, stoical acceptance of trial and tribulation, exhibited by the peaceful (but much victimised) dirt-poor Mexican ejiditarios; the lupine, which denotes the ever-present will to violence and domination which tends to predominate in McCarthy's view of human nature; and the equine, which is less present here than in *All the Pretty Horses*, existing as the merest echo of some kind of idealised union with the natural world (significantly the plot once again revolves around the retrieval of horses as a means of reasserting some sense of essential order in the world).

Nature then is part other (alien, indifferent, unknowable) and part mirror for the atavistic soul of man. In the opening section of *The Crossing*, Billy is 'twinned' in the 'antique gaze' of both the Indian found prowling his parent's farmstead ('Eyes so dark they seemed all pupil' (*Crossing*, 6)) and the wounded she-wolf which he later both traps and rescues – a transparently racist use of the idea of a racialised 'other'. There are thus obvious parallels with John Grady Cole's mystic union with horses in the previous novel, but this 'twinning' seems less benign, the lupine less pastoral epiphany than an acknowledgement of the wolf's inevitable struggle for survival.

Nevertheless, at this stage of the novel we are still dealing with a link between the animalistic and the real; we are dealing with categories of being, whereas later the novel deals with categories of knowledge. McCarthy stresses the way in which the wolf is in the world, its con-crete, physical, sensory existence; unlike exiled, abandoned mankind, 'the wolf would be always corroborate to herself and never wholly abandoned in the world' (*Crossing*, 79), never abstracted, separate or false. The novel intimates an invisible world of scents, smells, traces; olfactory knowledge insensible to humans, the corporeal realm in which man lives but which he never truly occupies or perceives:

> Between their acts and the ceremonies lies the world and in this world the storms blow and the trees twist in the wind and all the animals that God has made go to and fro yet this world men do not see. They see the acts of their own hands or they see that which they name and call out to one another but the world between is invisible to them. (*Crossing*, 46)

This separation between language ('they see that which they name') and physical being, is, of course, at the heart of DeLillo's and Auster's concerns examined in the previous chapters. Physical reality – the movement of the wind, the feel of the sun, the indefinable odours of living things – all these things are beyond transcription, too specific, ephemeral and undefinable to be caught by the blanket categorisation of words. The old trapper explains this through the metaphor of *un copo de nieve*, a snowflake:

> But before you see it it is gone. If you want to see it you have to see it on its own ground. If you catch it you lose it. And where it goes there is no going back from. Not even God can bring it back. (Crossing, 46)

This notion that to catch a thing is to lose it obviously parallels Grady's horse-breaking and Parham's attempt to trap the wolf; it also suggests, in a cultural context, the turning of the wilderness into a commercialised replica of itself, tourism destroying its very reason-to-be – an engagement with untouched nature. It also suggests an aesthetic justification for McCarthy's eerily formless landscapes ('the cold and the dark and the silence' (*Crossing*, 112)) for the true landscape lies in what cannot be visualised and thereby reduced to stereotypical images, the property of being in the world which the wolf knows through sounds, smells, scents. Moreover, there is a link to the morbid reality suggested earlier. Each moment, or scent, is unique, specific, never to be repeated in exactly the same form (like the copo de nieve in fact); it is therefore transitory, mortal, unlike the endless repetition of identical words. As the trapper tells Billy, 'The wolf is a being of great order and . . . it knows what men do not: that there is no order in the world save that which death has put there' (*Crossing*, 45).

This characteristic conjunction of reality and mortality reappears later in the novel, through the story of the old revolutionary blinded in the war. This act of blinding – one of the most strikingly grotesque in the entirety of McCarthy's *oeuvre* – releases the man from the inevitably doomed enterprises of politics and revolution, and reveals to him the sphere of the invisible: touch, smell, palpable existence. Blindness is connected with wisdom in McCarthy s work (and this too can verge on self-parody) precisely because it obliterates the apparent and intimates hidden forms, absolute reality – a distrust of images which unites virtually all of the writers in this collection. Sightless and vulnerable, the wounded revolutionary is profoundly aware of his status as a physical thing in a world of other physical things – indeed, his continued survival depends on this knowledge. Slowly however, this sightlessness becomes the means of his salvation for 'the world unfolded to him in a way it had not before in his life' (*Crossing*, 285). The falsity of earlier beliefs fall away from him. 'He said that in his blindness he had indeed lost himself and all memory of himself yet he had found in the deepest dark of that loss that there was also a ground and that there one must begin' (*Crossing*, 291–2). This ground would seem to be that of the physical world and connects the blind man to the olfactory existence of the wolf; at the same time, however, this darkness also suggests a more dreadful, metaphysical knowing:

> He imagined that in his estate of eternal night he might somehow
> have already halved the distance to death. That the transition for
> him could not be so great for the world was already at some certain

distance and if it were not death's terrain he encroached upon in his darkness then whose? (*Crossing,* 280)

As so often in McCarthy, we seem to be on the very borderline between this world and the next, his fiction occupying a kind of transitional limbo where the familiar landscape falls away to suggest some awful reality impossible to put adequately into words. As with DeLillo and Auster, McCarthy's prose is concerned with tracing the virtually invisible outlines of this reality, 'hidden geometries and their orders which could only stand fully revealed . . . in darkness and ashes' (*Crossing,* 130). Such an idea is inherently Platonic. The everyday is not to be trusted, a mendacious illusion; hidden beneath this veil lie the true forms of the world, although we may not wish to perceive them:

> He spoke of the broad dryland barrial and the river and the road and the mountains beyond and the blue sky over them as entertainments to keep the world at bay, the true and ageless world. He said that the light of the world was in men's eyes only for the world itself moved in eternal darkness and darkness was its true nature and true condition and that in its darkness it turned with perfect cohesion in all its parts but that there was naught to see. He said that the world was sentient to its core and secret and black beyond men's imagining and that its nature did not reside in what could be seen or not seen. (*Crossing,* 283)

This is perhaps as clear a statement of McCarthy's creed as we are likely to get, deathly to the core, as obsessed with mortality as Freud's notion of Thanatos, likewise agreeing that the reason for existence is extinction, the dark void to which we all unconsciously yearn to return; all are 'accomplices in their own death' (*Crossing,* 379) writes McCarthy. If death is our true state (but beyond representation) and life a matter of decay (such decayed forms being the only shapes we can make out in this void) then this is a bleak epiphany indeed. 'Because what can be touched falls into dust there can be no mistaking these things for the real,' the blindman tells Parham. 'At best they are only tracings of where the real has been. Perhaps they are not even that. Perhaps they are no more than obstacles to be negotiated in the ultimate sightlessness of the world' (*Crossing,* 294). *Tracings of where the real has been* – McCarthy's prose merely a marker for the dead.

So where then does this leave McCarthy as a writer? We can imagine his prose as a kind of trap for the real, the author mixing his own 'matrix' (*Crossing*, 22) of redolent smells, sights, perceptions, hunting the elusive nature of being, our sense of physical existence. Billy's capture of the wolf occupies a full seven pages of description in the novel (only the horse-breaking scene in *All the Pretty Horses* takes so long), intensely aware of its own linguistic struggle, striving to tether and represent the real. This act of subjugation, however, destroys the very essence of the thing sought, representation an act of destruction. McCarthy is also implicated in the gory spectacle of the dog-fight, the wolf turned into exhibit and commodity, the scene hawked by a demented pitch man yelling in the mud (*Crossing*, 104). His fiction is full of down-at-heel travelling shows, shabby carnivals, evil freak shows. Ultimately the whole notion of art is rendered absurd by the endless plains of dust and mud, the empty arenas which dwarf and extinguish the dilapidated pageants and stage-sets.

As we have seen, the theatrical operates as a simple synonym for the false in McCarthy's work; Billy is bored by the gaudy costumes and artificial acting during the play, but spellbound by the sight of the diva washing herself in the river the following morning, her naked body suggesting in some sense the undisguised real (*Crossing*, 220). This distrust of the dramaturgical also suggests a certain degree of self-criticism of course; if fictions are inherently false, seeking only to disguise and dissemble, then how should McCarthy himself write? After all, is he not reduced to the same absurd state of yelling and crying on some endless, dusty plain?

Such questions of truthfulness are foregrounded in the extended disquisition on maps and representation which takes place as the brothers leave the Mexican town of Keno for the high country (*Crossing*, 184). One old man draws a simple map in the dust. A second describes this map as a 'fantasma', a mere 'decoration' (*Crossing*, 184). A third states that no map is even possible, for the country is marked by fires and earthquakes and therefore is too unstable to chart properly. The only true guide is one's own experience, and this is only true for one's own, specific journey. The aged ejiditarios then take to squabbling, the tenses of their discourse oddly fractured. One argues that even if the map was false, 'it was a mistake to discount the good will inherent in the old man's desire to guide them for it too must be taken into account and would in itself lend strength and resolution to them in their journey' (*Crossing*, 185). Another disagrees, for 'to follow a false map was to invite disaster' (*Crossing*, 185); 'the map in question was a folly and that the dogs in the street would piss on it'. When the last old man argues 'that for that matter the dogs would piss upon their graves as well and how was this an argument?' (*Crossing*, 185), the elderly disputants finally concur. One notes 'in any event our graves make no claims outside of their own simple coordinates and no advice as to how to arrive there but only the assurance that arrive we shall' (*Crossing*, 186), and with this the symposium breaks up.

This exchange in itself draws together all the essential characteristics of McCarthy's writing: representation as mere markers in the dust, the connection between signs and graves, disputes over the nature of truth, and a stress upon the impossibility of adequately representing the real world and the landscape. But there is a shift here, and a differentiation between questions of absolute reality (which for McCarthy is death) and categories of knowledge, which are subjective, relative and individual. The old man's map is really a picture of his own voyage – after all, as McCarthy writes, plans are one thing and journeys another. If the absolute truth is hidden from man then one is thrown back upon one's own experience. There was 'but one reality and that was the living of it' states Billy near the novel's end (*Crossing*, 380). The focus of the novel thus shifts from notions of an absolute truth to the act of narrating, and this in turn alters McCarthy's very approach to the book.

In probably the most difficult exchange in McCarthy's fiction, the unnamed custodian who inhabits the precarious, ruined church instructs Billy Parham on the primacy of witness:

What was here to be found was not a thing. Things separate from their stories have no meaning. They are only shapes. Of a certain size and color. A certain weight. When their meaning has become lost to us they can no longer even have a name. The story on the other hand can never be lost from its place in the world for it is that place. And that is what was to be found here. The corrido. The tale. And like all corridos it ultimately told one story only, for there is only one to tell. (*Crossing*, 145)

Later, he goes on:

Acts have their being in the witness. Without him who can speak

> at all? . . . for what is deeply true is true also in men's hearts and
> it can therefore never be mistold through all and any tellings.
> (*Crossing*, 154)

All of this is not wholly dissimilar to the shift in DeLillo's prose from
a concentration upon the failure of writing to a stress upon the possibility of language; it also seems to link McCarthy to the main current
of Postmodern linguistic theorising:

> For this world also which seems to us a thing of stone and flower
> and blood is not a thing at all but a tale. And all in it is a tale and
> each tale the sum of all lesser tales and yet these are the selfsame
> tale and contain all else within them. (*Crossing*, 143)

– a near perfect dictionary definition of metafiction, one might argue.

Little wonder then that Postmodern-minded critics see this as a way
out of McCarthy's morbid dead end, his obsession with mortification
as a sign of the real. For Diane Luce, it rescues McCarthy for humanism, shifts his focus from an indifferent, alien universe, what John Beck
calls 'a mineral disdain for . . . the organic' back toward the narrating
subject.[18, 19] The meaning of our lives 'is the meaning we put there by
exercising our human gift for storytelling or narrating'.[20] Unlike the
absurd stage shows, art becomes meaningful again, the only guide
we have – perfect accuracy no longer enters into the equation. *The
Crossing* is full of anecdotes which contradict each other, irreconcilable
tales which are told over and over again in different forms – the opera
company's mule, the gypsies and the ruined aircraft, even the husband
and wife's account of the aforementioned blinding. This stress on
narration humanises the text by making its truth relative and local; it
also ultimately justifies the form of the novel.

The most important of these contested narratives is the death of
Parham's younger brother, Boyd. Boyd's shoot-out with the leader of
the La Babicora vaqueros and his later conflict with the Guardia Blanca
of La Babicora (mercenaries hired to protect wealthy American landowners' interests) lead to his transformation (via martyrdom) into la
hombre de la gente, a hero of the oppressed Mexican people. Boyd's
actions are celebrated – and wildly romanticised – in the folk corridos
of the scattered Mexican villages and settlements, events rewritten so
as to fit the tragic but defiant necessities of the form:

The corridero held the fretted neck of his instrument with one hand and raised his glass . . . and toasted aloud the memory of all just men in the world for as it was sung in the corrido theirs was a bloodfilled road and the deeds of their lives were writ in that blood which was the world's heart's blood and he said that serious men sang their song and their song only. (*Crossing*, 375)

Perhaps unsurprisingly, most critics have argued that McCarthy's novel pays tribute to this oral folk-tradition, an outlawed cultural position, in John Beck's words, which defends the weak and illiterate from the linguistic domination of the landowners and lawmakers.[21] Certainly the novel seems to adopt much of its flavour and high style, the taciturn spareness of *All the Pretty Horses* replaced in *The Crossing* by a much more magniloquent, declamatory style and diction, mystical and metaphysical to the core. But are we still dealing with questions of genre here, the corrido no more 'authentic' or 'true' than the horse-opera clichés of the previous novel? Charles Bailey argues that the 'truth' of the corrido is irrelevant; reiterating the story of the map, he suggests that what counts is the very act of witness, this witness being of a profoundly political and subversive nature.[22] The act of heroism inspires, arouses, resists, and in this notion of resistance resides its true value and worth. But does it matter how Boyd really died? His actions are turned by the corrideros into a series of clichés which only seem more authentic because they possess an exotic, ethnic nature; in actual fact, the corrido possesses its own formal and thematic necessities which do not allow for any deviation from the plot. Indeed ultimately the corrido is fatalistic to the core:

The corrido is the poor man's history. It does not owe allegiance to the truths of history but to the truths of men. It tells the tale of the solitary man who is all men. It believes that where two men meet one of two things can occur and nothing else. In one case a lie is born and in the other death.
That sounds like death is the truth.
Yes. It sounds like death is the truth. (*Crossing*, 386)

McCarthy's own fiction crosses over the border (from American Western to Mexican ballad one might say, though the view of Mexico remains a stubbornly 'Anglo' one) because the corrido allows him to express his deterministic, mortal conception of man more clearly. But there is still a real sense of struggle here. Genre implies not just artificiality but a constricting sense of fate, the necessity to follow a predetermined plot; the corrido will always end in bloodshed and loss. Whilst Boyd (and in *Cities of the Plain*, Grady) succumb to this, the sceptical Billy struggles against such a position throughout. Nor is the question of representation and witness quite as simple in McCarthy's fiction as some of his critics would like to suggest. Against the notion that the world is but a tale, life a matter of its oration, McCarthy states that 'the world has no name . . . The names of the cerros and the sierras exist only on maps' (*Crossing*, 387). 'And it is because these names and these coordinates are our own naming that they cannot save us . . . they cannot find for us the way again' (*Crossing*, 387). Are men's maps (which is to say, the act of representation) then our only truth or a form of counterfeit? Ultimately, the old men's struggle over the legitimacy of mapping remains unresolved.

Turning upon the teller: *Cities of the Plain* (1998) and the end of the Border trilogy

Whilst it's probably too early for any real kind of critical consensus on the final part of the Border trilogy, the book certainly feels like a disappointment and severe anti-climax. I don't think that it need worry us too much that the novel is a reworked version of an unused screenplay written some ten years earlier; after all, all this really suggests is that McCarthy has known the inevitable outcome of events all along.[23] But there is a problem with this inevitability and indeed with the inexorable fatalism of the trilogy as a whole. *Cities of the Plain* is structured around the same pattern of repetition as *All the Pretty Horses* and *The Crossing*: John Grady Cole must again follow the dictates of his heart in pursuit of a doomed love affair; Billy Parham must again cross over the border to lose the thing he prizes most. There is no room to manoeuvre within such predestined, doom-laden plotting. Everything happens as it necessarily must. And such relentless reiteration, however aesthetically justified, inescapably poses a problem for the reader.

Moreover, McCarthy here seems to lose interest in the generic, Western staples of the trilogy. *All the Pretty Horses* successfully used the whole notion of genre to explore issues of authenticity (which is more real, the boy's cowboy dream or the monotonous reality of modernity?) and free-will (are the boys blazing their own path or following a well-rehearsed script?) In *The Crossing* such questions took precedence over the narrative itself (hence the difficulty of the text), but the novel retained its vitality by shifting the whole generic form from the conventional Western to the less familiar corrido. By *Cities of the Plain* that balance (and critical tension) between generic form and thematic depth seems to weaken and collapse. For the unsympathetic reader the effect is not unlike walking into the cinema before the end of a film and then watching the whole thing go round again. It is hard not to feel that we have all been here before.

Indeed, there is something curiously posthumous about the novel, as if the work exists in a strange kind of afterlife or bleak Valhalla. Much of this is down to the deathly quality of McCarthy's protagonists, a quality present throughout the trilogy:

> He looked as if he'd been sitting there and God had made the trees and rocks around him. He looked like his own reincarnation and then his own again. Above all he looked to be filled with a terrible sadness. As if he harbored news of some horrendous loss that no one else had heard of yet. Some vast tragedy not of fact or incident or event but of the way the world was. (*Crossing*, 177)

Like Grady in *All the Pretty Horses*, Parham ends *The Crossing* as a living ghost, 'as if he had died in some way years ago and was ever after some over being who had no history, who had no ponderable life to come' (*Crossing*, 382). The detonation of the atomic bomb at the Trinity test site in New Mexico which ends the novel (*Crossing*, 245) signals the final closure of any kind of benign pastoralism in the trilogy.[24] The land in *Cities of the Plain* is grey, dusty, infertile, the last remaining ranchers simply waiting to be bought out by the military. Mexico is no longer an escape from modern commodification, but simply a shabby extension of it; as David Holloway points out, the sacred tokens of truth in *All the Pretty Horses* are now simply units of exchange – the novel opens with the 'all-American' cowboys buying a whore each (*Cities*, 3) – and the its primary setting – the notoriously corrupt and violent Mexican city of Juárez – is urban not rural: Mexico a dilapidated Sodom and Gomorrah rather than a site of pastoral redemption.[25] Unlike the previous two narratives, *Cities of the Plain* is not a road-novel: there is nowhere else to go, either for the protagonists or for the genre.

We are at the end of something here and 'when things are gone, they're gone. They aint comin back' (*Cities*, 126).

There are other reasons for this. *Cities of the Plain* is a novel full of dead women, haunted by the spectre of a vanished femininity: Mac McGovern's dead wife (Mr Johnson's late niece), Billy Parham's long-gone sister, even Magdalena whose epileptic state and pale other-worldliness mark her out as not long for this world. For all the book's celebration of male camaraderie, this feminine absence leaves the setting sterile and barren, promising no further descendants. The Old Testament Father of *All the Pretty Horses* is displaced here by an absent Virgin Mary, whose pale, lifeless iconography dominates the work. Curiously, *Cities of the Plain* feels the most feminine of McCarthy's novels, although there are almost no women in it.

In many ways the book acts as a pale echo of the works which came before it: the dog-hunt is a violently degraded version of the round-ups of *All the Pretty Horses*, the rescue of the pup parallels that of the wolf of *The Crossing*, Grady's fatal knife-fight is a replay of the first novel's pivotal management. Indeed, the key elements of the previous works occur over and over again as if in a dream: Parham's failure to rescue his brother, the appearance of a wise blindman and a kindly patriarch, McCarthy's recurrent stress on mirrors, reflection and distortion. When Grady sleeps he imagines himself 'alone in some bleak landscape where the wind blew without abatement and where the presence of those who had gone before still lingered on in the darkness about' (*Cities*, 104), a passage emblematic of the novel as a whole.

Indeed the trilogy ends in an enigmatic 'dream inside a dream' (*Cities*, 273) which rather than proffering any sense of thematic closure seems to mark the final unravelling of McCarthy's aesthetic. Billy, now an old man, sheltering beneath an underpass in the year 2002, is greeted by one last mysterious philosopher, a figure whom he first interprets as death (*Cities*, 267) but who then proceeds to relate a lengthy dream-narrative involving a strange primitive tribe and an enigmatic final act of atavistic sacrifice. In this most abstruse section of the tale, the figure in the narrator's dream in turn begins to dream, rendering the 'reality' of the tale even more conditional and unstable – especially given that this entire dialogue may well be taking place solely within Billy's imagination. The result is a dizzying loss of any kind of stable textual ground. Who is narrating? What level of reality (story, memory, dream, fantasy) are we operating upon? As with Auster, this is profoundly disturbing – after all, if the textual reality is so obscure and flimsy then maybe our own sense of the real is also vulnerable.

Of course, such doubts have been present throughout the trilogy and McCarthy's concern with representation. The unnamed narrator relates how he attempted to 'map' or represent the patterns of his life, but somehow produced a chart which was both unrecognisable and suggested the contours of his own face. Parham is unimpressed. Either the record was a true one, or else invention. Either the narrator's face appeared or it didn't. Billy is extremely suspicious of any suggestion that one 'narrates' one's own reality given the intractable realities of loneliness and loss which he has himself faced. In this sense, the epilogue can be read as a comic dialogue between Billy's cowboy pragmatism (which argues that some things are real and some things are not) and a solipsistic standpoint from which all reality is profoundly unknowable:

> Can I say somethin?
> Of course.
> I think you got a habit of makin things a bit more complicated than what they need to be. Why not just tell the story?
> Good advice. Let's see what can be done.
> Andale pues.
> Although I should point out to you that you are the one with the questions.
> No you shouldnt.
> Yes. Of course.
> Just get on with it.
> Yes.
> Mum's the word here.
> Como?
> Nothin. I'll shut up askin questions, that's all.
> They were good questions.
> You aint goin to tell the story, are you? (*Cities*, 278)

For all the absurd comedy on display here, there is also a real sense of philosophical dread. McCarthy seems to deconstruct his own creation to the point of destruction, a void of unknowing from which no stable footing can be found. What do we trust? Our perceptions? But perception is an active process whereby we order the world. Our experience?

Experience is a synonym for unreliable memory, falsification, and desire. The act of witness and narrating? But how do we judge such narratives if we possess no grounds on which to judge notions of truth? Our sense of self, then? But to what extent are we even our own authors, given that 'those stories which speak to us with the greatest resonance have a way of turning upon the teller and erasing him and his motives from all memory' (*Cities*, 277). We seem to have reached a philosophical impasse from which there can be no going on:

> For as the power to speak of the world recedes from us so also must the story of the world lose its thread and therefore its authority. The world to come must be composed of what is past. No other material is at hand. And yet I think he saw the world unravelling at his feet. The procedures which he had adopted for his journey now seemed like an echo from the death of things. I think he saw a terrible darkness looming. (*Cities*, 286)

Against this doubt, McCarthy offers us a glimpse of Christian faith ('That man who is all men and who stands in the dock for us until our own time come and we must stand for him' (*Cities*, 288)) and a final scene of feminine solicitude ('Well, Mr Parham, I know who you are. And I do know why' (*Cities*, 292)) as Billy finds a temporary moment of peace at last. Ultimately this 'darkness looming', the fear which haunts the trilogy, turns out not to be the shadow of mortality or the threat of atavistic violence, but rather the unbeknown nature of all things. So what next for McCarthy? At this stage it seems impossible to know. His dilemma is certainly close to that of Postmodernism as a whole, and a long way from the pastoral essentialism of the Western genre. A darkness made of darkness; there seems nowhere else for McCarthy's prose to go.

NOTES

1. Abbreviations and page references refer to the following editions of McCarthy's work: *Blood Meridian* (*Blood Meridian*, London: Picador, 1990), *Horses* (*All the Pretty Horses*, London: Picador, 1993), *Crossing* (*The Crossing*, London: Picador, 1998), *Cities* (*Cities of the Plain*, London: Picador, 1999).
2. The picture I have in mind here is Thomas Cole's 'Falls of the

Kaaterskill' (1826), part of the Warner Collection of Gulf States Paper Collection, Tuscaloosa, Alabama.

3. Peter Messant (1994), *All the Pretty Horses*: Cormac McCarthy's Mexican Western, *Borderlines* 2 (2), December, p. 97.
4. Barcley Owens (2000), *Cormac McCarthy's Western Novels*, Tucson: University of Arizona Press, p. 27.
5. Ibid.
6. Ibid., p. 8.
7. Denis Donoghue (1993), *New York Review of Books*, 24 June, p. 5.
8. Neil Campbell (2000), 'Liberty beyond its proper Bounds: Cormac McCarthy's history of the West in Blood Meridian', in Rick Wallach (ed.), *Myth, Legend, Dust, Critical Responses to Cormac McCarthy*. Manchester: Manchester University Press, p. 218.
9. David Holloway (2000), '"A false book is no book at all": the ideology of representation in Blood Meridian and the Border trilogy', in *Myth, Legend, Dust*, p. 192 (Note 8, above).
10. See John Sepich (1999), '"What kind of indians was them?": some historical sources in Cormac McCarthy's *Blood Meridian*', *Perspectives on Cormac McCarthy*, Jackson: University Press of Mississippi, pp. 145–58.
11. Eileen Battersby (1989), *Irish Times*, 16 June.
12. Sepich, p. 125.
13. Richard Godden (2000), '*Blood Meridian* and "the evening redness in the east"', unpublished paper.
14. Quoted by Owens, p. 8.
15. Owens, p. 26.
16. Patrick W. Shaw (2000), 'Female presence, male violence, and the art of artlessness in Cormac McCarthy's Border trilogy', in *Myth, Legend, Dust*, p. 262 (Note 8, above).
17. See Gail Moore Morrison (1999), '*All the Pretty Horses*: John Grady Cole's expulsion from Paradise', in *Perspectives on Cormac McCarthy*, pp. 178–9 (Note 10, above) and Owens, p. 63.
18. See Diane Luce (1999), 'The road and the matrix: the world as tale in *The Crossing*', in *Perspectives on Cormac McCarthy*, pp. 195–219 (Note 10, above).
19. John Beck (2000), 'A certain but fugitive testimony', in *Myth, Legend, Dust*, p. 210 (Note 8, above).
20. Luce, p. 202.
21. Beck, p. 215.
22. Charles Bailey (2000), 'The last stage of the hero's evolution: Cormac McCarthy's *Cities of the Plain*', in *Myth, Legend, Dust*, p. 74 (Note 8, above).

23. Edwin Arnold (1999), 'The last of the trilogy: first thoughts on *Cities of the Plain*', in *Perspectives on Cormac McCarthy*, p. 222 (Note 10, above).
24. Luce, p. 217.
25. Holloway, p. 189.
26. Orville Prescott (1965), 'Still another disciple of William Faulkner', *New York Times*, 12 May.

BIOGRAPHY

McCarthy was born in Rhode Island in 1933, but grew up in Knoxville, Tennessee, where his father served on the legal staff of the Tennessee Valley Authority. He attended Catholic High School in Knoxville, and started his liberal arts degree at the University of Tennessee in 1951 before leaving to join the US Air Force in 1953, where he was mainly stationed in Alaska. He returned to the university in 1957, won the Ingram-Merrill award for creative writing in 1959 and 1960, married fellow student Lee Hollemann (who published a series of poems about their short-lived marriage in her collection, *Desire's Door* (1991)) in 1961, and sired a son, Cullen.

Still without a degree, McCarthy worked as a salesman in an auto-store in Chicago and started to write his first novel, *The Orchard Keeper*, which was eventually accepted and published in 1965 by William Faulkner's editor, Albert Erskine, at Random House. By this point McCarthy's first marriage had broken down. He met his second wife, Anne DeLisle on a trip to England and Ireland (according to Edwin T. Arnold, the historic Cormac McCarthy was the king who built Blarney Castle; McCarthy was actually christened Charles). With the benefit of a Rockerfeller education grant, the couple toured Europe and settled for a time in an artists' colony in Ibiza, where McCarthy finished his second novel, *Outer Dark*, published in 1968.

The McCarthys relocated to Tennessee in 1967, living hand to mouth in a converted pig farm outside Knoxville. A Guggenheim fellowship enabled them to move to Louisville and allowed McCarthy space to write his most controversial novel, *Child of God*, which received extremely mixed notices in 1973.

McCarthy separated from DeLisle in 1976, and moved to El Paso, Texas, where he had already begun to research stories of the US–Mexican border. His last 'Appalachian' novel, *Suttree*, which McCarthy had been writing on and off for twenty years finally appeared in 1979, and still stands as his longest, most demanding, and most autobiographical work. In 1981 McCarthy was awarded a MacArthur fellowship, a scheme set up to aid impecunious geniuses, which allowed him to further his historical and geographical research, physically traversing the settings which would make up his astonishingly visceral Western, *Blood Meridian* (1985). At this stage in his career McCarthy was still pretty much unknown outside of academic or critical circles, although a full-length study by Vereen Bell appeared in 1988, and *The Southern Quarterly* devoted a special issue to him in 1992. All this was to change with Knopf's publication of the first of the Border trilogy, *All the Pretty Horses*, in 1992, which went on to sell over 100,000 copies in its first year, and was awarded both the National Book Award and the National Book Critics Circle Award. He also gave his first and to date only substantial interview to *The New York Times Magazine* in the same year. *The Crossing* appeared in 1994 and *Cities of the Plain* in 1998. Billy Bob Thornton's film adaptation was released in December 2000, but failed at the box-office; nevertheless the film rights to *Blood Meridian* and an unnamed screenplay have also been sold. McCarthy continues to protect conscientiously his private life from intrusion, and is rumoured to have remarried in 1998.

APPROACHES TO CORMAC McCARTHY

An Americanist Approach
Whilst McCarthy's admittance into the American literary canon has been slow in coming, in many ways it's hard to imagine a more quintessentially American writer. Critics have drawn attention to his formal debts to Herman Melville (in terms of his crazed, incantatory sermonising), Ernest Hemingway (the other pole of McCarthy's prose, a flat, pared-down matter-of-factness about physical things), John Hawke (delirious visions of a fully functioning Hell), Flannery O'Connor (a peculiarly Southern and Christian brand of black humour), and, of course, William Faulkner, who, for a great number of critics at least, seems to provide a model for McCarthy's stylistic swerves between high-faluting, arcane rhetoric and ornery, pungent detail. Add to this McCarthy's deployment of all-American archetypes – in particular, the well-worn paradigm of the frontier with its binary opposition between civilisation and savagery, the individual and society, and man and nature – and you have a writer who seems to fit almost too snugly into the traditional model of the Great American Novelist.

But is this proof of the abiding longevity of national myths regarding the American wilderness, or simply another example of Postmodern recycling, a reheated Tex-Mex for nostalgic urbanites? Or is it that in the race to pigeon-hole a difficult and formally demanding author, McCarthy has been systematically misread: certainly *Blood Meridian* in particular seems predicated upon very different philosophical, moral and aesthetic assumptions from Faulkner's great works. One could apply virtually any of the classic texts of American literary criticism, from *Studies in Classic American Literature* to *Love and Death in the American Novel*, and produce a perfect fit: but what would this really tell us about McCarthy? 'The ugly fact is that books are made out of books,' explained McCarthy in *The New York Times* in 1992: hence is it possible to write a 'straight' novel of the American West; to describe the wilderness as if for the first time? How 'knowing' or 'innocent' a writer is McCarthy?

A Revisionist Approach

A second, more politicised approach might argue that McCarthy engages with American myths only to debunk them, deconstructing the racist and imperialist assumptions which underpin traditional notions of the 'Old West'. John Sepich in particular, has drawn attention to how meticulously researched are even the most surreal scenes of uninhibited butchery which McCarthy employs – *Blood Meridian* a compendium of historical records, memoirs, confessions and anthropological data. Is McCarthy thus seeking to show us the West as it really was (a fairly straight forward assumption of historical realism) or is he engaged in a critique of manufactured clichés and specious assumptions? Neil Campbell links McCarthy's later work to movements in 'New' Western history, and argues that both deconstruct the ideology of the frontier and notions of national progress to reveal an ugly site of imperialist conquest. But is McCarthy's work simply too phantasmagoric, too hallucinatory, too strange really to fulfil such an explicitly political agenda? Does his work substitute an alternative mythus (an image of the West as an unremitting inferno of ceaseless violence) rather than reveal 'the truth', in any acceptably historical sense? Moreover, what are we to make of the seemingly non-ironic nostalgia for the codes of the Old West in the Border trilogy? This could be more game-playing and thus still essentially deconstructive, but such a reading seems to go against the essential spirit of the work. If McCarthy doesn't take his cowboys seriously, then *Cities of the Plain* is a ridiculously flat and empty conclusion to the trilogy.

A Regionalist Approach

On first inspection, McCarthy's *oeuvre* seems to fall into two convenient halves – the Appalachian novels which range from *The Orchard Keeper* (1965) to *Suttree* (1979), and his Western fiction which embraces *Blood Meridian* and the Border trilogy. McCarthy's actual move from Knoxville, Tennessee to El Paso, Texas, provides the geographical motivation for this shift, which in turn signals a marked change in setting, sensibility and approach – most apparent in the move from the garrulous impressionism of Suttree's memoirs, to the pared-down taciturnity of his later cowboys. However, such a bold distinction has already come under attack in recent McCarthy criticism. Whilst *The Orchard Keeper* and *Suttree* can be seen as the most Faulknarian of McCarthy's works, full of grotesque, tall-tales, eccentric erudition, a love of story-telling for its own sake, and an essentially melancholy view of history, *Child of God* (1973) seems to connect with *Blood Meridian*, stressing an ahistorical view of human nature as irredeemably violent. Nor do protestations of an abrupt change in style really stand up under close inspection; rather there is a remarkable continuity of symbolism, theme and authorial voice, with a kind of apocalyptic grandeur present in McCarthy's fiction from the onset. Moreover, McCarthy's links between South and West are fairly explicit. *Blood Meridian* is populated by a good number of displaced Tennesseans (including its lead character), and *Cities of the Plain* argues against any notion of the 'Wild West'.

> I think these people mostly came from Tennessee and Kentucky. Edgefield district in South Carolina. Southern Missouri. They were mountain people . . . They always would shoot you. It wasn't just here. They kept comin west and about the time they got here was about the time Sam Colt invented the sixshooter and it was the first time these people could afford a gun you could carry around in your belt. That's all there ever was to it. It had nothin to do with the country at all. The west. They'd of been the same it dont matter where they might of wound up. (*Cities of the Plain*, p. 189)

A Generic Approach
Although published by a major publisher (Random House) and edited by Faulkner's long-time editor, Albert Erskine, McCarthy's early work sold poorly and attracted only a very small coterie of supporters. Orville Prescott's summation of his work ('Still another disciple of William Faulkner') suggests a kind of exhaustion of the Modernist ideals and aesthetics which McCarthy sought to uphold: a stumble from experimentalism to indulgence, absurdism to sensationalist violence, textual richness to impenetrability.[26] *Blood Meridian*, supported by a MacArthur Fellowship, suggested a way out of this artistic dead-end, rooted in historical research, mythic archetypes, and a sustained engagement with a single theme: man's limitless propensity for violence. Though now regarded as McCarthy's masterpiece, the novel caused few ripples outside of the generally Southern and academic supporters of his previous work; as Madison Smartt Bell puts it, 'He shunned publicity so effectively that he wasn't even famous for it.'

The financial failure of the novel even threatened McCarthy's ability to continue as a writer; hence his unacknowledged but self-conscious decision to deploy generic fiction as a vehicle for his actual metaphysical and thematic concerns. Barcley Owens argues that McCarthy finally decided to give people what they want, 'the mythic stuff of their dreams', a generic approach deploying the usual formulaic staples: noble heroes, love at first sight, strict definitions of good and evil, a tourist's nostalgia for nature. *All the Pretty Horses* perfected this recipe, and sold over 100,000 copies in less than a year. *The Crossing* allowed more of McCarthy's genuine interests (in the nature of storytelling, language and matter, fate and free-will) to surface from beneath the Horse Opera template and therefore was less popular; *Cities of the Plain,* bar its incomprehensible coda, saw McCarthy's more shrewdly commercial instincts firmly in the saddle. However by this stage, McCarthy's loss of interest in generic conventions was clear to see. The novel, little more than a reworked version of the film script which McCarthy had been hawking for a good ten years, was an artistic failure, suggesting that his delicate balancing act between thematic interests and generic convention had finally given way. What now?

A Modernist Approach

Reading McCarthy through the lens of generic Western fiction is as foolish as reading *Moby Dick* in terms of the whaling industry: there are no breaks or jumps in McCarthy's fiction, either between South and West, or *Blood Meridian* and the Border trilogy, no 'selling-out', no empty exercise in parodying worn-out conventions. His obsessive concern remains the same: is it possible to know the world through language? Indeed, this struggle between vision/perception and the tangible absolutes of the world is at the very centre of Modern Art, philosophy and fiction: How does one square the 'I' and 'It', the subjective and the objective, linguistic abstraction and tangible matter? McCarthy believes in a reality which is ultimately outside of us and beyond us, but his struggle to represent such an absolute (an inherently religious idea) links his work to the most heroic ideals (and struggles) of Modernism. Hence his work has nothing in common with the stale repetition of the already said which forms Postmodernism's linguistic end-game. His furious engagement with Nature, Death, God and Fate is purely his own, out of step with the mediated banality which surrounds him. Such grandiose themes are no more exhausted or redundant for McCarthy than they were for Melville; rather they form the essential, ahistorical concerns of Art. Hence the variety of crazed seers, soothsayers, hermits and anchorites who occupy his work, a condition to which the intensely anti-social McCarthy aspires.

A Postmodernist Approach

Such protestations of holy innocence are impossible to uphold in the twenty-first century. McCarthy's landscape is made up of words not stones, signs rather than horses, texts not reality. His work sifts through various textual agencies – historical records, Modernist experiments (for Modernism, if repeated after the event, comes back in terms of recycled Postmodernism), generic scenarios, evangelical sermons – practising, in David Holloway's words, 'a kind of self-reflexive literary criticism' which is the work of a bibliophile rather than a cow-hand. Pynchon, rather than Faulkner, is a better reference point here: McCarthy knows that 'reality' is simply a textual strategy, 'fate' is a question of narrative-systems, 'God' the absent trace of our faltering belief in the veracity of 'the Word'. The metafictional elements of his work are apparent throughout his novels: his concern with issues of representation, narrative, documentation and legitimacy. Ultimately, his work is an exploration of how we think about language, as the extraordinary coda to *Cities of the Plain* makes clear. It is here that the generic scaffolding of trilogy is ruthlessly deconstructed, leaving, in a textual wilderness of endlessly receding words, a wilderness which can have no end. But would McCarthy agree with any of this?

LINKS TO OTHER AUTHORS

Don DeLillo/Paul Auster: Like McCarthy, DeLillo and Auster use spatial metaphors to connect ideas of map-making, space and representation. The notion of some kind of untouched wilderness is important to all three writers. DeLillo's *White Noise* (1984), like *Blood Meridian*, links the real with both death and violence, whilst Auster's *Moon Palace* (1989) also explores the idea of desert space in terms of what cannot be described.

Rolando Hinojosa: Hinojosa's prose offers a very different view of the US–Mexican border, its demotic humour puncturing McCarthy's use of the border as a metaphysical boundary.

E. Annie Proulx: McCarthy and Proulx both stress language as craft and skill, contrasting the practical or pragmatic with the romantic. Proulx's *Close Range* (1999) explores cowboy masculinity in extremely clear-eyed terms, stripped of any kind of mythical trappings.

Bret Easton Ellis: Both *Blood Meridian* and *American Psycho* (1991) could be read in terms of the connection between extreme violence and the Postmodern logic of numb repetition.

Thomas Pynchon: Both writers employ the movement westwards in terms

of its classical meaning: the movement toward death. Crazed seers, contradictory orators, and arcane mysticism link McCarthy's religious, metaphysical
work, to Pychon's.

BIBLIOGRAPHY

Primary Works
The Orchard Keeper (1965), New York: Random House.
Outer Dark (1968), New York: Random House.
Child of God (1973), New York: Random House.
Suttree (1979), New York: Random House.
Blood Meridian (1985), New York: Random House.
All the Pretty Horses (1992), New York: Knopf.
The Crossing (1994), New York: Knopf.
The Stone Mason (1994), Hopewell: Ecco Press.
The Gardener's Son (1996), Hopewell: Ecco Press (screenplay).
Cities of the Plain (1998), New York: Knopf.

Critical Sources
Ambrosiano, Jason (1999), 'Blood in the tracks: Catholic Postmodernism in *The Crossing*', *Southwestern American Literature* 25 (1), Fall, pp. 83–91.
Arnold, Edwin T. (2000), '"Go to sleep": dreams and visions in the Border trilogy.' *Southern Quarterly* 38 (3), Spring, pp. 34–58.
Arnold, Edwin T. & Luce, Dianne (eds) (1999), *Perspectives on Cormac McCarthy*, Jackson: University Press of Mississippi.
Bailey, Charles (1994),'Doomed enterprises and faith: the structure of Cormac McCarthy's *The Crossing*', *Southwestern American Literature* 20, Fall, pp. 57–67.
Bell, Vereen M. (1988), *The Achievement of Cormac McCarthy*, Baton Rouge: Louisiana State University Press.
Clarke, Brock (1999), 'Art, authenticity, and social transgression in Cormac McCarthy's *All the Pretty Horses*', *Southwestern American Literature* 25 (1), Fall, pp. 117–23.
Guillemin, George (2000), '"As of some site where life had not succeeded": sorrow, allegory, and pastoralism in Cormac McCarthy's *Border trilogy*', *Southern Quarterly* 38 (3), Spring, pp. 72– 98.
Guinn, Matthew (2000), *After Southern Modernism: Fiction of the Contemporary South*, Jackson: University Press of Mississippi.
Hall, Wade & Wallach, Rick (eds) (1995), *Sacred Violence: A Reader's Companion to Cormac McCarthy*, El Paso: Texas Western Press.
Harrison, Brady (1999), '"That immense and bloodslaked waste": negation

in *Blood Meridian'*, *Southwestern American Literature* 25 (1), Fall, pp. 35–42.

Holloway, David (2000), 'Modernism, nature, and Utopia: another look at 'optical democracy' in Cormac McCarthy's Western quartet", *Southern Quarterly* 38 (3), Spring, pp. 186–205.

Hunt, Alex (1998), 'Right and false suns: Cormac McCarthy's *The Crossing* and the advent of the atomic age', *Southwestern American Literature* 23 (2), Spring, pp. 31–7.

Jarrett, Robert (1997), *Cormac McCarthy*, New York: Twayne.

Luce, Dianne C. (2000), 'Ambiguities, dilemmas, and double-binds in Cormac McCarthy's *Blood Meridian'*, *Southwestern American Literature* 26 (1), Fall, pp. 21–46.

— (2000), 'The vanishing world of Cormac McCarthy's *Border trilogy'*, *Southern Quarterly* 38 (3), Spring, pp. 121–46.

Masters, Joshua J. (1998), '"Witness to the uttermost edge of the world": Judge Holden's textual enterprise in Cormac McCarthy's *Blood Meridian'*, *Critique: Studies in Contemporary Fiction* 40 (1), Fall, pp. 25–37.

Messant, Peter (1994), '*All the Pretty Horses*: Cormac McCarthy's Mexican Western', *Borderlines* 2 (2), December.

McBride, Molly (1999), ' From mutilation to penetration: cycles of conquest in *Blood Meridian* and *All the Pretty Horses'*, *Southwestern American Literature* 25 (1), Fall, pp. 24–34.

Owens, Barcley (2000), *Cormac McCarthy's Western Novels*, Tucson: University of Arizona Press.

Phillips, Dana (1996), 'History and the ugly facts of Cormac McCarthy's *Blood Meridian'*, *American Literature* 68, June, pp. 433–60.

Pilkington, Tom (1998), 'Fate and free will on the American frontier: Cormac McCarthy's Western fiction', *Western American Literature* 33 (1), Spring, pp. 7–25.

Poland, Tim (1994), 'And the word becomes horseflesh: the unheard discourse of Cormac McCarthy's *All the Pretty Horses'*, *Southwestern American Literature* 20, Fall, pp. 45–56.

Schopen, Bernard A. (1995), '"They rode on": *Blood Meridian* and the art of narrative', *Western American Literature* 30, Summer, pp. 179–94.

Scoones, Jacqueline (2000), 'The world on fire: ethics and evolution in Cormac McCarthy's Border trilogy', *Southern Quarterly* 38 (3), Spring, pp. 99–120.

Snyder, Phillip A. (2000), 'Cowboy codes in Cormac McCarthy's Border trilogy', *Southern Quarterly* 38 (3), Spring, pp. 147–66.

Spurgeon, Sara L. (1999), '"Pledged in blood": truth and redemption in Cormac McCarthy's *All the Pretty Horses'*, *Western American Literature* 43 (3), Spring, pp. 24–44.

Sullivan, Nell (2000), 'Boys will be boys and girls will be gone: the circuit of male desire in Cormac McCarthy's Border trilogy', *Southern Quarterly* 38 (3), Spring, pp. 167–85.

Twomey, Jay (1999), 'Tempting the child: the lyrical madness of Cormac McCarthy's *Blood Meridian*', *Southern Quarterly* 37 (3–4), Spring/Summer, pp. 255–65.

Wallach, Rick (ed.) (2000), *Myth, Legend, Dust: Critical Responses to Cormac McCarthy*, Manchester: Manchester University Press.

Useful Websites
http.//www.cormacmccarthy.com/
http.//www.mid.tec.sc.us/edu/ed/eng/biblio.html

ROLANDO HINOJOSA

Of all the writers under consideration here, the name of Rolando Hinojosa is perhaps the least familiar – to a British readership, at least.[1] But Hinojosa's ever-evolving *oeuvre* – which takes the form of a single interlinked, cross-generational cycle, the *Klail City Death Trip* – provides one kind of response to the contemporary attenuation of the word, precisely through its appeal to the novel's vocal range: fiction's ability to encompass a wide range of discursive forms – letters, reports, diary-entries, newspaper cuttings, historical records, conversations, tall-tales – and thereby to construct an endless dialogue between them, emphasising language as communication, repartee, banter and performance. In a sense, Hinojosa's best work – *The Valley* (1983), say, or *Klail City* (1987) – achieves that holy grail of socialist literature, the collective novel; but the voices are too richly idiosyncratic and irascible to satisfy any kind of ideological certainty or consensus. There is no monopoly on truth in Hinojosa's work; nor does his chorus stay in tune. But in the contradictory, quarrelsome, loquacious dialogue Hinojosa traces a connection between community and communication which lies at the heart of his linguistic generosity. Meaning is always shared, debated, orated in his work; indeed, one cannot imagine the *Death Trip* existing in any other medium.

Of course, the idea that the 'wisdom of the novel' (to paraphrase Milan Kundera) is to be found in its propensity for contradiction and uncertainty – the asking of questions rather than the provision of answers – chimes with much Postmodern thinking on how the novelistic form actually functions.[2] In particular, M. M. Bakhtin's notion of heteroglossia – the novel as an interweaving of various forms of speech, a polyphony of voices – provides a theoretical justification for Hinojosa's use of multiple narrators, plural interpretations, and conflicting evidence.[3] The truth in Hinojosa's work is never simply stated, but rather created through its ceaseless dialogue; since no character can claim sole property, this in turn forms the democratic basis of his work.

Not that such a notion is limited to Postmodern writing; other critics have linked Hinojosa's use of brief episodes, sketches and (fictitious) 'found' documents, to Modernism's stress upon a multiverse supplanting a conventionally realistic universe. John Dos Passos' multifaceted *USA* (1938) trilogy could be cited as one precedent, as could the querulous voices of William Faulkner's *As I Lay Dying* (1931) or *The Sound and the Fury* (1929), with one key extract from the latter ('They all talked at once, their voices insistent and contradictory and impatient, making of unreality a possibility, then a probability, then an incontrovertible fact, as people will when their desires become words') encapsulating Hinojosa's formal approach.[4] But it is also possible to trace less familiar and much older sources which inform the *Death Trip*.

The original Spanish title of *The Valley* is *Estampas del valle y otras obras* (1973), *Estampas* being a reference to eighteenth-century sketches of manners published in Spanish newspapers of the time: satirical, anecdotal vignettes whose brevity and wit provide a template for Hinojosa's twentieth-century prose.[5] Likewise the title of *Claros varones de Belken County* (*Fair Gentlemen of Belken County*) (1987) derives its source from fifteenth-century Spanish writing which sketched the physical, moral and social characteristics of Spain's ruling classes – frequently presented in a subtly ironic, even satirical vein.[6] Hinojosa extends this treatment to truck drivers, barmen and street-sweepers, juxtaposing the form's elevated prose (which in the twentieth century becomes the bureaucratic jargon of officials, politicians and bankers) with the vulgar vitality of everyday speech. Ideas of hierarchy or any sense of a single authoritarian meaning are thus questioned throughout the novels; Hinojosa's work is alive with the undisciplined clamour of a town-meeting or (more frequently) the bar-room. This comic mixture of different types of discourse, the elevation of the mundane into personal myth and the debunking of the pretentious through bathos, also serves to suggest another key source here – it is, perhaps, not entirely irrelevant that Hinojosa completed his masters degree studying Cervantes' *Don Quixote*.

But are there limits to the idea of the novel as 'the great democratic shout' as DeLillo puts it?[7] Critic Lennard Davis has poured scorn on Bakhtin's notion of the novel as many-headed, inclusive and plural; after all, isn't the voice always that of the author, no matter how well

disguised by ventriloquism or impersonation?[8] Claims of catholic inclu-
siveness – a kind of fictional universal suffrage, whereby everybody is
allotted their reasons – always lay the author open to counter-claims
regarding whoever might be marginalised or left out. And, yes,
Hinojosa's world is predominantly male, his milieu rooted in his
own experiences and upbringing, his voice immediately distinct, irrespective of which character is actually doing the orating. But the main
source of contention regarding Hinojosa's work has always been
political and linguistic – the two terms forever conjoined in the study
of Chicano literature.

Chicano writing always tends to be understood in terms of a conflict
between the encroachment of the dominant Anglo culture and the
threatened minority tongue of the region – a patois which is already
impure, being a mix of Spanish, Indian and older Anglo sources. The
very notion of Chicano literature therefore suggests a number of
specifically ideological connotations; a defence of a marginalised
people, the upholding of class pride, the notion of acting as a voice
(and memory) for the voiceless and forgotten. The characteristic tone
of Chicano literature is therefore not merely engaged but revolutionary; the lack of such ideological rhetoric in Hinojosa's work is therefore
all the more notable and for this reason controversial. Instead, his
position is closer to that expressed by François Truffaut's famous
dictum: 'I deeply mistrust everything that divides the world into two
groups: goodies and baddies, bourgeois and artists, cops and robbers.'[9]
Hinojosa's work consistently repudiates didactic themes, what he
terms 'boxed-in positions', secure notions of right and wrong. Instead
of staunchly defending the virgin purity of his mother-tongue,
Hinojosa stresses the linguistic immixture of his upbringing, its
complex blending of cultures, codes and language, its impurity and
richness. The Rio Grande Valley is hence to be treasured, not as the
last bastion of some untouched authentic folk culture, but rather as
the American melting pot in extremis – mongrel, interbred, and alive.
Certainly, Hinojosa remains aware of the threat of a blandly homogeneous 'outsider' culture, but he trusts in the innate vitality of the region
to resist, and indeed, actively to transform it.

Needless to say, such a position has its critics. As his *Death Trip* series
has progressed, so two central characters – Rafe Buenrostro and Jehú
Malacara – have emerged from the cast, slowly making their way in the
Anglo world, and thereby ever more explicitly distancing themselves

from their Chicano past. Joyce Glover Lee has described Hinojosa's central theme as 'the often wrenching transformation of the minority into a being who is, for all practical purposes, one of the majority.'[10] This process of acculturation is, of course, one of the central themes of American culture: the question of what is lost and what is gained in becoming an American, the endless, agonising negotiations between individualism and community, one's roots and one's possibilities – a narrative which America can never truly be done with. As Buenrostro and Malacara have penetrated the legal and economic establishment (one a police officer, the other a banker), so Hinojosa has switched from Spanish to English to represent their lives; a shift, Hinojosa argues, born out of linguistic honesty rather than expediency – this is the world in which they live, these are the terms by which they operate. For an instinctively bilingual writer such as Hinojosa, this transition carries few political connotations; but for some critics (Joyce Glover Lee in particular) the shift from the collective to the individual, from Spanish to English, and from the colloquial to the clipped functionalism of the police procedural or legal report, suggests an identification with the establishment which underlines the distance his characters have travelled – a journey which permits no going back.

Needless to say, Hinojosa disagrees. He sees ongoing activity of reworking his early novels into English as an opening up of his oeuvre, another mode of address which enters into an ongoing dialogue with his Spanish works (instead of a literal translation, there are major differences between the two), which is itself further evidence of the organic, ever-evolving nature of his work; its unfinished (and therefore living) quality. But has something been lost with the progression of the *Death Trip*, a forfeiture suggested by the very title of the series itself? Faced with Malacara's involvement with the murky financial imbroglio of Klail City's banking system, or sifting through Buenrostro's bureaucratic wrangling, it's hard not to miss Esteban Echevarrìa's tall-stories, to feel an elegiac sense of the passing of the authentic, or at least the loss of a kind of rude eloquence. Of course, there are many good, non-theoretical reasons why the past may appear more dramatic than the present. One might draw attention to Hinojosa's self-confessed preoccupation with the days of his youth and young manhood, or his sense that the struggle to be at least recognised by the dominant culture has now been achieved. There is also the simple fact that past events can be seen to have achieved a certain shape and form, at least when compared with the messy uncertainties of the present moment. But one might also feel that Hinojosa's guiding stars of Place and History seem less distinct as we travel through the twenty-first century – a loss which underpins the whole of *Klail City Death Trip*.

Rolando Hinojosa was kind enough to talk about these and other matters in the following interview, conducted in December 2001.

HINOJOSA ON HINOJOSA

AB: If I may, I'd like to start with a fundamental, and perhaps rather personal question: why write? To create something? To express some deeply-felt experience or emotion? To make public your views? Goethe believed that 'The beginning and end of all literary activity is the reproduction of the world that surrounds me by means of the world that is in me.' Would you agree?

RH: I suppose I'm no different from any other artist; one wants to express oneself, and, for me, writing is what I'm able to do. I also think that most people want to create something, and some of us are lucky enough to do so. As for deeply-felt experiences, or emotions, yes, and, as most writers, I should think, early experiences and emotions are how one begins when writing. Too, one writes to be read and thus to make one's views public. Otherwise, why write if not to express oneself? By so doing, of course, one also exposes oneself, but that's the trade-off. Some writers, I think, forget why they started writing in the first place and wander off to write stuff they may not particularly care for.

In my work, I try to recreate the world I was raised and lived in for the first seventeen years of my life: a small, hierarchical, rural community populated by Anglo and Mexican Americans living on the northern bank of the Rio Grande, some thirty miles from where the river empties into the Gulf of Mexico.

Later experiences and travels have enlarged the scope of what I write, but the early years, if not dominant, are present in the writing. Philip Roth, for one, was born and raised in Newark, across the river from New York, and writes of both places and its people. I imagine he could write about California and get away with it, but would he be satisfied with the work is the question.

AB: Is (as Hemingway claimed) the job of the writer to tell the truth?

RH: One does try to write the truth and usually at the beginning of one's career. While facts may not change, what one accepted as truths may have changed, and this, then, serves as an impetus to the writer. I don't think that one sets out to prove a truth but rather to present it, and then to develop it as one matures.

But one must remember that the word fiction stands for something, and thus one weaves the truth or several truths in a work. One does so to satisfy oneself but also to reveal those truths one has lived with through the years. Did Hemingway present the truth, or a truth, in his brief work *The Fifth Column*? We know which side he favoured and thus he told that truth, as he saw it. None of us has a monopoly on truth or on the last word, but such pronouncements are the type some writers make to beginning writers and to writing clubs.

AB: Do you see any kind of tension or conflict in your twin roles as writer and academic? I'm particularly interested in your thoughts regarding what might be loosely termed 'Postmodern critical theory'. By this I mean the notion that every writer writes books about books, that words only refer to other words, and any sense of 'reality' is just a textual mirage – much like the author him or herself. Does any of this influence how and why you write or do you consider such abstraction the antithesis of literary activity?

RH: I see no conflict or tension in my roles as an academic and as a writer. I teach courses in American literature, and since I'm ignorant regarding critical theory, I teach the course as a writer, that is, I show how the novels are put together, what the writer does to make the writing work. Then, as we read, I show how the writer creates a character, and why we may be or may not be satisfied with the characterisation. This brings in tone and attitude and their effect on them, the readers. I also point to the time in which the work takes place, the social classes which are presented, and focus on the language of the time and place the novel is set.

This leads to all manner of questions, and I find the students become involved since I'm not preaching or advocating one particular school of literary criticism. I also, from time to time during the term, remind them that we are not reading classical material; that what we are reading may be transitory, but that if read with care, they can then see what the writer is doing. They can, then, apply what and how we have been reading to other novels.

Language, the tool we work with, is what I emphasise in the papers they turn in. I am more interested in standard English usage than in swimming in what I call the streams of speculation. Flights of fancy is a fine, and as the students say, a fun way to pass the time in class. Well, I won't have that.

Despite what education I have come up with, I remain a working-class product. That I don't belong to that class because of the doctorate does not mean I've forgotten it or forgotten how I was raised.

AB: Do you feel that the formal possibilities of the novel have been pretty well mapped-out by now? Is the age of literary experimentation or invention now behind us?

RH: I very much doubt if we will ever map-out or run out of ways to write a novel. One can look at novel writing and compare it to the musical scale with its defined number of notes which are then quartered and halved and so on to produce thousands upon thousands of com-positions. Here, I think, is where the answer lies to why one writes. One admires past writers, but that does not mean one will write in that manner. Experimentation is a difficult trail, but that too is why one writes.

As for literary critics, I find them important if not essential. But I also think some of them have placed themselves in a box of their choosing, or of their professors's choosing, by favouring one literary school over another. I don't believe writers labour over this, nor is it our job to do so, since we have enough on our plate without worrying over what a special group may or may not like.

AB: Do you feel that literature has any kind of effect upon contempo-rary culture? Do books matter?

RH: I think books matter, but I also think that writers will continue to write even if books are not as popular as they once were, given electronic games and the rest of the entertainment industry. But books do affect contemporary culture and, in many ways, politics. Not that politicians welcome changes, but their constituents may be influenced by reading and in turn, will influence the elected officials.

I've no idea how many times I've heard of the difficulty of reading

Faulkner, but his writing has affected enlightened Mississippians and other Southerners as well. Faulkner's South has not completely disappeared, but it isn't the same South any more. His insistence on blood relationships and the South's unhappy history in this regard can neither be denied nor disregarded. The same goes for the writing of Flannery O'Connor, Eudora Welty, Katherine Anne Porter, and other Southern writers.

AB: To what extent do you consider yourself a specifically American writer? Do you have a sense of writing for a particular constituency or of acting as a spokesman for any kind of group?

RH: I'm nothing if I'm not an American writer. That I concentrate on the Anglo and Mexican American relationships and their history, on their commercial, cultural, and psychological ties up and down the border, is because I know the place and its people. Lynchings, deprivation of voting rights, discrimination regarding education, and being viewed as second- or third-class citizens was something I was raised with. Hence, when I write, the works are viewed as truthful, because these are historical truths. That the region has changed from the way it was at the beginning of the twentieth century and on through the Great Depression, World War II, and so on, and that those social and civil crimes are not as prevalent, or as obvious, is something I also write about. That may be part of Hemingway's truth, but the region has changed, and I also write about changes and alliances which previous generations of Anglo and Mexican Americans would not have dreamed of.

Society is a dynamic force, and the writer has to keep abreast of historical facts. For me to bang away now as if what happened then is still going on now, is to present a distorted as well as an inaccurate picture of the place, and of the United States as they are now.

Now, since I'm writing a series of works, I present the best and the worst of the place. The early novels of the *Klail City Death Strip* reveal the discrimination and crimes I mentioned for it's one's responsibility not to go around painting pretty pictures. It isn't paradise, as I've written elsewhere, and I don't write for one special group. There are devils and angels, victims and betrayers and characters who are full of abnegation, and so on. That both Anglo and Mexican American readers see themselves in the work is part of what I have set out to do. That they may not like what they see, or read, in this case, is up to them. My readership consists mainly of university students and professors, and they, as I, will not stand for cheap shots.

We talked earlier about my being an American writer. Well, I was born in this country, and I write about what my friends and I experienced socially, economically, and educationally. This includes the Chicano political and military experience. In part, it remains an untold story. What some of us have set out to do is to write from the inside. For my part, I write about the good and the bad in Anglo and Mexican American society. To do that, I use monologues, dialogues, the epistolary novel, reportage, the detective procedural and imaginary newspaper articles. In brief, whatever literary technique will help me.

I also use humour and carnivalesque situations because without humour, what one writes is not literature but propaganda tracts.

Unlike the old Europe where France was mainly populated by the French or the UK populated mainly by the descendants of the four areas which comprise the United Kingdom, the United States, in some ways, is not unlike the old Austro-Hungarian Empire: a mishmash of people ruled by seats of government more and more removed from its people. One would hope for a better rule than that under the Hapsburgs. In the United States, the government one gets is the one that is voted to power by a small number of its citizens. Interestingly, it's also a small number of people who contribute the most money.

At present, I'm mapping out a novel that is to reflect Belken County as it is now with the Mexican American population for the most part teachers, principals, superintendents, police chiefs, elected on boards of education, and in various small and larger businesses. This looks like a rosy picture, but there is a marked absence in bank ownerships or in car agencies, both great sources of economic power, or in the ownership of the rich agricultural land, the third major source of economic power in the area.

There have been changes in local, regional, state, and federal positions with a Mexican American presence. They're getting what they've always wished for with the attendant dangers in those wishes. Humour, of course, will be the vehicle, it couldn't be otherwise.

AB: In one interview you said that you didn't think you could ever write a novel without referring to some form of history. I wonder what your students think of this, given that contemporary culture is often accused of having no consciousness at all. Is history a thing of the past? Has some sort of continuity with previous generations snapped?

RH: I use history as a signpost; an inescapable reality. For my students, those droplets of history present in the novels, not only in mine, but also in the other novels of the American Southwest, principally Texas, are revelations they hadn't counted on. Texas, as most places, has its myths, but ours are an exaggeration as are most things Texan. Unless undergraduates are history majors, they bring to class what their parents and their fellow undergraduates hold onto; myths. Many believe that Texas can be divided into five states at any time. They forget, perhaps never understood, that the Constitution provides for a union of indissoluble states; this was questioned shortly after the Civil War, but the US Supreme Court in *Texas v. White* again affirmed that we are a union of indissoluble states. There are many other myths but the reality is that as a state, we inherited and maintain an inferiority complex. We're loud, and we're boisterous braggarts. At times, this is a pose, but too often it isn't. Texas Mexicans haven't forgotten the Alamo completely, but they also have little idea what the battle was about. When I mention that those inside the mission were Mexican citizens and thus rebels, Texans recoil. This is ignorance mixed with racism. We remain a Southern state: we seceded from the Union, we were a slave-holding state, we instituted Jim Crow laws, disenfranchised large portions of the population – black, poor white, and Mexican – with the poll tax, provided inferior and separate educational facilities, and on and on. I don't mean to give a history lesson here nor that that is all I lecture on; I bring these facts in when the novelists mention them and thus allow the students their say. But these students are not their parents nor do they carry the baggage their parents did. They do, however, need reminding.

Finally, at one point in the semester, I ask for a show of hands [of] those who have travelled to Europe. When asked how they identify themselves to Europeans, they, to a man and woman, say they're from Texas. Not the United States, but Texas. That is how deeply rooted our myths are.

AB: Do you think that the American idea of history is very different from the European? In a lot of European writing, history appears as a blind force of nature, occasionally erupting to destroy all in its path. The

Czech writer, Josef Škvorecký, once said that what he really wanted to write about was love, but that the horrors of history and politics always got in the way. I would assume that your own idea of history is very different. In what sense do you see yourself as a historical writer?

RH: Škvorecký is right regarding the horrors of history and politics. One can't ignore them, and I'm reminded of Eustace Budgell who wrote that facts were bothersome things in that they refused to go away. For those who write frivolous literature, if literature is the word, this is of small moment, but one cannot ignore the world.

As to my ideas of history, since I grew up during World War II, I have read as much as I've been able to regarding World War II – Versailles, the Great Depression, the Weimar Republic, and Hitler. When I die, and the books are collected, I don't doubt some fool will write that I was fascinated by the Nazis. Appalled is the word. You have David Irving, and I can't believe he is taken seriously. Of course one has to combat such people, but I can't accept that he negates proven, pictorial, and physical facts. As I said, history is a usable signpost for me much like the Civil War was for Faulkner. One mustn't forget or deny injustice, and what better way to present it than through literature which uses history as a foundation?

AB: Your own biography, in a sense, charts the relationship between Chicano and Anglo culture since the war. Did you ever feel that your subject matter was inescapable?

RH: When I started to write in high school, I was naturally influenced by American writers. I did not look around me although I was living and experiencing my daily life as a Texas Mexican. I took it for granted, but that didn't mean I accepted it. A lifetime of reading and coming from a family of readers, formed part of my adolescent education. Years later, when Tomás Rivera published his . . . *y no se lo tragó la tierra*, I discovered that that was what I wanted to do: present us, the Texas Mexicans, and the Hispanics in the Southwest, with a historical perspective. Unlike Rivera, I was born and raised on the border, and, as I have said repeatedly, not far from where the Rio Grande empties into the Gulf of Mexico.

For this I turned to tales and stories by the old people in my home town of 6,000. I caught the variants, but the message was always the same: we were here, they (the Anglos) came, and took whatever they wanted. This was mostly the case, but some Texas Mexicans did retain land. Not much, but it was something from which to build on.

I also read the Texas versions of Texas and Mexican history; in time, I discovered serious Texas Anglo historical writers who presented a version different from that of those who wrote hagiographies on James Bowie, David Crockett, William Travis, but who ignored the many positive, but unpopular, stances taken by Sam Houston.

So, armed with oral and all manner of historical works, I set off to write about my part of the world. While Texas Mexicans were victimised, I also noted that they victimised their fellow Texas Mexicans. This led to more digging, and I used that to help me to write not a single novel but rather a series, each part separate from the other, but which presented a cohesive whole.

It was, then, inescapable, although history was not the sole aim. It is, though, an *aide mémoire*. I used the Valley anthropology and geography as well as its culture, and, as always, reading, speaking, and writing in both languages.

AB: Is it harder to write about contemporary society? Is there a sense that the periods of greatest tension or struggle are in the past? Has the fight to force a cultural recognition of Chicano culture been won?

RH: Since I play with time in the series, I prefer to lag some twenty-five years behind the times. Much that was considered important at one time has now passed along with the welter of history.

I was born in 1929 and thus grew up during the Great Depression. This has marked me in many ways as was my teenage life marked by World War II and subsequent events. Reading European, North and Hispanic American literature as well has both helped and influenced me. This and my education and my three years in the military have also helped in my formation as a writer.

That I experienced, in childhood and as a teen[ager], what Texas provided socially and educationally as a Southern state has proved invaluable. I've lived a long life, enjoy reasonable health, and return to the Valley frequently, thus the new problems keep me going. Among these are drugs and violence; the false economy with the money that traffic brings; the break-up of some of the old families, such as ours which came to the area in 1747 and 1748, due to the drug economy; and the continuing the loss of language and thus culture among some social groups of Texas Mexicans which will continue to provide me with material.

AB: Following on from that, I'd be grateful if, for the benefit of British readers, you could define what you see as Chicano literature. Sorry if this seems a tall order in a sentence or two!

RH: The term 'Chicano' was a household word although most Americans of Mexican descent who had reached some level of the middle class did not use the term. And if they did, they referred to someone below them socially; conveniently forgetting the class they came from. The term did not catch [on] in Texas because Texas Mexicans preferred the term 'Mexicano'. The Anglos called us 'Messicans' – a put-down which led to fights on the playground.

In the late '60s with the war in Vietnam, the various civil rights movements, and a more educated class thanks to the Veteran's Entitlement Act, popularly known as the GI Bill, many Chicanos, to use that term for now, earned high-school diplomas and university degrees.

The term moved to the universities and was used, principally, by us, the privileged classes: students and professors. The Texas working classes preferred to refer to themselves as they always had: 'Mexicanos'. Some young Chicanos scoffed at the old people's use of the term; a mistake, of course, but then they were young. By the mid-'70s and now, the term, again in Texas, remains in the academy and among some students; although not in the general population. There are a number of clubs at the University of Texas in Austin, and they call themselves Mexican American, Hispanic, and, trailing, Chicano Cultural Centers. The Mexican American Studies Center is in the College of Liberal Arts.

The term 'Chicano' is popular among students, professors, and the bulk of Mexican Americans in California, Arizona, Colorado, and New Mexico. Hispanic and Hispanic American, perhaps due to the US census self-references, are also popular among the current generation.

When the publishing house Quinto Sol in Berkeley, California, began operation in 1967, its journal, *El Grito*, carried on its masthead 'A Journal of Mexican American Thought'; this at a time and place where the term 'Chicano' was strong. In 1970, Tomás Rivera won the first Quinto Sol Prize for . . . *y no se lo tragó la tierra*, and this then resulted in research on literature produced by Americans of Mexican descent; the centre for this recovery programme is at the University of

Houston. The academic establishment, always loath to adopt new entries into its offerings and curricula, did not welcome Chicano literature. That was then; it is now possible to earn [a] BA, [a] masters, and [a] doctorate in that field in many universities, particularly in the Southwest.

What, then, is Chicano literature? A categorical statement is not only wrong, it is also misleading. Generally, it is literature written in English or Spanish about Mexican American history and experience in the United States. Who writes it? Mexican Americans, Chicanos, or whatever they use as a self-referent. Some of the themes are rural or urban; the urban population now outnumbers the rural, and this has led to a speedier assimilation and acculturation which often lead to the loss or change of language and culture.

AB: How did you develop your characteristic style, yoking together disparate voices, sources, texts and references? There seems to be a constant play between integration and disintegration in your work. Was is it a case of the material determining the form, or was the idea of creating a polyphonic, multi-headed work central to your conception of the *Klail City Death Trip*?

RH: I think the style of yoking together voices, sources and all, came about in two ways. First, I wanted to present a panoramic view of Mexican Americans [and] their culture which includes history; not necessarily intensively but rather extensively. This, then, gave rise to the fragmentary novel which allowed me to present the various social strata of the Texas Mexicans; their history is most different from that of New Mexicans or Californians. The second novel was also fragmentary which afforded me more room to follow up on families and to establish identities of the multiple characters. This last produced additional voices. Secondly, after the first work and with a view toward the second, I decided to do a series. The models here were the Spaniard Benito Pérez Galdós, Balzac, and finally Anthony Powell. Each part would then spill over to the next one and so on. Of these, Powell is consistent with Nicholas Jenkins as his narrator. I wanted none of that; I wanted to present various classes, ages, and sexes. Their behaviour would allow for integration and disintegration which made my life easier; the characters would carry the ball, and the narrator, at times, would disappear. This last is most evident in *Becky and her Friends* [1990] where the characters speak to the narrator who gives the barest of biographical facts about the characters. As a result, the intervention by the narrator is slight.

Since I remain highly interested in form, the make-up of that society fits in with the polyphonic, multi-headed work I set out to do. It's no secret that form is a great determinant and a key to what one can do with the material at hand.

AB: What's the best way for new readers to go about reading the series? Is there an obvious jumping-off point?

RH: The series, from the first novel on, plays with time and thus space. This continues to the present day with two exceptions, the two detective novels which are procedural and thus linear. The point there was to give the narrator no privileged position in the telling of the story.

I would recommend beginning with *The Valley* which introduces many of the characters and the place. The second, *Klail City*, also works with time and space as the older generations begin to disappear and social and economic changes continue. Since I use wars as signposts, one sees emerging generations who may or may not continue the old ways of viewing the world. This sounds as if I had an order in mind; I didn't. I was lucky to have come up with the series.

AB: How do the Rafe Buenrostro mysteries fit into the overall shape of the series?

RH: The Rafe Buenrostro series are a fit because of the social and economic changes in the Valley. Land has always been a theme and some of it which had been lost has been regained through sales, marriages, and accommodation. I needed the two detective works because of the false economy in the Valley. The introduction of major drug contraband has brought to the place much money and its corollary, violence. And, since the money is illegal, it is not easily invested or disposed of unless it undergoes laundering. A consequence of this is that some of the founding families who came to the Valley in the eighteenth century have succumbed to big money. This, naturally enough, would foster all manner of changes in any society. The genre allows one to show violence and betrayal, but also steadfastness and the maintenance of values among the stalwarts. One should not read feel-good writing here, since fools and knaves are also presented.

I also eschewed the brawling detective; Buenrostro is a Chief Inspector and knows how to delegate, but he also does legwork. He is not a brilliant Holmes-type, but he has a keen memory, and he puts it to use.

Both works are in keeping with an old agenda; to use all manner of narrative prose: fragmentary, epistolary narrative verse as in the case of *Korean Love Songs* [1978], and reportage along with uninterrupted monologues and dialogues which form the bulk of *Rites and Witnesses* [1982] as well as long journals as in *The Useless Servants* [1993].

AB: The most significant change of direction in the series has been a movement from Spanish to English. To what extent do you accept the argument that such a shift possesses a political as well as an aesthetic dimension?

RH: This is the year 2002, and I noticed thirty years ago, that, with few exceptions, college-educated Mexican Americans are not as fluent as their parents and grandparents were in the '60s, '40s, and before. Their reading of Spanish is also weak, and weaker still, is their writing. Assimilation, acculturation, the rise of the middle class, in large part due to the Veterans' Entitlement Act, popularly known as the GI Bill, produced hundreds if not thousands of educated men and women who served in World War II and Korea.[11] Their children and also their grandchildren came from the middle classes due to their parents' education.

Since most parents spoke mostly in English to their offspring and used Spanish as a code, many of the children relied on their grandparents for their Spanish. Even now, in the Valley, with Valleyites having blood kinships on both sides of the Rio Grande, many of those who live on the northern bank don't speak Spanish fluently. The same pattern follows to a greater degree with the urbanites who need to assimilate and acculturate in the second and subsequent generations if they wish to compete in professions and in the work place. Their urban parents, first generation, say, encourage this so the children can better themselves.

I don't believe this is any different from what happened and happens in the large urban areas of the East and West Coasts among Greeks, Italians, and others. The Eastern European Jews who have contributed so much to American culture were in the same boat, as it were, when they came from Russia and Germany and elsewhere.

For some fifteen years, say between 1970 and 1985, the majority of publishing houses, with few exceptions, considered [producing] Mexican American literature. They thought it was all written in Spanish, or that it was an intramural literature, as were most emerging American literatures in their early form. It was also a matter of the market-place. Since 1985, and the academy has helped in this regard, houses such as Macmillan, HarperCollins, and Harcourt Brace Jovanovich began to publish anthologies of American literature which was, in its truest sense, American literature. They also publish literature for Hispanic children.

Most Mexican American writers today, right now, can't write in Spanish, but this isn't a sin or a betrayal as was looked upon by the older generations. I've not said that it's a fine literature, because, as in any literature, some is good and some isn't. Time, as always, is the judge.

AB: Do you think that your stress on the verities of Place and History position your work in opposition to the spirit of the time?

RH: No, I don't. I hold, along with many others, what Hume said about human nature that the mind is a collection of sensations; events, too, which produce those sensations as they are remembered, forgotten, recreated and so on as one writes and thinks about the past.

The spirit of the time is no different, I don't believe, from the way people behaved and thought in the old days. That they believe that people in the past were much better behaved than we are today betrays little knowledge of history and psychology; in brief, knowledge of our fellow human beings.

Part of the series shows the characters without knowledge of television, for one contemporary gadget, but they substituted other forms of entertainment; not to sound a cynic, one as brutal and as mindless as the other. Cheating and betrayal and conflict then is the same as today. Sacrifice, abnegation, and bravery are the same as they were then, as are cowardice and self-centredness. I may not buy everything Hume put out, but his overall view holds today, and especially for writers since we live now, are influenced by contemporary events and sensations, and we may set these at the time we are writing in years past.

AB: The title of your series suggests an elegiac sense of loss and the passing of time. To what extent would you see your work as nostalgic, even given the fact that the position of the Mexican American in Texas society has much improved materially?

RH: The first two parts, *The Valley* and *Klail City* suggest an elegiac sense of loss and the passing of time, and critics have written on this. But that's the problem of setting that down on paper: it is frozen and some may think that the series sticks with this. The speakers who hark to the past are of the old generation which disappears, except in the conversations of those who knew them. The young live in the present and are participants in wars, the university, family doings, their professions, to name a few instances where they find themselves.

The monologues given by an eighty-seven-year-old man reveal part of the old history and leave an oral record of what went on. This is part of the young's legacy, but the old do not counsel that the young should live in the past.

I mentioned earlier that many young men and women are not as fluent in Spanish as their forebears. This is true, but their opportunities for education and for political life are much different from what they were. They retain residual memories of what was told and passed on to them. That they didn't experience the harsh racism is one thing, but that racism exists is nevertheless true although not, thank God, to the extent that it once did in many areas.

I mentioned the GI Bill earlier. This was a great boon for the United States; the majority of Anglo-Americans prior to World War II did not enjoy the benefits of higher education. Congress's act opened the doors. Cynically enough for higher education, when *Brown v. Topeka Board of Education* in 1954 ruled separate but equal as unconstitutional, thus overthrowing *Plessy v. Ferguson*, this allowed many blacks, after much travail, and some deaths, to enrol in colleges and universities. When they proved their high athleticism, this formed another part of the cynicism in higher education.

This bolstered alumni contributions and enlarged stadiums, creating a special class of student, the athlete. All this took place with overwhelming public approval but also with a sense of apathy toward the mission of higher education. Still, who knows what shape this country would be in now without the Brown decision.

AB: The other writer in this book whose work explores the US–Mexican border is Cormac McCarthy. What are your feelings

regarding his Border trilogy? Who, in your opinion, are the most interesting American writers working today?

RH: I've not read Cormac McCarthy. I usually wait for time to pass; for
the hoopla from New York, and Texas, of course, to die down. I confess
I'm not a reader of contemporary American literature. I know who they
are, and what they are about, but that's about it. I also read *The New
York Times* Sunday section and *TLS*. When *The New Yorker*, say, publishes
a critical essay or a long review by Updike, then I will take time to read
him. I also read some Joan Didion and some, not much, Susan Sontag;
this last has nothing to do with likes or dislikes. I like Alan Bennett's
work, but he isn't American. What's to be made of this? Well, there's
so much to read and so much claptrap that amounts to log rolling that
I choose not to join the parade.

NOTES

1. Astonishingly, for a writer widely considered to be the foremost Chicano
   novelist, Hinojosa has no UK publisher. In the US, his works are mainly
   published by Arte Publico Press, which operates out of the University of
   Houston, Texas.
2. See Milan Kundera (1990), 'The depreciated legacy of Cervantes', in *The
   Art of the Novel*, (transl. Linda Asher), London: Faber, pp.3–20.
3. See Mikhail M. Bakhtin (1981), *The Dialogic Imagination* (ed. and transl.
   Michael Holquist & Caryl Emerson), Austin: University of Texas Press. José
   David Salvídar applies these ideas to Hinojosa's prose in 'Rolando Hinojosa's *Klail City Death Trip*: a critical introduction', in José David Salvídar
   (ed.) (1985), *The Rolando Hinojosa Reader*, Houston: Arte Publico, pp. 44–63.
4. William Faulkner (1989), *The Sound and the Fury*, London: Picador, p.101.
5. See Rosaura Sánchez (1985), 'From heterogeneity to contradiction in
   Hinojosa's novel', *The Rolando Hinojosa Reader*, p. 78 (Note 3, above).
6. Ibid., p. 80.
7. Don DeLillo (1991), *Mao II*, London: Jonathan Cape, p. 159.
8. See Lennard J. Davis (1983), *Resisting Novels: Ideology and Fiction*, New
   York: New York University Press, pp. 177–8.
9. François Truffaut (1987), *Truffaut on Truffaut* (transl. Robert Erich Wolf),
   New York: Harry N. Abrams, p. 216.
10. Joyce Glover Lee (1997), *Rolando Hinojosa and the American Dream*,
    Denton: University of North Texas Press, p. 203.
11. Franklin Roosevelt's Serviceman Readjustment Act (1944) paid for
    access to higher education for millions of veterans after World War II.

BIOGRAPHY

Romeo Rolando Hinojosa was born in Mercedes, Texas, in 1929. On his father's side, he is descended from the Spanish colonists who first claimed the area for New Spain in the eighteenth century; on his mother's side, he is related to the early Anglo settlers who arrived in the Rio Grande Valley in 1887. Hinojosa was educated in both Mexican and American schools, and raised, like most Mexican Americans, bilingually.

After leaving high school Hinojosa served a term in the US army, and was called back to fight in the Korean war whilst a student at the University of Texas in Austin – a conflict which forms a significant reference-point in his work. Thereafter, he taught Spanish, History, and Government at Brownsville High School, worked for a Texas chemical company, took a civil-service post with the Social Security Administration, and eventually returned to higher education, producing a masters dissertation on *Don Quixote* and a doctorate on the novels of Pérez Galdós.

After his move to Texas Academy and Institute University in 1970, where he later became Chair of the Modern Language Department, he started to publish his first pieces of prose (mainly anecdotal short stories and satirical essays on local politics) in *El Grito*. His first novels, *Estampas del valle y otras obras* (1973) and *Klail City y sus alrededores* (1976), both written in Spanish, each won major prizes: the Premia Quinto Sol and the highly coveted Casa de las Américas, respectively. Hinojosa was now recognised as one of the leading figures of the 'Chicano' literary movement, and claimed sole property of the (fictional) Belken County and its environs, using it as the setting for his hugely ambitious *Klail City Death Trip* – an organic sequence of novels, detailing the Mexican American experience in Texas in the twentieth century.

All of Hinojosa's fiction feeds into this vast work, although the direction of his 'death trip' (a sense of mortality and the passing of a way of life underpinning the often riotous comedy of his work) has taken a number of unexpected twists and turns since then. His first work in English was a collection of poetry, *Korean Love Songs* (1978), also part of the *Death Trip* series; Hinojosa explained that as he experienced the war in English, as part of the US army, it would have been false to write about it in any other way. Similarly, as the setting for his fiction has moved ever closer to the Anglo, rather than Mexican, world, English has supplanted Spanish as his central tongue – a shift seen by some in the Chicano fraternity as a controversial and highly political decision.

In the '80s, he 're-created' his best known works, *The Valley* (1983) and *Klail City* (1987) in English, and opened up a surprising side-road from the *Death Trip* series, with *Partners in Crime* (1985), the first of the 'Rafe Buenrostro

Mysteries'. After serving terms as Dean of Arts and Sciences and Vice-President for Academic Affairs at Texas A&I, Hinojosa moved to the University of Minnesota for several years, before returning to the University of Texas at Austin in 1981, where he now serves as both Professor of English and Director of the Texas Center for Writers. Suspicious of dogmatic ideologies, didactic themes and 'boxed-in assumptions', Hinojosa's work in some ways sits uneasily alongside the more politicised wing of the Chicano canon, or at least that part of it which urges authors to (in the words of Felipe de Ortega y Gasca) 'praise the people, identify the enemy, and promote the revolution'. Hinojosa's tone is ironic, tolerant, and dismissive of the conceit of separating the world into simple categories of right or wrong; no-one possesses the truth in Hinojosa's writing, but everyone has the right to be understood. 'What I worked on, as far as my life was concerned, was toward a personal voice which was to become my public voice', he once noted: never stridently didactic but heterogeneous, multi-vocal, and sardonic.

LINKS TO OTHER AUTHORS

Don DeLillo: Hinojosa's stress on language as communal, the creation of shared narratives, can be placed alongside the ending to DeLillo's *The Names* (1982):

> This is a place to enter in crowds, seek company and talk. Everyone is talking. I move past the scaffolding and walk down the steps, hearing one language after another, rich, harsh, mysterious, strong. This is what we bring to the temple, not prayer or chant or slaughtered rams. Our offering is language. (*The Names*, p. 331)

Cormac McCarthy: McCarthy's Border trilogy is also set upon the US–Mexican border, and draws upon many of the same historical sources as Hinojosa's early work, albeit from an explicitly Anglo perspective.

E. Annie Proulx: Hinojosa links his work to those writers who 'impart a sense of place, and a sense of truth about that place, and about the values of that place'. Proulx's stress on the regional – what many Americans dismiss as 'fly-over country' – suggests a connection to Hinojosa, as does her notion of the local acting as some kind of defence against the placelessness of Postmodernism. *Accordion Crimes* explores the themes of acculturation and Americanisation – the traumatic shedding of one's ethnic identity in order to get ahead materially – in strikingly similar terms to Hinojosa's *Death Trip*.

Douglas Coupland: Hinojosa's stress on the lodestones of History and Place position his work in vital opposition to the spirit of our times. In an interview in 1992, Douglas Coupland noted 'It's a conceit on the part of older people to assume younger people have to know everything they know. Something's got to go. Unfortunately, young people seem to have deemed history and geography irrelevant, and to me, they're extraordinarily important.'

Thomas Pynchon: Hinojosa's roiling rhetoric, his use of poetic digression, and his love of good talk for its own sake – his garrulous gift of the gab – link his work to eighteenth-century models such as *Don Quixote* (1605) and Laurence Sterne's *Tristram Shandy* (1759), and thus provide an unexpected link to Pynchon's loquacious *Mason & Dixon* (1997). The book's connection between borders, capital, and commercial interests also suggests a link to Hinojosa's exploration of the murky world of Belken County finances.

READING THE *KLAIL CITY DEATH TRIP* SERIES

For the neophyte reader, coming to Hinojosa in English for the very first time, *The Klail City Death Trip* presents a number of daunting obstacles: its convoluted publishing history (with some works first written in Spanish and then 're-created' a decade later, others translated or published first in English but out of sequence), the saga's organic, unfinished nature, its multiple time lines and recurrent characters spread out over ten books, and, of course, its mixture of prose, poetry, journalistic *feuilleton*, mock interviews, detective yarns and historical record. But as long as one doesn't expect all aspects of the mosaic to be filled in instantaneously, and is willing to countenance an anecdotal, loitering liberty of thought, Hinojosa's writing is by no means difficult: rather, it is generous, humane and richly digressive.

The best place to start is with Hinojosa's funniest and most attractive works, *The Valley* (reworked in 1983) and *Klail City* (1987), both of which offer a colourful, serio-comic picture of Mexican-American life from the turn of the century, through to the '20s and '30s. Hinojosa's characteristic mode here is the bar-room tall-tale, the well-polished family anecdote, the oral folk-culture of the region. His sense of irony prevents these works from turning into whimsical local colour; the endless tales contradict each other, frequently indict their narrators, and lazily circle around a number of key 'legends' – recounted as song, joke, yarn or fact. Plot is replaced by voice here; an endless chorus of personal testimonies, grievances, arguments and fabrications, at once democratic, collective and eccentric. The title, however, hints at the elegiac tone of the series; this segregated world, where Anglos are conspicuous by their absence, is already a thing of the past, recounted as memoir, marginalia and scrap-book. The 'break' comes with the two wars which disrupt the Valley's indolent sense of isolationism; for several key characters, including Hinojosa's central protagonists, the recalcitrant Jehù Malacara and the taciturn Rafe Buenrostro, conscription marks their entry into the Anglo world, and thereafter the world of the bar-room swashbuckler will never again be enough. The sense of fragmentation is more jagged and painful in these works, a struggle to represent rather than loquacious idleness: military jargon sits uneasily with lyrical reflection, surreal exaggeration, and blank-faced reportage, Hinojosa's repetition-compulsion akin to shell-shock.

His blank-verse cycle, *Korean Love Songs* (1978) counts as one of his finest works, whilst the first part of *Rites and Witnesses* (1982) and *The Useless Servants* (1993) reflect a more sober treatment of the same material. *Dear Rafe* (reworked in English in 1985) is a complex meditation on the question of 'Americanisation', the first half of which is composed of letters sent by Malacara to Buenrostro whilst the latter recovers from his injuries in a military hospital. Malacara now works for the Klail City Bank, and the novel acts as a satirical exposé of widespread corruption and political and economic malpractice, in which Jehù is both amused observer and active participant. His cynical initiation into Anglo ways concludes with his flight, although whether this is due to financial or sexual irregularities, is never made clear; the second half of the book is a mock investigation into Tehù's activities, in the form of a number of contradictory interviews and statements, and serves as a kind of symposium on the role of the upwardly-mobile Mexican American in an Anglo world. Likewise, the second half of *Rites and Witnesses* is composed of fictitious interviews with a wide cross-section of Anglos, documenting their responses to the complex racial mix of the region: the testimonies are, as always with Hinojosa, contradictory, ironic and satirical, but by no means present a monolithically racist view of the Anglo world. Indeed, most of Hinojosa's Mexican Americans at some point make an active decision to accede to the dominant culture, though such acculturation is not without a sense of loss or nostalgia; nevertheless, the strong succeed whilst those whose ties are strongest to the fading world of Hinojosa's early work slowly wither. *Becky and her Friends* (1990) represents an interesting attempt to explore this issue in terms of the role of women in the Valley, but suffers from a curiously attenuated narrative.

Hinojosa's recent excursions into the genre of the police procedural – *Partners in Crime* (1985) and *Ask a Policeman* (1998) – retain his satirical and political edge, but flatten his linguistic virtuosity into a matter-of-fact pragmatism; a curious direction given Hinojosa's astonishing talents of impersonation, vernacular lyricism, and his ability to record endlessly fascinating, magnificently garrulous, everyday speech.

BIBLIOGRAPHY

Works in English

Korean Love Songs (1978), Berkeley: Justa Publications.
Rites and Witnesses (1982), Houston: Arte Publico.
The Valley (1983), Tempe: Bilingual Press.
Partners in Crime (1985), Houston: Arte Publico.
Dear Rafe (1985), Houston: Arte Publico.
Claros Varones de Belken (1986), (transl. Julia Cruz), Tempe, AZ: Bilingual Press.
Klail City (1987), Houston: Arte Publico.
Becky and her Friends (1990), Houston: Arte Publico.
The Useless Servants (1993), Houston: Arte Publico.
Ask a Policeman (1998), Houston: Arte Publico.

Critical Sources

Broyles, Yolanda Julia (1985), 'Hinojosa's *Klail City y sus alrededores*: oral culture and print culture', in José David Salvídar (ed.), *The Rolando Hinojosa Reader*, Houston: Arte Publico, pp. 109–32.

Bruce-Novoa, Juan (1980), *Chicano Authors: Inquiry by Interview*, Austin: University of Texas Press.

Calderon, Hector (1985), 'On the uses of chronicle, biography and sketch in Rolando Hinojosa's *Generaciones y semblanzas*', in José David Salvídar (ed.), *The Rolando Hinojosa Reader*, Houston: Arte Publico, pp. 133–42.

Cota-Càrdenas, Margarita (1985), '*Mi querido Rafa* and irony: a structural study', in José David Salvídar (ed.), *The Rolando Hinojosa Reader*, Houston: Arte Publico, pp. 158–69.

Dasenbrock, R. (1988), 'An interview with Rolando Hinojosa', *Translation Review* 27, pp. 3–8.

Eger, Ernestina (1982), *A Bibliography of Criticism of Contemporary Chicano Literature*, Berkeley: University of California Press.

Flores, Lauro (1985), 'Narrative strategies in Rolando Hinojosa's *Rites and Witnesses*', in José David Salvídar (ed.), *The Rolando Hinojosa Reader*, Houston: Arte Publico, pp. 170–9.

Leal, Luis (1979), 'Mexican-American literature: a historical perspective', in Joseph Sommers and Tomás Ybarra-Fausto (eds), *Modern Chicano Writers*, Englewood Cliffs, NJ: Prentice-Hall, pp. 18–30.

— (1985), 'History and memory in *Estampas del Valle*', in José David Salvídar (ed.), *The Rolando Hinojosa Reader*, Houston: Arte Publico, pp. 101–8.

Lee, Joyce Glover (1997), *Rolando Hinojosa and the American Dream*, Denton: University of North Texas Press.

Mejía, Jamie Armin (1993), 'Breaking the silence: the missing pages in Rolando Hinojosa's *The Useless Servants*', *Southwestern American Literature*, 18 (2), pp. 1–6.

Neate, Wilson (1990), 'The function of Belken County in the fiction of Rolando Hinojosa: the voicing of the Chicano experience', *American Review*, 18 (1), pp. 92–102.

Paredes, Raymund (1978), 'The evolution of Chicano literature', *MELUS*, 5 (2), pp. 12–26.

Randolph, Donald (1986), 'Death's aesthetic proliferation in the works of Hinojosa', *Confluencia*, 1 (2), pp. 38–47.

Salvídar, José David (ed.) (1985), *The Rolando Hinojosa Reader*, Houston: Arte Publico Press.

Salvídar, Roman (1990), *Chicano Narrative: The Dialectics of Difference*, Madison: University of Wisconsin Press.

— (1985), '*Korean Love Songs*: a Border ballad and its heroes', in José David Salvídar (ed.), *The Rolando Hinojosa Reader*, Houston: Arte Publico, pp. 143–57.

Sànchez, Rosaura (1985), 'From heterogeneity to contradiction: Hinojosa's novel', in José David Salvídar (ed.), *The Rolando Hinojosa Reader*, Houston: Arte Publico, pp. 76–100.

dos Santos, María I. Duke & de la Fuente, Patricia (1985), 'The elliptical female presence as unifying force in the novels of Rolando Hinojosa', in José David Salvídar (ed.), *The Rolando Hinojosa Reader*, Houston: Arte Publico, pp. 64–75.

Torres, Héctor (1986), 'Discourse and plot in Rolando Hinojosa's *The Valley*', *Confluencia*, 2 (1), pp. 84–93.

Zigal, Tom, & Jasper, Pat (1983), 'A conversation with Rolando Hinojosa-Smith', *Texas Arts*, Summer, pp. 8–9.

Zilles, Klaus (2001), *Rolando Hinojosa: A Reader's Guide*, Albuquerque: University of New Mexico Press.

E. ANNIE PROULX[1]

I would like to start with what would seem to be an uncontroversial truism – namely that most contemporary writing remains essentially realistic and readers read, not just to be entertained, but in order to learn something about the world around them – the way people live, the vagaries of human nature, hard-won truths about seemingly inexhaustible varieties of experience. Admittedly, such a proposition perhaps implies a number of rather fuzzy assumptions – that the writer essentially writes about his or her own experiences, that an act of imaginative empathy allows the reader vicariously to experience these too, and that fiction provides a more personal, and thereby somehow more accurate, reflection of the way things really are; but on the whole, our critical yardstick remains honesty, truth and wisdom. Implausibility and exaggeration raise our hackles; bias and distortion are suspect.

And yet traditional, canonical criticism argues that American writing is founded upon the principles of the romance rather than pragmatic reportage, this despite – or rather, *in spite* – of the practical, material nature of America itself. From *Moby Dick* (1851) to *Gravity's Rainbow* (1973), the main current of American literature has dealt with the great metaphysical and existential questions – God, Nature, Free-Will – and even those works which might seem to be more conventionally 'realistic' – *Huckleberry Finn* (1884), say, or *The Great Gatsby* (1926) – can be read as allegorical investigations of the same essentially spiritual concerns. For many critics, realism, or naturalism, which aims at a kind of pseudo-scientific objectivity, remains a minor strain in American literature, condemned to the parochial margins. Of course, American authors have always written about ordinary life, provincial settings and insular, humdrum existence, but unless one employs the grand tools of mythic symbolism, thereby making the great imaginative leap from the local to the universal, it remains a kind of second class local colour, chiefly interesting for anthropological rather than literary reasons.

One might feel, however, that such concerns are purely academic, in the most pejorative sense of the word. After all even the most cursory survey of contemporary fiction suggests that the recurrent themes are profoundly personal and small-scale – growing up, coming of age, the death of a loved one, mid-life crises – such fiction reliant upon a shared sense of mutual experience, in the terms of Oprah's 'Book of the Month Club', fiction one can relate to. Creative writing courses continue to pump out graduates who have imbibed that hoariest of literary shibboleths: to write about what one knows; always to create from within one's own experience. Since the aim of such fiction is direct emotional communication, it is stylistically dependent upon very conventional modes of writing – detailed description, straightforward narration, an immediately apprehensible social context – a style which everyone understands as more or less formally 'realistic'. After all, communication requires shared assumptions, expectations and understandings and it is in this sense that realistic fiction acts as the literary norm. High-brow critics may well denigrate such fiction as safe, conservative and narrow, an avoidance of 'big issues' and 'deeper concerns', but such a trend is also in keeping with Postmodernism's mistrust of metanarratives: who still believes in Great Art, Universal Themes, metaphysical concerns? Literature has lost such pseudo-religious epithets; what we desire is the here and now, lived experience, local, secular, domestic truths. Forget the visionary Modernist in his or her ivory tower; who can relate to such a genius? Realistic fiction, at some level, acts as a kind of literary 'self-help book' steering us through the problems and perils of the everyday, albeit in a conventionally dramatised manner. In this sense, what we require from our reading is vicarious experience to weigh against our own. Nor is such an agenda in itself politically conservative. After all, the personal is the political, and even the most domestic of settings raises questions about gender, economics, class, and race and ethnicity. Moreover, if one wishes to propagate an ideological point of view, to convey a political message to as wide an audience as possible, then surely mutual, democratic communication rather than idiosyncratic experimentation, suggests the most efficacious means to do so.

However, it is at this point that we run into a whole new series of theoretical problems, and what we might term 'the realistic consensus' begins to break down. As Elizabeth Ammons puts it, 'In any discussion of 'American Realism', one must always ask 'Whose reality?' and

'Whose America?"[2] If we continue to assume a link between realism and lived experience, then how do we deal with experiences which are either wholly outside of conventional middle-class existence (say, 'ordinary' (but to me, extraordinary) life in America's inner-city ghettos) or else subtly, linguistically separate from the WASP mainstream – and here one might think of Chang-rae Lee's *Native Speaker* (1995) or Gish Jen's *Typical American* (1991). How far does a democratic faith in mutual comprehension – that cornerstone of realism – ultimately stretch? Do we all assume the same conventional definition of what is 'realistic'? But if one gives up on notions of literary empathy, then how does one avoid the creation of linguistic enclaves wholly incomprehensible to outsiders? In the most stereotypical of terms, can a middle-class white man really understand the experiences of a poor, working-class black women? Or, to play devil's advocate for a moment, what if we reverse such terms – would one say ever say that because of her upbringing, Maya Angelou will never truly understand *Tender is the Night* (1934)? Moreover, if we feel that there is a problem with (to choose a famous example), William Styron writing as an African-American in *The Confessions of Nat Turner* (1967), then is this because of questions of authenticity (he has not experienced that life) or language – the terms by which Styron's protagonist would understand his life are different to the literary codes which in turn structure the novel.

Postmodern theory, of course, would have no truck with any notion of the authentic. High Art denigrates realism because it lacks any notion of transcendence; its feet remain stubbornly upon the ground. Political critics dislike the term because its stress upon subjective experience militates against any understanding of the big picture – global capitalism, patriarchy, ecological catastrophe or whatever. Post-Structuralism distrusts realism because of its verisimilitude – its illusory imitation of the textures of real life. Whereas traditional realism prides itself upon honesty, accuracy, and the pursuit of unvarnished truth, Post-Structuralist critics argue that such moral righteousness is exactly what is so pernicious about the term: its claim to capture some kind of self-evident rightness.

Post-Structuralism argues that realistic works of fiction do not simply document the world 'out there', but rather construct a *trompe-l'oeil* imitation via a series of recognisable (but most of the time, wholly invisible) stylistic conventions. For Post-Structuralists, this is the 'mimetic fallacy', the notion that any kind of straight reproduction of external reality is possible. The writer may well indulge in a number of literary tricks intended to convince the reader of the veracity of his or her creation – indeed, many of the seminal works of eighteenth- and nineteenth-century literature pass themselves off as letters, found diaries and the like, in order to substantiate their claims toward serious-ness rather than imaginative indulgence – but this imitation of life serves to disguise a specific ideological agenda under the guise of 'the way things are'. Moreover, the definitions and conventions of realism obviously change over time and vary from culture to culture.

In terms of post-war American letters, Raymond Carver can be seen as the *éminence grise* of the recent return to realism, a brilliant writer who has suffered the misfortune of having his technical devices and stylistic innovations broken down, taught, and reproduced by lesser talents: the clipped, unadorned prose; ear for mundane speech; his use of a use of a strangely surreal banality.[3] This specific brand of 'dirty' realism itself becomes a series of reproducible clichés and conventions; reality becomes generic. Carver's work creates an instantly recognisable (and for that reason profoundly depressing) milieu, but for Post-Structuralist critics this 'aura' of reality has less to do with capturing the material essence of his surroundings than with its divergence from previous definitions of realism. As Richard Lehan writes, 'A realistic text draws no more directly on life than any other kind of writing'; rather, language forms an 'encoded barrier' to reality, and writers therefore toil within self-enclosed semantic systems.[4]

Of course, such a revelation, that writers self-consciously employ words rather than simply taking notation from reality, rather like the fact that the word 'cat' has no necessary connection with a real feline, can be seen as a matter of stating the obvious. After all, what writer would claim otherwise? But to argue that there is *no* connection between prose and lived experience seems equally facetious. As even Lehan notes: 'Life is too much with us, and realism as a literary perspective is too vital to our sense of being, to be shut up for long in the airless room of linguistic self-reflexivity.'[5]

Post-Structuralism's quarrel with realism is ultimately founded upon its mechanisms of illusion, realism's attempt to convince us it is displaying the genuine article; but to argue that therefore the true subject of literature is wholly linguistic, also seems self-defeating. What about the world beyond the text? Surely nobody truly expects perfect correspondence – but does this really mean that we can't even talk about it – or can only talk about the fact that we can't talk about it?

Whilst critics such as Jerome Klinkowitz and Michael Anesko can talk about the death of realism in our time, such deconstruction appears very remote from why writers write and why readers read; whilst one can accept that the course of Modern Art marks a shift from the reproduction of the everyday world to the creation of a purely formal (shape, colour, composition, scale) dimension, it seems much more difficult – and not a little redundant – to try and separate the art of fiction from mimesis.[6] Equally, however, one might argue that what seems the most 'realistic' can in fact be the most generic; indeed, Post-Structuralism would argue that any such distinction is itself facetious. Can we say that some writers reveal previously undiscovered aspects of the real world whilst others simply recite conventional formulae? Are all our notions of what we accept as realistic in fiction ultimately generic rather than existential? 'Realistic' speech in books, for example, is very different from how people really converse, but common-sense tells us whether a line of dialogue is believable or not. Having said that, common-sense also tells us that the sun revolves around the earth.

This chapter explores the contested notion of realism through the work of E. Annie Proulx, and in particular explores how such positions are related to issues of class and regionalism, and to ideas of naturalism (the unadorned truth) and fabulation (the tall-tale) in American letters – which indeed, seems a relevant place to start.

'Reality's never been of much use out here.'

(Close Range, 13)

As a subject, American Studies is particularly prone to over-generalisation, but for the purposes of this discussion, I'd like to propose two different mythic notions of the continent. The first, and perhaps for European readers the most resonant notion, is the idea of America as imagined space, the site of that most intangible (but frequently most materialistic) of concepts, the American dream. In this reading, America is manifested as a utopian site of possibility, promise and desire. This is the America of literary romance, the America of the Edenic wilderness, of starting again and becoming someone new, cleansed from the sin of previous civilisations. But against such idealism, one can also configure an America of material pragmatism, an America which sees land as struggle rather than inspiration, practical, utilitarian and commodious. Such an America has little time for insubstantial illusions; what counts in its dour, stoical heart is getting by, going on, material survival. 'If you can't fix it then you've got to stand it,' as Proulx writes (*Close Range*, 318), a sober rejection of any kind of escapism.

In her key work, *The Social Construction of American Realism* (1998), Amy Kaplan connects the realistic literary tradition with the economic and material realities of America's social development; against an America founded by dreamers, believers and idealists, she posits an America of farmers, businessmen and proto-industrialists.[7] Kaplan argues that a key strain in American writing is anti-idealistic, a rejection of America's patriotic boosterism and propensity for grandiose self-advertisement. After all a promised Utopia cannot help but create discontent, and the early history of European migration saw a stark distinction between idealistic promises of the continent (accompanied by sentimental treatises on the beneficence of Mother Nature) and the appalling hardship involved in trying to wrest a living (and also some degree of profit) from the harsh and recalcitrant land. The genteel tradition was broken on the back of pragmatic exertion, and against the transcendental impulse to view material things as merely the outward manifestation of spiritual realms, Kaplan posits an American writing concerned with objects, work, matter and physicality, secular and anti-intellectual to the core. Things rather than ideas count here, and its *modus operandi* is an empirical form of realism, founded upon a (puritanical) denial of fancy or frivolity.

Certainly E. Annie Proulx's prose has its dour side. At times it suggests Alfred Steiglitz's famous photographs of painter Georgia O'Keeffe: lean, bare, bony, imposingly austere. For the most part, Proulx's view of nature and the land is completely free of any hint of romanticism; things are simply things, their value utilitarian (does it work?) rather than metaphorical (what does it stand for?). What similes she does use tend to be stark, commonplace and concerned with physical detail: 'his thin back bent like a branch weighted with snow' (*Heartsongs*, 3), 'his eyes moving over her like an iron over a shirt' (*Close Range*, 31). Nature reflects neither man's spiritual fears nor his aspirations; hers is a universe of things and work, seemingly pragmatic, sober and common-sensical. Whilst tourists may comprehend the environment in terms of inspirational views, sights or landmarks, Proulx's understanding of the land is based upon physical labour; it bears the fingerprints not of God (as discussed in the chapter on McCarthy) but of human industry and drudgery:

The work of his hands had changed the shape of the land, the weirs in the steep ditch beside the lane, the ditch itself, the smooth fields were echoes of himself in the landscape, for the laborer's vision and strength persists after the labor is done. (*Postcards*, 85–6)

For the majority of Proulx's characters, Postmodern pronouncements of the death of the 'real' or nature simply don't make any sense; there are holes to be dug, fences to be fixed, food to be cooked. Her characters don't occupy the sphere of the image, the system, the consumer-event; Postmodern solipsism is a luxury they simply cannot afford, its free-floating abstraction inimical to rural life. Nostalgia for the real? Proulx's characters are surrounded by reality all day long, often needing to be heaped up, dug round, or waded through. Hence the native's disdain of those who come in search of sentimentalised ideas of the pastoral, a quaint ruralism. Ultimately, the land is toil and that's about all there is to say about the matter. Most of the rural characters in her short stories profess a 'disdain for art and intellect' (*Close Range*, 112), or else 'hated books . . . despised everything except the wood' (*Heartsongs*, 3). Practicality is all. The land – especially in the Wyoming stories of *Close Range* – is obdurate, stony, barren and unforgiving. Aside from the constant struggle to wrest some kind of subsistence from it, there seems precious little existence to go round.

Proulx's first novel, *Postcards* (1992), deals with the break-up of the Blood family and their subsequent expulsion from farm and land, but the tone of the book contains only a trace element of pastoral elegy. After the suicide of her husband, Jewel Blood is quite happily transplanted from farm-house to trailer-park, enjoys its amenities, finds the space easier to clean, and for the first time in her life starts to take rides to look at 'views' (*Postcards*, 145). The farm may have been 'in the Blood family since the Revolutionary War days' (*Postcards*, 128), but Proulx stresses less a sense of organic belonging than the land as a locus of unceasing toil, travail and slavery, a black ditch which swallows the life of each generation. For Marvin Blood, like so many of Proulx's characters, mutilated by the land, it is somewhere to escape from; only the second son, the significantly named Loyal Blood, believes that the soil will provide his salvation ('the work of a farm would set him right' (*Postcards*, 211)) but he too dies unredeemed and unforgiven, guilty of the murder which opens Proulx's sanguine narrative. One thinks of the poet Robert Frost, who also sought in honest rural toil a form of secular grace, deliverance from past transgressions. Proulx, however, repeatedly denies the notion of redemption through nature; rather, as in Tom Waits' song 'Murder in the Red Barn' has it, 'There's always some killin'/You got to do around the farm'.[8]

Proulx's early stories in particular stress the idea of nature (and agrarian life) as red in tooth and claw, employing hunting as an overarching metaphor for the eternal paradigm of predator and victim. The Stone clan of 'Stone City' are irredeemably animalistic, instinctively violent, antisocial and untamed:

> They had all these little shacks with broken-down rusty cars out front, piles of lumber and empty longnecks and pieces of machinery that might come in handy sometime, the weeds growin' up all crazy through 'em everywhere. The Stone boys was all wild, jacked deer, trapped bear, dynamited trout pools, made snares, shot strange dogs wasn't their own and knocked up every girl they could put it to. Yessir, they was some bunch. (*Heartsongs*, 29)

The story ends with the narrator moving out, selling his house to 'a retired couple from New Jersey' who were 'innocently enthusiastic about the country' (*Heartsongs*, 40). The land, however, belongs to the Stones and to the foxes and bears they are constantly compared with, the realm of wild beasts and aggressive physicality. Such regressive imagery connects Proulx to the naturalistic tradition in American realism, which is likewise concerned with the primitive and the animal-like in man: characters who are blindly unselfconscious, driven by base biological impulses and dimly understood needs. Loyal Blood, for example, can be profitably compared to Frank Norris' violently irrational *McTeague* (1899) (immortalised by Gibson Gowland in Erich von Stroheim's 1923 masterpiece, *Greed*) or the murderous Jacques Lantier of Zola's *La Bête Humaine* (1890), the destiny of each determined by a hereditary inclination to violence or insanity, sadistic sexuality, and an aggressive (if paradoxical) impulse toward both self-destruction and the survival of the fittest. Flesh and Blood (Proulx's naming is iconic here) are everything; free-will or rational thought doesn't enter into it.

Naturalism is primarily understood as a nineteenth-century literary concept, rooted in Darwin, eugenics and a profoundly mechanistic (and materialistic) notion of human nature. Its pessimism justified by 'objective' biological models, Naturalism proclaimed the essential bes-tiality of man, his kinship with the violent forces of natural selection. Man was brute, not angel, it averred; physicality rather than spirituality was the driving force of human development. Of course, there was an ideological element in all of this too. It was the lower orders who were most prone to degeneration and atavism, whilst the middle classes sublimated such physical drives (to borrow Freudian terms which would later, in turn, inform this philosophy) in material greed, barter and competition; the upper classes, free from hypocritical bourgeois morality, simply indulged their carnality under the guise of decadence. In all of this, civilisation appears as but the thinnest of garments covering man's naked physicality, masking our status as things driven by compulsive forces (genetic, environmental, instinctual) beyond our control.

In terms of formal characteristics, Naturalistic writing at the turn of the century can be seen to be precariously positioned between two conflicting modes of writing. Governed by the guiding principle of realism (to reflect the unvarnished truth about man (and, more shockingly, woman), no matter how unflattering the resulting portrait may be), Naturalism aimed at a kind of pseudo-objectivity, which in turn demonstrated the empiricism of the various scientific theories which informed it. Hence it is characterised by reams of conscientiously researched data, an obsessive attention to physical detail, and a fidelity to real place-names, actual locations, and documented settings. Naturalism argues that the environment determines the individual, and hence there is a striking reversal of foreground and background, whereby 'characters' become merely the sum of impersonal determi-nants. Context is all. Such a belief in literary objectivity means that all things are relevant, an undifferentiated reportage free from bias or discrimination; the boring, the ugly, the mundane, everything goes in, the constituent particles of everyday life.

However, pitted against this sober stress on the factual, lies a very different compulsion, namely the need to illustrate and thereby 'prove' Naturalism's central thesis regarding the inherently violent, animalistic nature of man. Hence, Naturalistic novels of the period also tend to be (to modern tastes at least) wildly sensationalistic and prurient, dealing with extreme states of madness, perversion and butchery. This didactic drive to prove humanity's bestiality obviously creates a tension here; after all, as Saul Bellow has argued, boredom rather than barbarism is the bête noire of most of us, and few individuals could (or would) point to their lives and claim that savagery was the norm (though of course the abattoir of history could be raised as witness for the prosecution here). This mixture of sober reporting and lurid *grotesquerie* in turn suggests another source of literary naturalism, namely journalism (especially crime-reporting), which is also predicated upon a juxtaposition of plain data and violent ruptures of this norm. Indeed, nineteenth-century Naturalism can be seen as a thematic and stylistic rapprochement between literature and journalism. Both are reliant upon the 'evidence' of facts, detailed descriptions, and extensive research; equally the 'reality' which they capture is in turn determined by their audience, reception and public taste for sensation. Literary Naturalism is always pushing against common-sense understandings of what is or isn't 'realistic' toward a kind of expressionism – a concern with extreme states of being, inherent ugliness or evil, macabre incidents, grotesque exaggeration, the bad news about who man really is. All this is still carried out under the flag of truth, but notions of objectivity are (to say the least) extremely compromised here: which best illustrates the truth, the extreme or the mundane norm? And which truth are readers interested in anyway?

All of which leads us back to the close of the twentieth century and E. Annie Proulx. Certainly Proulx's prose shares several key characteristics with the tenets of literary Naturalism. Her work is exhaustively researched (her latest novel, *Accordion Crimes* (1996), possesses nearly four pages of acknowledgements), ambitiously wide-ranging (Proulx is famously dismissive of the notion that one should only write about one's own experiences) and – most obviously, perhaps – incredibly detailed, especially on the topics of work (how things are done) and goods (how things are made). Her work is full of extended disquisitions on farm-work, trapping, fishing, mechanics, weaving, rope-making, ship-building and the like, and frequently displays an archivist's weakness for lists; *Postcards* in particular is guilty of a compulsive need to provide the correct name for everything – shrub, car, tool – irrespective of the effect this has on the ongoing narrative. In essence we feel that Proulx knows what she's talking about, and this pragmatic knowledge bestows on her writing a considerable authority, free from pretension, fancy or dissemblance. Ultimately, the key-notes of her work are those two terms which Postmodernism has so much trouble with: honesty and authenticity.

This drive to document, to name, is put to work in the service of a back roads America which rarely makes it into print; a kind of regionalism determined more by class than place. Whether the setting be Vermont, Wyoming or Newfoundland (the last of which moves us outside America, I admit!), Proulx's milieu is predominantly blue-collar, rural, dilapidated and facing hard times. This is not the desperate poverty of, say, Steinbeck's *Grapes of Wrath* (1939), nor the well- defined parameters of Faulkner's Yoknapatawpha county; rather it is a contemporary America of just off the interstate, small towns reliant on a fading rustic charm to pull in the tourists, struggling farms, run-down stores, depressingly forlorn diners, plots of land which lack scenic vistas but where a particularly stubborn and spiky kind of vegetation persists. Proulx calls them 'the back places. Bad Route Road. Whoopup Creek Road. Cracker Box Road' (*Postcards*, 254) situated on a specifically American junction between the homely and the dreary. We are a long way from the hyper-real highways which Jean Baudrillard speeds along in *America* (1988), or the alternatively shining and crime-ridden metropolis of so much American fiction; a down-home, country-living America which, (at least at first sight) the simulacra haven't bothered to copy.

One could argue that the whole *raison d'être* of *Postcards* is to nail down and represent this working-class, agrarian setting. Reminiscent of Dos Passos, and his idea of the 'camera's eye', Proulx dedicates whole chapters of the book to virtually uninterrupted description (designated simply 'What I See'), and it is here that the novel is at its most evocative, melancholy and clear-sighted:

> Loyal, going along the roads, the shadows of white poplars like strips of silk in the wind; pale horses in the field drifting like leaves; a woman seen through a window, her apron slipping down over her head the hairnet emerging from the neckhole, the apron faded blue, legs purple mosquito bites no stockings runover shoes; the man in the yard nailing a sign onto a post; RABIT MEAT; a plank across Potato Creek; a swaybacked shed, the doors held closed with a heavy chain, white crosses, windmills, silos, pigs, white poplars in the wind, the leaves streaming by as he drove. A fence. More fence. Miles and miles and miles of fence, barbwire fence. (*Postcards*, 68)

One might also think of the snap-shot imagism of early William Carlos Williams, a kind of revelation of the ordinary, whereby the run-down quotidian seems to be captured for the very first time. The descriptive brilliance of these passages – their feel for down-at-heel textures and materials, their eye for mysterious detail, their sensitivity toward the specific rather than the generic – itself acts as a justification of realism; we feel that this is a world outside of bland generalities or media 'types', an instantly recognisable world that somehow we've never quite seen before, minutely observed and thereby uncovered. Of course such 'straight' description doesn't simply translate scenery into words, thereby perfectly recreating Proulx's (or Blood's) point of view, but nevertheless without what Post-Structuralism derides as the mimetic fallacy, one misses the whole point of such passages, and their astonishingly evocative power. *Postcards* stresses the notion of description as part art and part craft; the opening scenes in particular are full of painterly terms (drawn, varnished, etched, stippled) which draw attention to the specific act of writing and the sheer labour involved. One of the key themes in the novel is literacy itself, but we are never in doubt as to what Proulx is writing about, or about the fact that in her view skill and accuracy are conjoined.

However, alongside this feel for micro textures, the weft and weave of physical things, lies a central narrative which appears wildly exaggerated, gruesomely grotesque, and nightmarishly threatening. Proulx's back-roads America is anything but the small-town USA where nothing ever happens; rather the novel is peppered with recurrent accidents, murders, suicides, natural disasters and (a Proulx speciality) decapitations. This is a wildly inhospitable land, where hazards lurk in every ditch, junk-yard and turn of the road, culminating in the mass-grave of itinerant workers which Blood uncovers near the end of the book (*Postcards*, 319). This juxtaposition of the macabre and the mundane, the aberrant and the ordinary, again links Proulx to Naturalism, as does the fact that the various, seemingly surreal ('sur-rural' in Tom Waits' words) deaths are all drawn from real events recorded in newspapers, county records and the like. Proulx's latest novel, *Accordion Crimes* (which takes in decapitation by roofing, electrocution by worm-probe, and one poor individual sown up inside a cow, amongst its unending accidents, illnesses and atrocities) in particular attracted a great deal of negative criticism regarding its taste for macabre excess, but Proulx remains stridently unrepentant regarding her acknowledgement that 'violence is a fact of life in our country' especially amongst the poor.[9] Again she stresses that none of the violent episodes in the book was actually invented, but instead uncovered in diaries, safety statistics and medical reports; reality is stranger and more minatory than our generic models, she argues, and hence we regard actual events as unrealistic because they fail to conform to convention.

Nevertheless, there is something slightly disingenuous about Proulx's position here. The sheer relentlessness of the mutilation, the use of hyper-condensed (and thereby heightened) secondary material to create an idiosyncratic and bleakly skewed vision, again all point to the legacy of Naturalism with its distinctive coupling of the minutely observed and the wildly embellished. I am very much taken with Jane Shilling's characterisation of Proulx's latest collection of short stories, *Close Range* (1999) as 'the rural equivalent of urban myths' – tall-tales and camp-fire yarns (in 'The Blood Bay', a bunch of dumb-cluck cowpokes believe that one of their number has been eaten by a horse) told with a wink and a grimace.[10] This is most obvious in 'The Half-Skinned Steer', which, Proulx's notes tell us, is an old Icelandic legend transplanted to the Wyoming plains (*Close Range*, 8). The story consists of two narrative strands, one involving the return of old man Mero to the family ranch to attend the funeral of his brother, the other a half-remembered yarn recounted many years earlier by his father's girlfriend. In the latter, a half-crazed rancher with a metal plate in his bonce skins a steer for supper, only for the creature ('raw . . . bunchy and wet' (*Close Range*, 38)) to recover and shuffle off onto the plains where the rancher last sees 'the raw meat of the head and the shoulder muscles and the empty mouth without no tongue open wide and its red eyes glaring at him, pure teetotal hate' (*Close Range*, 38). This half of the story is recounted through the girl's rich colloquial accent and foregrounded as a completely unbelievable shaggy-dog story, albeit one in which the listener is willingly taken in:

It was her voice that drew you in, that low, twangy voice, wouldn't matter if she was saying the alphabet, what you heard was the rustle of hay. She could make you smell the smoke from an unlit fire. (*Close Range*, 35).

For some reason this story stays with Mero all the days of his lfe, and at the moment of his death (he stumbles down a steep incline in the snow) he is revisited by its awful visage, realising 'that the half-skinned steer's red eye had been watching for him all this time' (*Close Range*, 41).

The story is in many ways emblematic of Proulx's style, juxtaposing painfully grim realism (the old man's downfall is all too believable and commonplace, and recalls Jewel Blood's death in *Postcards*) with ostentatious gore. The violent shifts in tone (flat accounts of the old man's car trouble alongside gruesome relish) are only resolved at the end of the story when the two strands dove-tail; the violent exaggeration of the tall-tale turns out to be an accurate representation of the inherently hostile nature of the land. However, there is also a second, metaphorical level at work here. As a boy, old man Mero is told that the sexual organs of women are like an Indian stone he has found, a stone vulva shaped like a horse-shoe. Thereafter 'no fleshy examples ever conquered his belief in the subterranean stony structure of female genitalia' (*Close Range*, 27), and the revelation of the exposed wetness of the skinned steer carries a macabre sexual charge – against his will, Mero is extremely aroused by his father's girlfriend telling the tale. Mero dies amongst the rugged harshness of the stony plain, symbolic of the barren nature of his own dour emotional life, but 'reality', Proulx argues, is the dripping, steaming sinews of the corporeal, the bodily real which lies just beneath the skin, the visceral truth which can burst forth from the mundane at any time.

The tradition of the tall-tale – racy, hysterical, fantastical – is very different from the type of puritan pragmatism I have been talking about, and suggests in turn a very different American folk tradition, namely that of redskin humour.[11] Proulx has argued that poverty and deprivation actually have a salutary effect on the imagination, feeding creativity rather than choking it through deadening labour:

> People who are poor or who are in 'socially disadvantaged' situations are forced by circumstance to use their imagination more vigorously than people in more comfortable positions . . . If you have nothing and no place in the world, the imagination is an engine of incredible power, both to lift you out of where you are and to impel you into another reality.[12]

Stubborn practicality and perfervid delirium co-exist in Proulx's world. Hence the epigram to *Close Range*: 'Reality's never been of much use out here' (*Close Range*, 13). 'The elements of unreality, the fantastic and improbable, color all of these stories as they color real life,' she writes (*Close Range*, 9), but they also speak of her continuing debt to Naturalism and its very specific sense of the real. The agrarian imagination of which Proulx speaks also has a dark side, a bleak and terrible cabin-fever, a madness and hysteria instilled by extremes of isolation and loneliness. The girl seduced by her father's tractor ('The Bunchgrass Edge of the World') or the cattleman's ranch decorated with desiccated corpses ('55 Miles to the Gas Pump'), suggest less flattering expositions of the rural psyche, and once again hint at an expressionistic edge to her realism, its concern with extreme states of mind and being.

This ever-present Gothic tinge to Proulx's writing has led to accusations of anti-humanism, of a kind of gleeful giggling at the misfortunes of her blue-grass grotesques. Naturalism is often accused of a lack of humane sympathy, of a nihilistic stress on ugliness for its own sake, but I would also like to suggest that there are times when Proulx's writing has got nothing in common with the concept at all. Her prose lacks the lofty scientific distance which characterises, say, Zola's *Rougon-Maquart* (from 1871) cycle. Her characters are anything but specimens in a laboratory, and her stories lack any kind of didactic purpose, or any heavy-handed warning of social degeneration or social atavism. What is perhaps most striking about them is their utterly secular, prosaic nature. Terms such as transcendence, redemption or salvation simply do not apply to her writing (Blood isn't forgiven for the murder of Billy, but neither is he damned; he simply goes on and on and then stops), and this disdain for abstraction also extends to Naturalism's pseudo-scientific jargon.

One way of approaching her first two novels, *Postcards* and *The Shipping News* (1993) is through the gradual humanising of their lead characters, Blood and Quoyle; their transformation from unpresupposing human dough (Quoyle, 'a great damp loaf of a body . . . a freakish shelf jutting from the lower face' (*Shipping*, 2), Blood 'lumpen' and 'rubbery' (*Postcards*, 11)) to recognisably complex characters. Blood in particular moves from taciturn menace to become a garrulous (and boring) old fogey. Hence, Naturalism's Pavlovian view of identity – selfhood as an illusory conduit of impersonal forces – seems to have little in common with Proulx's self-conscious deepening of personality from comic-strip monstrosity to fully realised singularity. Interestingly,

Accordion Crimes reverses this process, discarding characters through the disorientating device of the flash-forward: they suddenly disappear from the text as we learn of their eventual fates, which, more often than not, are of the darkly humorous or bizarrely tragic variety. This sense of ultimate fate – a kind of unavoidable accident – may account for the fact that the book seems Proulx's cruellest work to date, reducing the individual to merely the sum of their gross misfortune. All the characters come to bad ends because (Proulx implies) we all come to a bad end if you apply a broad enough perspective; however, the overall effect is that unavoidable loss of dignity or significance which such mortal slapstick implies. For many critics this use of the grotesque remains a problem, creating a sense of readerly superiority toward the dirt-poor, sometimes illiterate, lives of Proulx's broken-down characters; a literary problem which ultimately revolves around what seems to be the very un-American issue of class.

'Do you like shooting them? The birds, hunting for birds I mean, do you like it?'

(*Postcards*, 90)

Of course, in many ways class is a non-issue in US society, rendered invisible by its rhetoric of rugged individualism, social mobility, and democratic opportunity. Since class-consciousness is so weak, notions of identity tend to be defined via other referents – ethnicity, region, employment or wealth. Nevertheless issues of class are central to much of Proulx's writing, and give an interestingly bitter flavour to some of her best work.

One of the central themes of *Heartsongs* (1988), for example, is the incursion of 'summer people' into blue-collar, rural communities; empty-headed tourists ('you look like a character out of a Rupert Frost poem' states one (*Heartsongs*, 7)) in search of a little pastoral pick-me-up – shootin' for the men, quilt-making for the gals. There is much sardonic fun to be had in mocking the wealthy back-to-nature urbanites, with their gullible enthusiasm for handicrafts, folklore and 'the land', but Proulx is perfectly aware that rural communities, in the face of devastating agricultural depression, desperately need such vacationers' dollars in order to survive. In her fiction, however, the transformation of working communities into seasonal holiday-villages has a strange and pernicious effect, suggestive of the notion that the Postmodern ailment of simulation has infiltrated these communities after all. For those who have been brought up in such an environment, the presence of outsiders bestows a kind of debilitating self-consciousness, whereby ordinary rural life turns into a strange brand of performance-art, natives acting up for the rubber-neckers. Working farms are mummified into preserved museums, rural practices turned into 'quaint' displays, local goods sold not for use but for ornament; in essence, agrarian life is fetishised as an example of the 'authentic' or 'natural' but this very process in turn falsifies its blue-collar nature, transforming 'the land' into a kind of ersatz theme park. Whilst some inhabitants willingly submit to this process, hamming it up for the out-of-towners or hawking cheap junk as holy relics of Americana, others find them-selves confused by this new dramaturgical state, unsure as to whether they are simply going about their business or acting out some kind of a role – hunters, fishermen and farmers as the bucolic equivalent of Micky, Donald and Goofy. In 'The Unclouded Day' a hunter is oddly paralysed by the presence of a paying tourist, suddenly aware of himself as the subject of another's gaze, his activities a spectacle, his skills a kind of pantomime. Unbidden, a theatrical element slips into his life, whereby he captures himself acting out his own life, a postur-ing which in turn stops him dead in his tracks.

Of course, it is the quaint, picturesque qualities of rustic life which are easily assimilated into this kitsch pastoralism; the raw edge of rural existence is not so simply commodified. But even poverty and isolation can seem ornamental if approached from a suitable distance. In 'Electric Arrows', the pretentious Moon-Azures – fabulously wealthy practi-cians who play at being weekend farmers – try to buy out Old Aunt Rebu's photographs of the Clew family; bleak, haunted, sober prints of stern patriarchs, sick babies and dilapidated barns, the faces 'round plates above dark shoulders', 'the shadows of the clapboards like black rules' (*Heartsongs*, 137). Even extreme austerity can be rendered desirable through its association with 'the authentic' and 'the real'. Aunt Rebu, though, is not for selling:

> What Aunt is afraid of is that the Moon-Azures will pass the pictures around among their weekend guests, that they will find their way into books and newspapers, and we will someday see our grandfather's corpse in his homemade coffin resting on two sawhorses, flattened out on the pages of some magazine and labelled with a cruel caption. (*Heartsongs*, 146)

She fears a process of objectification and thereby commodification, representations plucked from any sense of context to become (paradoxically) artefacts of some fuzzy notion of 'the real'. The people pointing the camera have all the power here; the subjects are passively caught, tagged and labelled – a different kind of hunting all together.

In 'Negatives', a famous photographer, Walter Welter, comes to stay with his friend, Buck B., 'a forcibly retired television personality attracted to scenery' (*Heartsongs*, 171). Buck is tiring of his rural idyll, now it is out of season – the weather is bad, the roads poor, the isolation depressing, but Welter becomes obsessed with Albina Muth, a semi-literate piece of white trash spotted outside the supermarket with her gaggle of children, 'thick-lidded eyes and reptilian mouths' (*Heartsongs*, 172), a dirty, damaged, clichéd, incarnation of his favourite subject matter, 'the rural downtrodden':

> The fingers on both hands couldn't count the dinners Walter Welter ruined with his stories of Albina Muth. Friends came up from the city for a mountain weekend, had to listen to grisly accounts: she had left her awful husband for a deranged survivalist who hid knives under tin cans in the woods; she lived with an elderly curtain-rod salesman made such a satyr by rural retirement that Albina had been rushed twice to the emergency room; she was being prosecuted for welfare fraud; her children had headlice; she sported a vestigial tail. (*Heartsongs*, 172)

Like some kind of stray, Welter takes her into Buck's home, cleans and feeds her, allows her to sleep in Buck's car. Her destitution renders her exotic whilst her desperation makes her suitably quiescent. Ultimately he photographs her naked in a ruined poorhouse, first squatting over broken-glass, then backing out of a filthy oven; and then finally rapes her. To him she is subject-matter, nothing more, nothing less, reduced by her poverty to a state of animal otherness, simultaneously transfigured and abused by the lens.

Interestingly, smart-talking photographers and reporters also pop up in *Postcards* (Arlene Greenslit writing up tragic loss as a 'human interest piece') and *Accordion Crimes* (where the photo-journalist is blinded by a nine-year-old with a semi-automatic rifle before going onto the chat-show circuit as a celebrity victim). Even the local rag, *The Gammy Bird*, in *The Shipping News* is sold on the back of child-abuse

stories and gruesome snaps of car-crashes. While such characters are
for the most part unsympathetic, it is perhaps worth questioning
whether this is perhaps some kind of profession of bad faith on behalf
of Proulx. After all, she too is in the representation game, and as a
writer she is inescapably drawn to the extreme and the bizarre.
Ultimately, one might argue, can one position her writing outside of
either bucolic commodification (telling tall-tales for city-folk) or
sensationalistic freakishness?

One of the problems for self-consciously working-class writers is
that the (liberal) audience for such material is so unquestionably bourgeois; as the old joke goes, who needs stories of poverty, heart-ache
and destitution when you can get all that at home? Of course this is
not to say that, in Proulx's case, no New England farmer or Wyoming
rancher would ever pick up her work; but certainly, common-sense
would tell one that most readers of her work would identify with the
vilified out-of-towners, even if, as at the end of both 'The Unclouded
Day' and 'Electric Arrows', they wind up the butt of Proulx's jokes.
Much of her recent short fiction was originally published in *The New
Yorker*, and if one is to insert her into her own narratives, inescapably,
she appears as the one pointing the camera. So what does this mean
to a writer concerned with representations of the poor, the marginalised
and the dispossessed?

In *Postcards*, Proulx foregrounds literacy as one of the central themes
of the book. Alongside her own struggles as a writer – the sometimes
tentative nature of her prose, the search for painterly metaphors ('as a
scene drawn in powerful ink lines'; 'like a perspective painting') in
the opening chapters of the book, or the self-conscious exercise of the
'What I see' sections – Proulx includes examples of Blood's own hand-
writing; scrawled, stumbling, misspelt, awkward. His transformation
as a character is chronicled in part by the journal he keeps in the
stolen 'Indian's Book' ('Things he planned to do, song lyrics, distances
travelled, what he ate and what he drank' (*Postcards*, 109)), just as
Quoyle's metamorphosis in *The Shipping News* is signalled by his shift
from tabloid headlines to loquacious oratory. Admittedly Proulx is more
obviously articulate and linguistically resourceful than her characters,
but are we then right to attack her for condescension? After all, should
one check a writer's cv to see if she has the right to talk about working-
class, rural life? Interestingly, Proulx has been attacked for both selling
a prepackaged version of pasteurised ruralism, and for peddling a

brand of anti-country Gothic (the last line of her serial-killing vignette is 'When you live a long way out you make your own fun' (*Close Range*, 280)), as if she can somehow be simultaneously *Little House on the Prairie* and *The Texas Chainsaw Massacre*. What is at stake here is Proulx's claim to be what Brian Jarvis calls 'a counter-hegemonic' writer, an author whose stress on the 'authentic' and the 'real' is in vital opposition to the commodified, artificial tenor of our age.[13] In this context, perhaps a better way of framing such suggestions can be provided by examining the connection between Proulx's realism and her regionalism.

'Nothing but rock and sea, the tiny figures of humans and animals against them for a brief time.'
(The Shipping News, 196)

Regionalism – which is to say, writing grounded in a specific and particular sense of place – has often appeared the poor provincial cousin of great literature and its exploration of grand themes, universal truths and the like. Instead, regionalism offers us only local quirks and parochial peculiarities, a little close-to-home exoticism for those who don't want to travel too far; indeed, for some metropolitan critics, regionalism appears as a sign of insular limitation, a provincialism exhibited in both form (conventional realism) and content (local, peripheral concerns, remote from the national interest). Such critical condescension, however, has been recently shaken; firstly by Postmodernism's denial of the 'universal' (and attendant stress on the marginal) and perhaps more importantly, by the idea that a sense of grounded space can provide some kind of resistance to the abstract placelessness of global capitalism.[14]

The central argument here is a familiar one. Global capitalism manifests itself (albeit hidden behind the banner of consumer choice) as a bland homogeneity, the local or specific swallowed up by ubiquitous brand-names, corporate slogans and homogenised space. As we saw with DeLillo, the placelessness of the shopping mall or airport lounge displaces geographic specifics. Idiosyncratic practices, local traditions, and a specific sense of belonging are all eroded to the point of extinction by the relentless march of global marketing, information and corporate stylistics. Whether it be at the hands of the media, fashion, news, branding, or advertising, the specific is vanishing like the ozone layer; customs, practices and differences eviscerated by the global mall which has replaced the notion of a global village. In this context, the once much-maligned and reactionary tradition of literary regionalism assumes a new relevance, acting as a kind of grounded, organic buffer to internationalism, deracination, CNN, the WWW, Nike, Gap and the like (one of the subtle signifiers of change in *Postcards* is the spread of McDonald's). In essence, the local acts as our last line of defence against the homogeneous.

Unfortunately there is a problem with such romantic lionising of the peripheral – namely that marketing chiefs have been there before us. Capitalism can quite happily absorb and artificially perpetuate examples of the local, rebranding and selling them as commodified signifiers of the 'natural' or 'authentic'. Our nostalgia for the real – whether it be home-cooking, clean air, or outdoor pursuits – provides a key market for capitalism to exploit via life-style choices, leisure options and idealised images. In short, the urge to flee the all-pervading influence of the global market-place is built into the system itself, a fact reflected in vacation-sites, advertising strategies, and a general fetishising of the organic or the real. Capitalism is quite happy to market its own antithesis – as long as you are willing to pay for it.

Interestingly, Proulx can be positioned on either side of this debate. Her clear-sighted stress on specific details, accurate reportage, vernacular speech and local eccentricity place her writing in stark opposition to the non-territorial abstraction of the mediascape. Equally, however, one could argue that the idea of readers of *The New Yorker* lapping up stories of agrarian desperation (not unlike the Moon-Azures poring over the bleak black and white prints) indicates her true degree of commercial incorporation. Unfortunately the only way to resolve this argument is by recourse to deeply unfashionable notions of honesty, accuracy and truth. And here, of course, we encounter the same old problems.

In many ways the Pulitzer-Prize/National Book Award-winning *The Shipping News* (1993) is Proulx's most controversial text for precisely these reasons. The Newfoundland setting of the book places it far beyond the usual settings for North American fiction, the novel's rich, metaphorical prose rendering its locale stark and unfamiliar. Proulx relentlessly stresses the bleak, ferocious weather, the harshness of the labour, and the isolated extremity of the storm-lashed communities, but in doing so she also transforms this sense of communal tenacity into something to be desired; not for no reason have the publishers included on the book-jacket a quote by *The Times* suggesting that 'To read *The Shipping News* is to yearn to be sitting in the Flying Squid Lunchstop, eating Seal Fin curry, watching icebergs clink together in the bay.'

Mark Shechner has attacked the novel's setting for being too obviously therapeutic, its ideas of belonging and connecting expressed via the novel's central (and over-stressed) premise of knotting or binding one's life to others.[15] In this reading, the lead character's salvation takes the form of what seems to be a very conventional, even Hollywood narrative-arc, whereby he learns Very Important Life Lessons through his exposure to Back to Basics Values. In a sense we are back to the puritan paradigm discussed earlier, whereby the very harshness of the setting makes communal responsibility a necessity. As Robert Scott Stewart writes, 'Though jobs are scarce to non-existent, Newfoundlanders continue to have a firm and settled sense of self, of who and what they are, and where they come from', and this sense of cohesion proves capable of stamping Quoyle's 'damp loaf of a body' (*Shipping*, 2) into a practical and pragmatic shape.[16] Ultimately, Quoyle defines himself through his commitment to others, a communitarian form of self-realisation which is very different to bohemian notions of self-expression (or ideas of transcending provincial insularity) but which also might suggest a kind of reactionary conformism.

Indeed, the politics of the novel have been hotly debated. Many commentators have simply taken the following speech by *The Gammy Bird*'s hard-bitten editor, Jack Buggit, as indicative of Proulx's own stance:

> There's two ways of living here now. There's the old way, look out for your family, die where you was born, fish, cut your wood, keep a garden, make do with what you got. Then there's the new way. Work out, have a job, somebody tell you what to do, commute, your brother's in South Africa, your mother's in Regina, buy every goddamn cockadoodle piece of Japanese crap you can. Leave. Go off to look for work. And some has a hard time of it. (*Shipping*, 286)

Certainly this idea of Newfoundland as a kind of retreat from contemporary insanity is reinforced near the end of the novel, when Quoyle receives an agonised phone-call from his old buddy Partridge:

Quoyle, they shot at Mercalia on the freeway last week. Show you how crazy the scene is, I made a joke about living in California, about LA style. Fucking bullet holes through her windshield. Missed her by inches. She's scared to death and I'm making jokes. It hit me after Edna called, what a fucking miserable crazy place we're in. There's no place you can go no more without getting shot or burned or beat. And I was laughing. (*Shipping*, 291)

Where can one find relief from contemporary artificiality, violence and desire? In work, family, community, craft, belonging; an austere rebuttal of Postmodern images of fame and consumer-gratification. Proulx leaves out religion (according to Scott Stewart a particularly divisive issue in Newfoundland), but otherwise seems to be suggesting a fairly straightforward conservative programme.[17] However, pro-Proulx critics take great pains to divorce the book from 'the loathsome set of 'family values' sentimentality which infects many current discussions . . . particularly as employed by certain right-wing political parties'.[18] Ken Millard, for example, argues that the book puts forward a very unconventional, inclusive notion of what constitutes a 'family', and what belonging ultimately entails.[19] However, it should be noted that, with the best will in the world, isolated rural communities are not generally noted for their liberal open-mindedness, and it is significant that Quoyle's aunt must still keep her lesbianism under wraps given the fiercely parochial nature of her surroundings.

Even more troubling in any discussion of the politics of the book is Proulx's constant stress upon child-abuse, which indeed forms the staple ingredient of the local rag for which Quoyle works. Millard argues that this disturbingly flippant motif is used to satirise any notion of 'Newfie' life as a kind of pastoral retreat or bastion of family values; here is insularity writ large, denoted in explicitly sexual terms.[20] Indeed, Proulx's throwaway use of black comedy has upset a number of otherwise sympathetic reviewers; at the start of the book Quoyle's wife attempts to sell his children to a paedophile ring (a scene played almost wholly for laughs) and Proulx includes a number of lurid *Gammy Bird* stories, which belong to her favourite tradition of the grotesque tall-tale (of these, 'Filthy old Dad rapes children's horse' (*Shipping*, 270) is perhaps the most notable). Of course at this point (and probably not for the first time, either) we may well feel that when it comes to representations of American life, Proulx is damned if she does and damned if she doesn't. After all if Proulx offers an attractive portrayal of rural life then this is seen as prettifying for the tourist-trade, whilst if she deigns to explore the darker aspects of isolation and insularity she is accused of trading in demeaning Gothic stereotypes. Similarly, one could argue that it is only the enormous critical and commercial success of the book which has led to accusations that Proulx has been appropriated by the heritage industry; if our analysis of the worth of a text is dependent upon its resistance to commercial values then obviously we aren't going to get very far with mainstream American writing. All writers are part of the system in that they are in the business of selling their books; but having said that, it doesn't necessarily follow that issues of integrity, honesty or accuracy are therefore invalid.

As Millard notes, there is plenty of evidence in the text to refute any simplistic notion of a kind of rural idyll or privileged zone, uncontaminated by capitalism. Trade agreements, fishing quotas, and the discovery of rich off-shore oil deposits all exert a fundamental commercial influence upon Newfie life, and most of the islanders, it seems, cannot wait to cash in and ship out. Indeed, Proulx argues that there are as many inhabitants longing to leave as characters looking for some sense of home. As one such character, Nutbeem, notes, 'I'm going to remember this place for many things . . . but most of all for the inventive violence' (*Shipping*, 247). Certainly, the description of Quoyle's ancestors as 'Loonies . . . wild and inbred, half-wits and murderers' (*Shipping*, 162) suggests something different from the usual American ancestor-worship. 'They was a savage pack' states one salty sea-dog. 'In the olden days they say Quoyles nailed a man to a tree by 'is ears, cut off 'is nose for the scent of blood to draw the nippers and flies that devoured him alive' (*Shipping*, 139), a passage which encapsulates the novel's sense of itself as an extended fisherman's yarn.

This degree of deliberate confabulation indeed makes any critical assessment of Proulx's realism ultimately rather problematic. Whilst her acknowledgements page thanks various individuals and institutions for assisting her in the extensive research necessary for such a book, the usual copyright disclaimer is replaced by a note describing her characters as 'fancies' and the setting 'an island of invention'.

In many ways, *The Shipping News* is the most cartoon-like of Proulx's works, populated by eccentric sketches ('Face like cottage-cheese clawed with a fork' (*Shipping*, 57)) rather than conventionally rendered characters. One can again draw attention to the Naturalistic strain in

Proulx's writing, the ink-stains of her characters dwarfed by the over-whelming magnitude of the setting ('small figures against the vast rock with the sea behind' (*Shipping*, 196), and also to the 'Newfie joke' which trades on stock figures and likewise subordinates character to the demands of the gag; 'Not a word of truth in it . . . But how she makes you think there was! Oh, she's terrible good!' (*Shipping*, 280).

Ultimately, the final justification for Proulx's distinctive brand of realism may be provided by *The Gammy Bird* itself, a kind of model for Proulx's own prose. Sensationalistic, gossipy, possessed by a prurient interest in car-crashes and deviant sexuality, the paper nevertheless possesses its own sense of rough and ready integrity; it 'was a hard bite. Looked life right in its bloodshot eye' (*Shipping*, 63). Its reporting may not be 100 per cent accurate, and demonstrate a definite lean toward the colourful and the exaggerated, but, Proulx suggests, reality is not to be kept within generic bounds, and the paper embodies a kind of provisional truth which is hard-won, unsentimental and ultimately communal. When old man Card types up the copy, he adds his own misreadings, vernacular spellings, and Newfie accent, and even these typos (much beloved by *The Gammy Bird*'s readers) serve a local verity which has less to do with hard facts than with the relationship between paper and reader. None of the islanders takes *The Gammy Bird*'s colourful oratory, libellous assertions, and biased invective as gospel truth, but the reality it embodies is a workable one, recognisable even in its distortions – especially in its distortions – and fulfils a pragmatic need. The 'reality' the paper represents has ultimately more to do with the act of communication than with any sense of strict imitation. One might also say the same thing about the relationship between mimesis and the novel.

Postmodernism and the spectre of 'authenticity'

What do we mean by the word authentic? Post-Structuralism would argue that any aura of 'authenticity' in fiction is an illusion, a textual trick conjured by the self-legitimising nature of certain kinds of discourse, an effect of language. Whenever a branch of language seeks to justify its claims by recourse to notions of the authentic, we should be on our guard, for the authentic is never an organic or natural 'given' but always ideologically inscribed. Only con artists harp on about the genuine nature of their goods.

When discussing the concept of realism, however, notions of

authenticity remain the prime justification for the form: notions of accuracy, validity, veracity, honesty remain at the fore. In *Accordion Crimes* (1996), Proulx employs accordion music – ethnic, folk musicology – as an authentic badge of immigrant, working-class experience; the riotous release of Friday night following a week of toil and servitude. Proulx repeatedly stresses the music as earthy, libidinal, and employs explicitly bodily metaphors to capture the music's sound – breathing, sighing, screaming, air squeezed through the lungs, part death-rattle, part orgasm, the earthly pleasures which form the only recompense of the poor. At the same time however, she separates this notion of authenticity from any idea of racial purity: the instrument passes from Italian to German to Cajun to Pole to African American, the music never distilled, but mongrel (and competitive) , like America itself. The twin enemies here are a bland assimilation, a watering-down of the ethnic flavour for a bland homogenised audience; and mummification, the music slipping from the hands of 'the people' (though Proulx is extremely unsentimental on this point), into the deadening claws of historians, curators, academic specialists and the like. The betrayal of the music by its audience – who just want fast tunes and a good time – mirrors the larger Americanisation of immigrant culture, but Proulx denies the existence of any untouched, privileged 'pure' culture; rather, everything is absorbed, mixed, exploded, an inherent turbulence which is inscribed into the text of the novel itself.

Unusually then for an American novelist, the idea of authenticity is rooted in class rather than race, poverty rather than ethnicity. The tentative prose of *Postcards* has long since vanished; as Mark Shechner has noted, Proulx foregrounds her prose as a virtuoso performance, swapping accents, settings, gender and tone at will, character again subordinated to a naturalistic stress on pattern, energy and form.[21] The brilliant audacity of this impersonation and improvisation has, of course, its critics: she 'does' Basque shepherds, Texan cowboys, black teenagers, Catholics, evangelists, patriarchal figures and abused spouses, but in what sense can such a barnstorming pantomime be authentic? She can nail the accent, and flesh out her minutely detailed research, but in what sense can this imitation be seen as 'true'? By recourse to Proulx's own immigrant (French-Canadian) background? To the material hardships of her own life? To the veracity of her knowledge and background information? To our own common-sensical view of life (although surely there are surely too many decapitations for the novel to be seen as 'realistic')? To our generic understanding of what constitutes a realistic read?

In a sense, all realistic fiction is a lie in the service of truth. Post-Structuralism, though, would argue that any shock of recognition, any assumption of perceiving real life lived in the raw, is simply a textual sleight-of-hand. *Accordion Crimes'* seething formlessness, its refusal to furnish us with finished 'plots', Proulx's brilliant ethnic ventriloquism, her stress on institutionalised racism as one of the central facts of American life; all suggest an unsentimental honesty, but this is just a carefully constructed textual mirage, Post-Structuralists would argue. After all, what does the reader really know about the life of German farmers or Hispanic musicians to judge whether a representation is true or false? But if one is only left talking about – and to – oneself, if language is only concerned with its own legitimisation, then why read at all? Without some faith in communication, some sort of belief in mimesis, without the aura of the authentic, it is hard to see how the novel can continue to exist. Proulx's specific brand of realism is grounded in a specific literary tradition (Naturalism), employs generic codes borrowed from both 'dirty' realism and the folk tradition of the tall-tale, and is dependent upon a specific ideological stress on class; but none of this prevents our ultimate evaluation of its worth resting upon the subjective values of honesty and authenticity. Indeed, without the humanist belief that we are learning something true about other peoples' lives, 'realism' becomes just another way of stacking words up on a page.

NOTES

1. Abbreviations and page references refer to the following editions of Proulx's work: *Postcards* (*Postcards*, London: Flamingo, 1994), *Heartsongs* (*Heartsongs*, London: Fourth Estate, 1996), *Shipping* (*The Shipping News*, London: Fourth Estate, 1994), *Close Range* (*Close Range*, London: Fourth Estate, 2000).
2. Elizabeth Ammon, in Donald Pizer (ed.) (1995), *The Cambridge Companion to American Realism and Naturalism*, New York: Cambridge University Press, p. 95.
3. For a fine introduction to Carver, see Nick Hornby (1992), *Contemporary American Fiction*, London: Vision Press, pp. 30–52.
4. Richard Lehan, ibid., p. 67.

5. Ibid., p. 70.
6. See Jerome Klinkowitz (1992), *Structuring the Void*, Durham: Duke University Press.
7. Amy Kaplan (1998), *The Social Construction of American Realism*, Chicago: University of Chicago Press.
8. Tom Waits (1992), 'Murder in the Red Barn', *Bone Machine*, London: Island Records.
9. Proulx, quoted by Katie Bolick (1997), 'Imagination is everything: a conversation with E. Annie Proulx', *The Atlantic*, 12 November, pp. 56–61.
10. Jane Shilling (1999), *The Times*, 17 October.
11. Philp Rahv's famous essay on 'Palefaces and redskins' was first published in his *Image and Idea* (1949; rev. 1957), Westport: Greenwood Press .
12. Proulx, in Bolick, *The Atlantic*.
13. Brian Jarvis (1998), *Postmodern Cartographies*, London: Pluto Press, p. 88.
14. For an excellent discussion of this idea see Herb Wylie (1998), 'Ransom revised: the aesthetics of regionalism in a globalized age', *Canadian Review of American Studies*, 28 (2), pp. 97–117.
15. Mark Shechner (1997), 'Until the music stops: women novelists in a post-feminist world', *Salmagundi*, 113, Winter, p. 227.
16. Robert Scott Stewart (1998), 'Tayloring the self: identity, articulation and community in Proulx's *The Shipping News*', *Studies in Canadian Literature*, 23 (2), p. 54.
17. Ibid., p. 69.
18. Ibid., p. 62.
19. Kenneth Millard (2000), *Contemporary American Fiction*, Oxford: Oxford University Press, pp. 22–30.
20. Ibid., pp. 23–4.
21. Shechner, p. 229.

BIOGRAPHY

E(thel) Annie Proulx was born to French-Canadian parents in 1935, and grew up in rural New England, later living in North Carolina and the Far East. Married and divorced three times, she raised three sons 'pretty much alone', supporting herself through waitressing, postal work, handicrafts, but primarily by writing freelance articles and how-to-manuals on an astonishing range of subjects, 'from grape-growing to fence-mending to bartering'. She gained a masters in History from Concordia University, but abandoned her Ph.D. on European economics and, in the early '70s, moved with a friend to start an extremely remote rural existence in Vermont, part of what she terms the 'back-to-the-land' movement of the period. During this time she founded a small-town newspaper, *The Vershire Behind the Times*, and increasingly turned to the writing of fiction.

Early short stories appeared in *Gray's Sporting Journal* and *Ploughshares*, and she published her first novel, *Postcards*, in 1992, at the age of fifty-seven. The award of a Guggenheim Fellowship enabled her to undertake the extensive research necessary for her subsequent novels, *The Shipping News* and *Accordion Crimes*, and in 1994 she finally moved from Vermont to 'the long, wonderful, empty silence' of Wyoming, the state to which she had previously retreated to fine-tune her work. 'The long sight lines, that long shoot of the eye to a distant horizon for some reason frees thoughts and images for me more than anywhere else,' she wrote. The state also provides the setting for her second short-story collection, *Close Range* (1999).

PROULX ON PROULX

Readers often ask me why don't you write about women, implying that if you are a woman, that's all you can write about. Writers can write about anything they want, any sex they want, any place they want. The worst piece of advice given to young writers is to write about what they know.

When you measure one person's life, say, against the teeming millions and billions that are on earth today, it shrinks in magnitude, quite stunningly. I always place my characters against the idea of *mass*, whether landscape or a crushing social situation or powerful circumstances.

I always wanted a brother and I liked the things that men did; when I was growing up, women didn't go skiing, or hiking, or have adventurous canoe trips, or any of that sort of thing . . . I find male characters interesting. Because much of my writing is set in an earlier period, they do the things that women could not appropriately do.

Those who say the book is moribund often cite the computer as the asp on the mat. But the electronic highway is for bulletin boards on esoteric subjects, reference works, lists and news – timely utilitarian information, effectively pulled through the wires. Nobody is going to sit down and read a novel on a twitchy little screen. Ever.

LINKS TO OTHER AUTHORS

Don DeLillo: DeLillo's stress upon the tactile presence of the world (as opposed to the immaterial absence suggested by information technology) provides a surprising link to Proulx's art.

Cormac McCarthy: Proulx's exploration of masculinity and violence offers an interesting comparison with McCarthy's heroism. Both writers are concerned with a link between the land and the authentic.

Rolando Hinojosa: Like Hinojosa, Proulx switches from comically terse newspaper journalese to the storytelling rhetoric of raconteurs who speak as if 'declaiming from a stage'. Both writers shift from conventional 'realism' to a specific kind of larger than life regional oration, and the clash of various kinds of discourse.

Douglas Coupland: Both writers are interested in tourism as a metaphor for some kind of falsification of nature and the real.

BIBLIOGRAPHY

Primary Works
Heartsongs and Other Stories (1988), New York: Scribner.
Postcards (1992), New York: Scribner.
The Shipping News (1993), New York: Scribner.
Accordion Crimes (1996), New York: Scribner.
Close Range (1999), New York: Scribner.

Critical Sources
Baum, Geraldine (1993), 'A mind filled with stories', *Los Angles Times*, 15 November.
Bell, Millicent (2000), 'Fiction chronicle', *Hudson Review*, 52 (4), Winter, pp. 37–40.
Bolick, Kate (1997), 'Imagination is everything: a conversation with E. Annie Proulx', *The Atlantic*, 12 November.
Bray, R. L. (1992), 'The reader writes most of the story: an interview with E.Annie Proulx', *New York Times Book Review*, 22 March.
Conarre, J. (1999), 'Heart-songs: a response to Richard Eder's review of Annie Proulx's *Close Range*', *New York Times Book Review*, 13 June.
Crimmel, Hal (2000), '"*Close Range*": Wyoming Stories', *Western American Literature*, 35 (3), Fall, pp. 320–2.
Eder, R. (1999) '*Close Range*', *New York Times Book Review*, 23 May.
Flavin, Louise (1999), 'Quoyle's quest: knots and fragments as tools of narration in *The Shipping News*', *Critique*, 40 (3), Spring, pp. 239–47.
Gray, Paul (1996), 'Striking the wrong chord', *Time*, 24 June.
Klinkenberg, Verlyn (1994), 'The princess of tides', *New Republic*, 30 May.
Mantel, Hilary (2000), '*Close Range*', *New York Review of Books*, 11 May.

Millard, Kenneth (2000), *Contemporary American Fiction*, Oxford: Oxford University Press.

Norman, Howard (1993), 'In Killick-Claw everybody reads *The Gammy Bird*', *New York Times Book Review*, 4 April.

Rackstraw, Loree (2000), 'Painful irresolution', *The North American Review*, 274 (3), Winter, pp. 67–9.

Shechner, Mark (1997), 'Until the music stops: women novelists in a post-femenist age', *Salmagundi*, 113, Winter, pp. 220–38.

Stewart, Robert Scott (1998), 'Tayloring the self: identity, articulation and community in Proulx's *The Shipping News*', *Studies in Canadian Literature*, 23 (2), pp. 49–70.

Walter, Natasha (1993), 'Newfoundland kisses', *Times Literary Supplement*, 26 November.

Wylie, Herb (1998), 'Ransom revisited: the aesthetics of regionalism in a globalised age', *Canadian Review of American Studies*, 28 (2), pp. 99–117.

BRET EASTON ELLIS[1]

'We have spoken of the hostility to civilization which is produced by the pressure that civilization exercises, the renunciations of instinct which it demands. If one imagines its prohibitions lifted – if, then, one may take any woman one pleases as a sexual object, if one may without hesitation kill one's rival for her love or anyone else who stands in one's way, if, too, one can carry off another of the other man's belongings without asking leave – how splendid, what a string of satisfactions one's life would be!'
Sigmund Freud.[2]

How to be a subversive in a society where everything is permitted? Or, how can one choose to be a bohemian when non-conformity is the norm? Can one still be revolutionary when everything – including the very spirit of revolt – is absorbed by the system and turned into new opportunities for profit and growth? The French philosopher, Jean Baudrillard, defines the Postmodern in terms of 'a post-orgy world', spent and sleepy, a kind of cultural refractory period, luxuriating in the obscenity of total availability.[3] His version of the Postmodern is a world where nothing is censored, repressed or taboo, a world in which moral values have been wholly superseded by commercial concerns. For Baudrillard, the 'American miracle is that of the obscene', marked by unprecedented wealth, instantaneous gratification, an almost unbearable profusion of consumer choices.[4] In short, 'an air-conditioned paradise . . . But a very slight modification, a change of just a few degrees, would suffice to make it seem hell'.[5]

We are a long way beyond the Freudian drama of repression here, that seemingly eternal struggle between individual desire and social prohibition. For Freud, the instinctual drives of mankind – sexual, violent, anti-social – are perpetually at war with the basics of civilisation – civic duty, social responsibility, moral order. At times (and this is,

195

of course, one of the central themes of early Modernism) the lid is
screwed down too tightly, and society inflicts wounds upon the individual psyche in the form of neuroses. Behaviour is strictly regulated.
Specific bodily functions are deemed inappropriate and controlled via
guilt and shame. Sexuality is constrained by a tight corset of injunctions
and inhibitions. But, Freud argues, one should not romanticise these
libidinal forces, which are profoundly selfish, amoral and destructive. If
unchecked, if one were permitted to follow one's natural inclination
toward rape and murder (and note how thoroughly unsentimental
Freud's view of Nature is here), then barbarism would result.
Civilisation is built upon the sublimation of these energies, channelling
such forces into socially acceptable manifestations: ambition, progress,
art and science. Nudity is turned into art, unlicensed sexuality into
monogamy, aggression and conquest into capitalism and technological
progress. Hence, for Freud, sexuality is always a threat to the social
order. For this reason pornographic images are taboo, promiscuity is
frowned upon, the libidinal is the essential basis of the obscene. No
matter how painful this renunciation of desire may be, repression is
the price we must pay for civilisation.

But what if Freud is wrong? After all, the restrictions, hypocrisies
and prohibitions of turn of the nineteenth century Vienna appear very
distant – even quaint – from our twenty-first century viewpoint. Indeed,
one might argue that the current vogue for nineteenth-century novels,
literary adaptations, and heritage cinema is a kind of paradoxical nostalgia for repression. In the tightly corseted world of Victoriana, the
mere glimpse of pale flesh is enough to inspire a swoon; nudist
beaches, on the other hand, are profoundly unerotic because of the
lack of any form of restriction. Everything is immediately on show.
Desire requires a sense of longing which instantaneous gratification
simply doesn't have time for. Similarly, the truly scandalous nature of
Freud's theories is virtually inexplicable to us now. This is the stuff of
day-time talk shows, magazine articles and primary school education;
sexually explicit images, song lyrics and celebrity gossip make up the
daily texture of our mediated lives. Of all of Freud's ideas, the most
old-fashioned seems to be that of the Super-ego, the harbinger of
guilt, conscience and moral contrition. For Freud, the Super-ego was
the internalisation (or introjection) of the child's view of its parents:
what would my mother and father think if they could see me now?
But this assumes a stern patriarch; a castrating paterfamilias; a vengeful,

Old Testament father. For the bratty kids of liberal, baby-boomer parents, such an idea seems unutterably foreign, especially if one realises that one's swinging progenitors led a much wilder life than oneself. What's left is a vague sense of embarrassment (as in, say, *American Pie* (2000)), a strange listlessness in which there's nothing left to rebel against. Both Bret Easton Ellis and Douglas Coupland stress the predicament of being born after the '60s. Just as Freud's contentious writings on sexuality now seem as quaint as a Victorian keepsake, so too does the sexual braggadocio of '60s' radicals such as Herbert Marcuse and Norman O. Brown.[6] For Marcuse, building upon the theories of Wilhelm Reich, the liberation of Eros would spell the end of capitalism. Sexual energies currently diverted into the workplace, commodity fetishism, and a false sense of progress, needed to be turned back to their original source, he proclaimed – in essence, Make Love Not Work. Sexuality was subversive (totalitarian régimes are always puritanically prudish), pleasure a threat to the Protestant work ethic, post-coital drowsiness the antithesis of capitalism's relentless labour. But Marcuse, like Freud, seems to have underestimated the system.

Contemporary culture seems to suggest that libidinal forces and a capitalist economy can quite happily co-exist after all. In place of Freud's old-fashioned notion of sublimation – the imprisonment and forced redirection of the sexual iinstinct – it now seems as if the pornographic is everywhere. Desire still exists, but in a curiously attenuated and free-floating form. We still want things (namely consumer goods) but in turn, they seem instantly available. In order for us to keep on wanting, we must never feel wholly satisfied or gratified – a strange, libidinal twist on the idea of built-in obsolescence – we must always want the next thing. In the world of late capitalism, whatever we want we can buy – but there are always too many things out there finally to sate our appetite (as the ad for *Pokémon* says, 'Gotta catch 'em all'). Instant gratification is always accompanied by a queasy sense of emptiness. Desire is no longer about forbidden areas of life, but rather having the space to put things.

One might therefore argue that sexuality is even more severely harnessed to the system (and thereby, in Marcuse's terms, constrained) in late capitalism, but it is neither suppressed nor sublimated – rather the mechanics of desire seem incorporated within the very nexus of commodity culture. Commodified sexuality is no longer a threat; it provides an extremely lucrative source of income. Is there anything still taboo in our society? Why, yes: the uncommercial, the undesirable, the dull – everything else is grist to the mill, including, of course, the idea of rebellion itself. Modern Art caused scandals, riots, arrests, convulsive social repercussions. It saw itself as a spit in the face of bourgeois taste, a blasphemous provocation, a call to arms. When Luis Bunuel and Salvador Dali filmed *Un Chien Andalou* in 1928 they genuinely believed that its violent, morbid, irrational imagery – the slitting of a woman's eye-ball, priests tied to a dead donkey, a breast that turns into an arse – would disturb its audience to the point of madness. And indeed early viewers were offended, horrified, disturbed – and came again and again in ever greater numbers.

What can the avant-garde do, when their subversive work proves unexpectedly commercial? Novelty, controversy and sexuality sell; Surrealist imagery is now the stuff of advertising campaigns and rock album covers; subversion and an aura of rebelliousness simply add to its market value. Thus, huge corporate conglomerates will quite happily sell The Sex Pistols (whose album title *The Great Rock and Roll Swindle* is emblematic here), NWA (including marketing violent acts of resistance such as 'Cop-Killer'), Marilyn Manson, Slipknot, William Burroughs, Marx and Engels's *Communist Manifesto*, the collected works of the Marquis de Sade, *Driller Killer*, Herbert Marcuse, Hans Bellmer's pornographic dummies, *Hustler*, Salvador Dali colouring-in books . . . all available in a store near you. As Elizabeth Young puts it, 'Art no longer contests everything – if it ever did.'[7] Everything is incorporated – and the more extreme the better. This seems to leave us only with the position of being neo-conservatives, which is, of course, uncomfortable; we'd like to be bohemians, subversives, upsetting the prudish and scandalising the bourgeoisie, but instead we find ourselves calling for some kind of order, restraint, condemning the morally blank cultural scene. But even this position – with its implied sense of critical distance and moral objectivity – seems somehow unavailable to us. Satirists condemn their age, because they can still imagine something better, some kind of moral norm with which to contrast the current depravity; it is this idea of distance, of being outside of things, which no longer seems tenable to us today. Nobody illustrates this better than Bret Easton Ellis; 'This is not an exit' he writes at the end of *American Psycho* (*Psycho*, 399) and this motto could be seen as emblematic of the Postmodern dilemma: there's simply no way out of the mall.

'Fear never shows up and the party ends early.'
(*Less than Zero*, 87)

For many readers, the defining characteristic of Ellis's prose is just how boring it is. Elizabeth Young describes it in terms of a 'flat, stunned quality', soporific, toneless and glazed.[8] The effect is that of a petulant teenager too bored (or stoned) to communicate, blank, indifferent, apathetic. Your eyes glaze over; after a while, even skim-reading seems too much effort. Interchangeable, zombified dudes sleep-walk through endless parties; dialogue degenerates into a kind of anaesthetised mumbling; the very narrative seems on heavy medication. Only the most extreme acts of violence or explicit pornographic detail penetrate this fog, and even then it's hard to summon up the energy either to tut or shrug. Exhaustion, indifference and ennui are the constituent elements of Ellis's somnambulistic universe. Hedonism has never seemed so little fun.

Which is not to say, of course, that Ellis's writing is simply bad. Indeed, as a representation of blissed-out, affluent, lackadaisical LA youth, *Less than Zero* (1985) represents a near perfect convergence of content and form. Identical tans, blonde locks, perfect bodies, doped incoherence; it is impossible to work out who anyone is (or rather, impossible to motivate oneself to care), and the narrative progresses through short, disconnected fragments lacking in any sense of continuity or progression. People never meet up, appointments are never kept, nobody ever answers the phone; time is too liquid, or rather too viscous, for any kind of resolution. Yet another party, drug deal, sexual conquest: nothing registers, nothing matters. Each day is hot, sunny, perfect, but this endless reproduction drains it of any kind of meaning. This is a David Hockney print as X-rayed by Andy Warhol, revealing only hidden shallows at the bottom of the pool. As such it is utterly two-dimensional, like a kind of virtual reality hologram, stuck on perpetual rerun. No depth, no feeling, no change; the novel is becalmed in a kind of 'foetal tranquillity', a vacation that will never end.[9] One can imagine Dali's melting clocks here, the enervation of emptiness. It is impossible to imagine that anything else will ever happen.

Frederic Jameson characterises this as 'the waning of affect', a flattening-out of culture into an endless (and thereby meaningless) horizontality.[10] A permanent heat-haze hangs over the novel, destroying any sense of perspective and denying any chance of movement. Both the ocean and the desert are featureless (like this part of LA itself), flat planes of nothingness, reproduced, reproduced, reproduced. The rock and roll cliché of 'too much, too young' here acts as the novel's defining principle; even the pre-teens are incredibly jaded, have seen it all, are trapped in a cycle of endless repetition (nothing happens and then nothing happens again). The Postmodern notion that actual experience is replaced by representation – everything resembles a movie, a rock video, a line from a song – here implodes into an awful endemic lassitude; everyone has seen the movie, heard the song, watched the show, over and over and over again. There is nothing but re-runs. As Elizabeth Young puts it, everything is worn out, second-hand, monotonous, including the notion of youthful rebellion itself.[11] Once potent counter-cultural forces – rock music, drugs, permissive licentiousness – are simply absorbed by an indulgent consumerism. Astonishing affluence (the protagonists of *Less than Zero* are mainly the spawn of Hollywood executives, music producers, studio suits and rock stars) and disinterested tolerance effectively absorb any kind of recalcitrance. There are simply no laws left to break. When 'Teenage enema nurses in bondage' by 'Killer Pussy' comes on the radio, nobody blinks an eye (*Zero*, 25). Considerate parents will help their offspring score Coke. When Clay returns home to find 'some porno film on the Betamax', he idly wonders 'whose it is – my mom's? sisters'? Christmas present from a friend? the person with the Ferrari? mine?' (*Zero*, 75). But nothing excites, stimulates or provokes. Everyone has seen it all already.

Indeed, despite the explicit sexual nature of much of Ellis's writing, his is a peculiarly desire-less world – in essence, everything is too easily available for longing still to exist. Freud's controversial notion of bisexual polymorphous perversity – the idea that one's body is an enormous erogenous zone, whose sexual possibilities are severely restrained by society, brutally limited to reproduction – here becomes the norm, a kind of orthodox decadence. Ellis's characters are sexually omnivorous, virtually genderless, but there is no sense of transgression, or even passion. Tellingly, the longest sexual scene in the novel involves an act of mutual masturbation in which the participants never even touch (*Zero*, 121). Only the visual display (rather than the actual act) retains any sense of erotic frisson, but even this is distant, detached, indifferent; like watching TV or idly gazing out of one's car. The novel's repeated refrain ('People are afraid to merge on freeways in Los Angles' (*Zero*, 9)) characterises the degree of lobotomised non- communication at work here. Just as Los Angeles' freeways circle a downtown city centre which simply isn't there, the novel's characters mouth rock lyrics, repeat clichés, and mumble banalities but barely exist on the page. Only their words float across the paper, but even these don't seem to belong to anyone – or rather they belong purely to the culture at large:

> Benjamin says, 'The Human League are out. Over. Finished. You don't know what's going on, Kim.'
> Kim shrugs. I wonder where Dimitri is; if Jeff is still holed up with some surfer out in Malibu.
> 'No, I mean, you really don't,' he goes on. 'I bet you don't even read *The Face*. You've got to.' He lights a clove cigarette. 'You've got to.'
> 'Why do you have to?' I ask.
> Benjamin looks at me, runs his fingers over his pompadour and says, 'Otherwise you'll get bored.' (*Zero*, 96)

Interestingly, as the novel has got older, and the references and brand-names more obscure, the work has also become increasingly abstract. If you don't recognise the logo or the label, then the signs no longer signify anything (beyond being badges of pure consumerism) floating free across the page. With each passing year, the work becomes more weightless, intangible, evacuated of meaning. There are few passages of description; instead dialogue drifts ethereally, disconnected from any speaker. Similarly, Ellis's signature technique of first-person, present-tense narration, implies a sense of distance rather than immediacy. Clay is detached from even the present moment, absenting himself from the scene in order to narrate it, like a tourist seeing the world through the lens of a video camera. He records but isn't truly there. At times there doesn't seem to be any 'there' anyway:

> We park and then walk through the empty, bright Beverly Centre. All the stores are closed and as we walk up to the top floor, where the movies are playing, the whiteness of the floors and the ceilings and the walls is overpowering and we walk quickly through the empty mall and don't see one other person until we get to the theatres. There are a couple of people milling around the ticket booth. We buy our tickets and walk down the hall to theatre

thirteen and Trent and I are the only persons in it and we share
another joint inside the small, hollow room. (*Zero*, 100).

The movie doesn't even warrant a mention; the novel's attention span
isn't up to it anyway. Everything blurs, evaporates, erases. There is no
more terra firma to be had.

Or is there? Clay – his name suggestive both of his malleability as
well as a faint echo of something real – is obsessed with the desert
space which lies outside the city limits, the arid plains beyond the
mall and the freeway. Infernal winds howl in from the hinterlands,
uprooting palm trees and cutting power; flash-fires erupt without
warning; sudden earth tremors prophesy the end.[12] Occasionally,
fleeting glimpses of the real – poor folk, crashed cars, a dying coyote
(*Zero*, 142) – disrupt the hologram of endless leisure and ceaseless
indulgence which is Clay's lot. Not that this reality is in any way
redemptive, as it is for, say, Douglas Coupland or Paul Auster; rather
Clay responds with agoraphobic dread, fearing the return of a
repressed Nature, red in tooth and claw. The desert appears in the
guise of an Old Testament deity, the angry, vengeful Father missing
elsewhere, passing judgement on LA, as if on Sodom and Gomorrah.
And Clay knows that he deserves it, in some sense longs for it, the fiery
condemnation that will take away his listless sense of ennui. After all,
better Hell than nothingness – the novel's implicit self-loathing and
self-condemnation is nowhere more apparent than in these passages,
a desire for self-immolation, maybe the last desire left. But judgement
never comes. Moreover, the idea of Nature as the incarnation of the
real also falls apart. Clay's visions of apocalypse are rooted in disaster
movies, thrash-metal lyrics, tabloid fantasies; like the Gladney family
in DeLillo's *White Noise* (1984), Clay exhibits a longing for terrible
things, but this is not the same as the return of the authentically
real. What is Nature in the book? A werewolf prowling by the pool
(*Zero*, 75), a guilty fear of peasants storming the rich man's castle, a
vague intimation of mortality (but Clay and his friends are too young
to understand this – and besides, surgery means that one never grows
old). As Ellis puts it, 'Fear never shows up' (*Zero*, 87); non-resolution
robs us even of infernal purification. 'All that matters is that I want to
see the worst' (*Zero*, 172) admits Clay, a key sentence in the novel.

In a sense, the novel is a test of our moral indignation. We start with
mindless promiscuity and meaningless debauchery, and follow the

path of moral degeneracy down; Julian selling drugs to high-school kids (*Zero*, 126), an utterly vicious 'snuff' movie (which may or may not be real), the gang-rape of a twelve-year-old girl. Throughout all of this, Clay remains passive, ethically inert. His only act of condemnation is to walk out – from the (real?)castration scene of the porn-movie, and again from the apartment where the rape is taking place. The closest he gets to formulating some sense of outrage is the following exchange, regarding the twelve-year-old girl:

'It's . . .' my voice trails off.
   'It's what?' Rip wants to know.
   'It's . . . I don't think it's right.'
   'What's right? If you want something, you have the right to take it. If you want to do something, you have the right to do it.'
   I lean up against the wall. I can hear Spin moaning in the bedroom and then the sound of a hand slapping maybe a face.
   'But you don't need anything. You have everything,' I tell him.
   Rip looks at me. 'No. I don't.'
   'What?'
   'No, I don't.'
   There's a pause and then I ask, 'Oh, shit, Rip, what don't you have?'
   'I don't have anything to lose.' (*Zero*, 189–90)

Clay's quiescence forms the moral focus of the novel; in the light of his passivity, the reader is forced to assume an active moral position – to draw the line somewhere. But is this so simple? Elizabeth Young has written of Ellis's 'puritan disgust' and goes on to argue that 'the onus is on the reader to interject the moral values so conspicuously lacking elsewhere'.[13, 14] Peter Brooker, however, argues that the glazed, affectless tone of the novel also implicates the reader.[15] After all, the moral shocks of the novel soon subside; Ellis has to keep ratcheting up the degeneracy for us even to notice. Aren't we in a sense, complicit with the novel's obsession with violent extremes, the longing for something – and only the most abhorrent will do – to disturb our slumber, to satisfy our desensitised, jaded sense of horror? How much of *Less than Zero*'s claim to be a cool 'cult' novel is dependent upon its (carefully commodified and marketed) aura of illicit thrills? Rather than read the novel, why not (as countless readers have done with

American Psycho) fast-forward to the nasty bits, skim-read the dross until, like some bored cable-viewer playing with the remote control, one hits upon something that provides a momentary jolt of feeling? The dead bodies in *Less than Zero* suggest some level of visceral reality – but our longing for this implicates us in the acts of violence.

What is most interesting about Ellis's work is the way in which it fluctuates between acting as a diagnosis and a symptom of all that is wrong with the Postmodern. Indeed, it is this very lack of critical distance which produces its characteristic tone of self-disgust; it is the very thing it hates, which is to say that its defining characteristics form the very targets of its critique. The result is a very unstable form of satire indeed. It also helps to illustrate Frederic Jameson's claim that 'the cultural critic . . . like the rest of us, is now so deeply immersed in postmodernist space, so deeply suffused and infected by its new cultural categories, that the luxury of the old-fashioned ideological critique, the indignant moral denunciation of the other, becomes unavailable'.[16]

Certainly, it seems redundant to state that the novel is a critique of commodification, materialism, moral vacuity: of course it is. Equally, however, one cannot imagine things any other way. There are no viable alternatives available. Escape from LA? The East-coast education which seems to oppose West-coast indulgence, is revealed in *Rules of Attraction* (1987) to be simply its greyer, more overcast twin. Love? Clay's relationship with Blair suggests some kind of human feeling, but only as some kind of vestigial tail which evolution has left behind. Moreover, the signifiers of romantic attraction simply wither under the novels, reflexive, automatic irony. The romantic flash-back to their vacation at the Pajara Dunes near Monterey – an escape to simple pleasures such as walking along the beach, candle-lit meals, beach-combing, making love in the surf – is undercut by the speed with which they get bored, so that by the week's end all they can do is watch TV and get paralytic (*Zero*, 61). The closest one can get to real feelings is an unconvincing past tense:'I cared about you for a little while,' admits Blair (*Zero*, 204), which is as about as heartfelt as the novel gets.

One way of viewing the novel is to see it as a Postmodern reworking of Fitzgerald's *The Great Gatsby* (1925). Blair becomes Daisy, the girl he left behind; an Elvis Costello poster becomes the eyes of T. J. Eckleberg; the Valley of Ashes becomes the vast junkyard of crashed cars (*Zero*, 194). But the romantic idealism which, in a sense, absolves Gatsby of his materialism is utterly missing. For Gatsby, wealth suggests not just leisure or comfort or things, but possibility, a grander sweep of life. His desire remains pure as long as it remains unalloyed desire; it is the satisfaction of these urges which is tainted with material corruption. Hence, he gazes at the green light of Daisy's mansion across the bay, and the light symbolises eternal human longing. Ellis's characters, however, gaze into the headlights like stunned rabbits; instant gratification removes even that idealistic dream that things could be somehow other than how they are. In essence, they aren't innocent enough to dream. Nor does friendship provide any kind of emotional ballast. Again, traces of real feeling still exist, but only fleetingly; Clay visits his old school and momentarily remembers a childhood which is inconceivable now (*Zero*, 164); in the next scene, he accompanies his oldest friend, Julian, to a rendezvous with a middle-aged client (Julian is now a rent-boy and drug addict), but any sense of corruption or loss of innocence is immediately undercut:

> And in the elevator on the way down to Julian's car, I say, 'Why didn't you tell me the money was for this?' and Julian, his eyes all glassy, sad grin on his face, says, 'Who cares? Do you? Do you really care?' and I don't say anything and realize that I really don't care and suddenly feel foolish, stupid. (*Zero*, 172)

Ellis's characteristic mode is to proffer some vague memory of authentic, human emotion and then to mock ruthlessly our sentimental belief that such a thing might still persist. In this sense, the best one can say for Clay is that he is honest about being a fake, but even this implies a degree of self-criticism which borders on masochistic spite. Certainly, the scene between Julian and his fat, middle-aged client is engineered to illicit a kind of knee-jerk homophobia (*Zero*, 172–6), all the more striking because Ellis is himself gay. Degradation in *Less than Zero* still appears as the perversion of the past (watching the man grope Julian, Clay suddenly experiences 'an image of Julian in fifth grade, kicking a soccer ball across a green field' (*Zero*, 175)), but this nostalgic mode, so beloved of Coupland, gradually diminishes; after a while there are no memories, only video games, movie clips, MTV, Clay's 'only point of reference' (*Zero*, 208) and the source of the novel's apocalyptic (and self-consciously banal) imagery. But the past – and the dynamics of familial conflict – is not entirely absent here. The businessman disturbs because he is connected with Clay's father ('I keep wondering if my father knows this guy' (*Zero*, 174)), a fixation which Clay cannot shake. This shadowy father – no longer a symbol of parental authority, but somehow much more sinister – is central to Ellis's *oeuvre*, and provides a sense of dread which cannot be dismissed as artificial.

'You may think I'm a really disgusting yuppie, but I'm not, *really*.'
(*American Psycho*, 199)

In an interview with Jamie Clarke, Ellis admitted that Patrick Bateman was based partly on 'guys I met in Wall St, partly myself, and partly my father'.[17] He went on to explain that the book was, at some level, 'a criticism of the way my father lived his life, because he did slip into that void. He was the ultimate consumer. He was the sort of person who was completely obsessed with status and about wearing the right suits and owning a certain kind of car and staying at certain hotels and eating in a certain kind of restaurant regardless of whether these things gave him pleasure or not . . . And they were values that he passed on to me and I still can't say I've completely shaken them off.'[18]

The admittance that *American Psycho* (1991) is 'the most autobiographical of my novels', the product of a 'severe depression and black period' has, of course, been seized on by Ellis's many critics.[19] Interviews in which Ellis appears every bit as obsessed and *au fait* with designer labels and conspicuous consumerism as his characters, vaguely sinister descriptions of his black, minimalist apartment, and apparently unguarded expressions of masochistic despair regarding his vacuous, materialistic lifestyle, have all fed a dangerously naïve synthesis between Ellis's public persona and the figure of Patrick Bateman. After all, what kind of a healthy well-balanced person would come up with such stuff in the first place?

One of the fundamental debates regarding the novel is whether, given the unreliability of the text's narrator and the number of inaccuracies, contradictions and impossibilities involved, Bateman has actually committed the acts in the novel or simply fantasised about doing so; but this kind of debate brings us back to the vaguely unwholesome image of Ellis scribbling away in his notebooks, working out his sadistic scenarios in a fog of drugs, self-abuse and self-loathing. Certainly the novel plays with this collision between surface 'realism' and self-conscious fiction. Alison Poole is the lead character of Jay McInerney's *Story of my Life* (1988), whilst Boho-artist 'Stash' is borrowed from Tama Janowitz's

Slaves of New York (1986). Similarly, the corporation where Bateman 'works', Pierce & Pierce (also symbolic of his out-of-hours activities), is taken from Tom Wolfe's *Bonfire of the Vanities* (1987), and even Gordon Gekko, from Oliver Stone's 1988 satire, *Wall-Street* gets a passing mention (*Psycho*, 387). Though Ellis takes care to get the Wall-Street patois down pat (as Elizabeth Young characterises it, a kind of 'brochure-speak . . . part *GQ, Stereo Review, Fangoria* and *Vanity Fair*'), this keen-eyed observation is married to a self-conscious exaggeration and distortion, from Bateman menacing a co-worker, 'greenish bile dripping in strings from my bared fangs' (*Psycho*, 151), who somehow fails to notice, to delirious nonsense such as Bateman being followed home by a park-bench (*Psycho*, 395) or watching a cheerio being interviewed on live TV.[20]

Elizabeth Young argues that such incongruities set up a kind of 'authorial dissonance' which distances us from Bateman's relentless first-person tone.[21] Such a position allows her to argue that the book is 'straightforwardly judgemental and condemnatory': or, as Ellis puts it, 'I really didn't think that I had to say "killing people is wrong"'.[22, 23] But perhaps a more interesting reading stresses our collusion with Bateman's crimes. Just as the thought of Bateman endlessly watching Brian De Palma's *Body Double* (1984) back to back with Abel Ferrara's *Driller Killer* (1979) unavoidably triggers a conservative, censorious reaction (maybe this isn't a very healthy thing), so too does an image of lonely adolescents furtively pawing a copy of Ellis's book (Mary Harron's film-version is probably too tame) suggest that there is something implicitly unwholesome or illicit about the book. This is not to say that the book isn't serious or openly critical, but simply to argue that, as with *Less than Zero*, the text itself embodies the very characteristics which Ellis both recognises and despises. The more one reads it, the more one realises that this is a book which makes its own contents (and creation) the target of its critique, implicating the reader in the bad faith of being drawn to it in the first place.

What, after all, is one's response to the book's endless litany of atrocities? Ellis cunningly (and surprisingly, given the novel's infamous reputation) holds out on the first murder scene until some 130 pages in; rather like Hitchcock, he makes us want the crime to happen, and thereby makes us complicitous in the act. Do we read the brutality in full or automatically begin to draw back, noting only the surface extremity? Even if one allows one's brain to take in the details – eye-gouging, skin-peeling, genital mutilation – to what extent are we willing (or able) to imagine what this would actually feel like, to put ourselves in the position of the victim? The only way to get through such scenes is to abstract the violence, to register a dull sense of horror , but otherwise disengage. Take, for example, the infamous torture-by-rat scene which is probably the book's most vicious high (or low) point. One registers the extremity of the violence, the sheer sexual viciousness of the act, but otherwise blanks out the visceral detail. To make the scene bearable one has to dehumanise it, turn it into a spectacle (look, this is an even more terrible crime than the last!), disregard the victim – which is, of course, exactly what Bateman does in the first place. The murders in the book do become boring; the 'high' they induce in both perpetrator and reader lasts for a shorter and shorter spell. Endless reproduction renders everything meaningless, affectless; extremity is the only cure for boredom, but, as with Andy Warhol's 'Electric Chair' (see Chapter 1 (DeLillo)), even this is subject to the Postmodern law of diminishing returns. Lassitude always wins out in the end.

Ellis refuses to offer any 'realistic' or psychological motivation for Bateman's actions. Nor does he offer catharsis or condemnation; in short, no-one really cares. His repeated confessions – most explicitly to his lawyer, Harry Carnes (*Psycho*, 352) – trigger no repercussions or just deserts. As in *Less than Zero*, there is a longing for punishment, but no kind of moral framework which would make the mechanics of tragedy possible. We learn nothing about the idea of evil, remain unpunished for our own prurience. 'I gain no deeper knowledge about myself, no new understanding can be extracted from my telling' states Bateman at the end of the novel. 'There has been no reason for me to tell you any of this. This confession has meant *nothing* . . .' (*Psycho*, 377). The reader is left without any literary justification for their following Bateman down into the depths, as nothing can be learnt from his actions. During the early sections of the novel, one might fool oneself into thinking that some of the old psychological categories of repression or sublimation still exist. After all, doesn't Bateman actually act on the evil impulses which everyone feels? To kill the person who cuts ahead of you in the traffic, to humiliate the person who makes you feel small, to demonstrate your own brutal prowess in a corporate structure which stresses your disposability? This is Bateman as psychotic Everyman. Whilst other employees of Pierce & Pierce sublimate these drives, channel such aggressive impulses into the bellicose language of hostile takeovers, cutting a deal, or stiffing the opposition, Bateman takes these impulses literally – hence 'Mergers and Acquisitions' becomes 'Murders and Executions' (*Psycho*, 206). But in this brutal process of desublimation, contemporary culture is already ahead of him. Everything (and everybody) can already be bought, consumed, and disposed of – at a purely financial, rather than moral, cost. In a sense, there is no need to sublimate; Ellis's New York wears its appetite on its sleeve. In fact, one could very well reverse these terms: it is the financial or the mercantile impulse which is genuine, and Bateman's murders are but a visceral perversion of this. As John Walsh puts it, 'In his murky vision, a skewed and suicidal materialism is the sole currency of his young metropolitans, the only stuff of conversation, the single realm of thought, the measure of personal wealth and social health.'[24] Bateman's actions represent the capitalist instinct sublimated into violence.

Is there something to be learnt after all, then? James Annesley argues that 'Patrick Bateman's murders are crimes for which an increasingly commercial and materialistic society must take ultimate responsibility' and that 'it is his rampant consumerism that provides the key to understanding his activities'.[25] People represent just another commodity to be consumed; the experience only becomes real when it is filmed, taped and replayed as a commodified image, viewed as a TV show or a movie. On one level, Bateman's violent physicality represents an atavistic return to real things, an escape from the electronic abstraction of his job on the stock market (what does he actually *do*?) and the meaningless flow of signs all around him. But Patrick also narrates his brutality in terms of a film script, employing dissolves, zooms, and jump-cuts, lapsing into the third person for the 'action-sequence' where he is pursued by the cops (*Psycho*, 349). Turning people into things and events into images is at the heart of theories of late capitalism; Bateman is simply an *uber*-consumer, 'unable to distinguish between purchasing a camera and purchasing a woman'.[26]

Peter Brooker, meanwhile, offers a slightly different interpretation of Bateman's activities.[27] He stresses Bateman's fear that 'I simply am not there . . . I am a noncontingent human being' (*Psycho*, 377). One of the running jokes throughout the novel (reminiscent of Tristan Tzara's refrain that *dada* is a joke told again and again until it becomes a threat) concerns the notion that Bateman is completely indistinguishable from his co-workers. He wears the same suit, glasses and braces, carries the same brief case and business card, and beyond these surface accoutrements, there simply isn't anything else to him – no discrete identity, personality or unique sense of self. Bateman is Postmodern man: a featureless dummy waiting to be dressed in the costumes of consumer culture. He expresses himself through things – his apartment, clothes, stereo, his ability to get a seat at the most exclusive of restaurants; but if these should be taken away from him, then there simply wouldn't be anything left. Hence the existential fear that he won't be able to make a booking, that his looks are inadequate, that someone else's business card may be better; without such things Bateman is little more than a Wall Street version of *The Invisible Man*. Hence, also, his ferocious repudiation of the underclass, those who possess none of these defining objects. Their abject state reminds him of his own nothingness, his lack of any essential self. They represent the existential void which his conspicuous consumption papers over; but, as Brooker suggests, given the relentless unpredictability of the markets, they also represent a black hole into which he could stumble at any time.

Such ideas, surprisingly perhaps, link Ellis's concerns to those of DeLillo and Auster. As with some of DeLillo's early protagonists, Bateman also speaks in media tongues, reciting great chunks of received information lifted straight from magazine articles, political speeches or banal editorials. His early outburst on the importance of promoting 'general social concern and less materialism in young people' (*Psycho*, 16) and the terrifically poker-faced 'reviews' of albums by Genesis, Whitney Houston and Huey Lewis are all examples of this. At these points, he simply isn't there. He doesn't speak the words, they speak him. His existence is contingent on discourse rather than vice versa, turning Bateman into a kind of textual mirage, an effect of language. He is a product of the jargon floating through the air-waves, an intersection of various clichés, adverts and slogans, rather than a person. Even his explicit summing-up of the novel's concerns doesn't belong to him, but rather to the author who provides his autocue:

> Nothing was affirmative, the term 'generosity of spirit' applied to nothing, was a cliche, was some kind of bad joke. Sex is mathematics. Individuality is no longer an issue. What does intelligence signify? Define reason. Desire – meaningless. Intellect is not a cure. Justice is dead. Fear, recrimination, innocence, sympathy, guilt,

waste, failure, grief, were things, emotions, that no one really felt anymore. Reflection is useless, the world is senseless. Evil is its only permanence. God is not alive. Love cannot be trusted. Surface, surface, surface was all that anyone found meaning in . . . this was civilization as I saw it, colossal and jagged. (*Psycho*, 375)

But this is not civilisation as Bateman sees it; there *is* no Bateman. The speech isn't his. He is simply the mouthpiece, a kind of after-effect or echo of language. As Frederic Jameson notes, 'there is no longer a self present to do the feeling'.[28] There is no inner life, only public oration; no characters, only codes. Hence, Young contends that 'individuals can no longer exist'.[29] Goodbye then, to desire, love and emotion. These things still persist, but only as ghosts, floating through the ether as pop songs, movie quotes, clichés and stereotypes. Feelings don't originate in us; they are beamed from satellite to satellite, occasionally coming to rest on our lips but always as a repeat, a reproduction. The logic of the system dictates that Bateman must exist, rather than any convoluted psychoanalytic diagnosis. He is the inevitable product of the raw material (porn, MTV, the *Wall Street Journal*, *Driller Killer*) circulating within contemporary culture. But, as I suggested in the introduction, there is problem with this point of view. If the idea of an inner life is over now, replaced by a kind of material display (these things *are* me), if subjectivity is a thing of the past, revealed to be a strange illusion of discourse or a quirk of language, then how can one formulate these thoughts in the first place? If language is so authoritarian, then how can literary critics spend so much time attacking it? Moreover, it seems one thing to claim that a figure in a novel is a language effect and quite another to apply this idea to oneself.

Interestingly, Elizabeth Young still clings to the idea of subversion, and argues that the furore generated by *American Psycho*'s initial release proves that this is a 'dangerous' text, 'unable to be assimilated' by the dominant culture.[30] Other critics (admittedly, with the benefit of hindsight) argue that the system has dealt with the book quite comfortably, thank you: a perpetual best-seller, critically-acclaimed film adaptation, a prominent feature on college American Fiction courses – the idea of the *poète maudit*, starving in his garret, scorned by the prudish Philistines, just doesn't seem relevant here. Moreover, one can easily see why the book has become such an obvious literary sensation. It's ultra-violence furnishes it with a frisson of the forbidden – but the book is available on the high street, rather than being impounded by the (thought) police. It offers a bleak, utterly unremitting critique of consumerism, but the book is itself a fashionable accessory, a hip consumer item. The fact that the book was, for a time, *de rigueur* amongst both student radicals and Wall Street professionals, testifies to its commercialism. Ellis's books already seem like products of the world he is ostensibly decrying (Oliver Stone's satire on media violence, *Natural Born Killers* (1994) also comes to mind); in a sense then, it's unsurprising that Peter Brooker concludes that 'It is hard to avoid the hollow feeling that *American Psycho* is a commercial ploy, more a calculated assault on the market than a wilful smack in the face of the bourgeoisie.'[31]

And yet, in a sense, this is precisely what is so interesting about Ellis as a writer – the way in which he is implicated in the system, his failings as a satirist. For all the talk of Patrick Bateman's non-existence, his voice stays in one's head for weeks afterward, both emotionally numb and unbearably hysterical, a stunned, monotone, 'howl of pain'.[32] If read doggedly, conscientiously, repetitively, *American Psycho* doesn't permit one the luxury of critical distance; rather, it accentuates the illness, exaggerates the symptoms, brings one to the point of self-disgust. One could argue that Ellis's work is a kind of homeopathic medicine, inculcating the diseases, curing us by making us aware how sick we really are – though, of course, that would assume that there is some kind of a cure in the first place.

Maybe in a paradoxical way then, the text's self-loathing is a sign of life – or at least a sign of self. After all, Bateman doesn't need to work – his father occupies some inconceivably lofty corporate position at Pierce & Pierce, and hence his position is virtually meaningless ('What work do you actually do?' asks his fiancée. 'You practically own that damn company' (*Psycho*, 221)). Patrick, however, clings to his position as the only thing which provides him with any sense of a 'credible public persona' (*Psycho*, 297). 'I . . . want . . . to . . . fit . . . in' he tells Evelyn (*Psycho*, 237), as if only his tailored business suit will hold him together as a character. Ellis's characterisation of Bateman's father as slipping into a 'void' thus seems particularly telling; rather like buying a product which promises individuality only to find everyone else in the office wearing the same thing, self-definition becomes confused with self-erasure.[33] Other people finish Bateman's sentences; colleagues mistake him for another anonymous clone. His father is associated less with paternal authority (although, he does in a sense embody the shadowy corporate system) than disappearance (Bateman's father is dying in *The Rules of Attraction*, as was Ellis's at the time of writing *American Psycho*).

For Freud, the father was an agent of prohibition, his strictures determining the limits of acceptable behaviour. One's sense of self grows out of frustration and dissatisfaction; one learns what one cannot do, and this determines where 'you' end and the world begins. In Ellis's post-Freudian, Postmodern world, however, the father doesn't define, but dissolves. His wealth makes all things possible, whilst his absence makes all things meaningless – just like Bateman's position at P&P. In a sense the malign father is as central to Ellis's work as he is to, say, Kafka's, but in a radically different way. The Father in Ellis threatens the self not by censure, but by vacancy. Bateman's voice can only be differentiated from the media monotone when he gazes into the abyss. Only Bateman's self-loathing suggests that there is still a self left to save.

NOTES

1. Abbreviations and page references refer to the following editions of Ellis's work: *Zero* (*Less than Zero*, London: Picador, 1986), *Psycho* (*American Psycho*, London: Picador, 1991).
2. Sigmund Freud (1953), *The Standard Edition of the Complete Psychological Works of Sigmund Freud*, London: Hogarth Press, vol. XXI, p.15.
3. Jean Baudrillard (1988), *America*, London: Verso, p. 46.
4. Ibid., p. 8.
5. Ibid., p. 46.
6. See Herbert Marcuse (1966), *Eros and Civilization*, Boston: Beacon, and Norman O. Brown (1968), *Life against Death*, London: Sphere.
7. Elizabeth Young and Graham Caveney (1992), *Shopping in Space*, London: Serpent's Tail, p. 261.
8. Ibid., p. vii.
9. Baudrillard, p. 45.
10. Fredric Jameson (1992), *Postmodernism*, London: Verso, p.10.
11. Young, p. 22.
12. See Joan Didion (1993), 'Holy water', in Joan Didion, *The White Album*, London: Picador, pp. 59–67.
13. Young, p. 26.
14. Young, p. 100.

15. Peter Brooker (1996), *New York Fictions*, Harlow: Longman, p. 144.
16. Jameson, p. 46.
17. Bret Easton Ellis, interviewed by Jamie Clarke, http.//www.geocities.com/ Athens/Forum/8056/Ellis/clarkeint.html (p. 10).
18. Ibid., p. 11.
19. Ibid., p. 7.
20. Young, p. 101.
21. Ibid., p. 94.
22. Ibid., p. 100.
23. Ellis, interviewed by Andy Beckett (1999), 'Leader of the Bret Pack', *The Guardian*, 9 Jan.
24. John Walsh (1991), 'Accessories before the facts', *The Sunday Times*, 21 April.
25. James Annesley (1998), *Blank Fictions*, London: Pluto, p. 13.
26. Ibid., p. 14.
27. Brooker, pp. 143–4.
28. Jameson, p. 15.
29. Young, p. 20.
30. Ibid., p. 89.
31. Brooker, p. 144.
32. Young, p. 40.
33. Ellis, in Clarke, p. 11.

BIOGRAPHY

Bret Easton Ellis was born in Los Angeles, California, in 1964. He grew up in the middle-class area of Sherwood Oaks, in the San Fernando Valley, his father a successful property-developer. His family's increasing affluence, however, masked a deeper sense of domestic dysfunction; Ellis described himself as 'a horror, a really bad kid', and the family atmosphere as 'poisonous'. His grades were poor, he failed to fit in at school ('a very corrupt Beverly Hills-type high school where you could actually bribe the principal by taking him out to lunch at Ma Maison'), and the pale, petulant Ellis felt an awkward outsider, flat-footed and gangling, lacking in any kind of social grace. Writing seemed to be the only thing he took seriously – indeed, he had completed a 'very violent and sexually aggressive' fairy-tale and presented it to his parents as a Christmas present at the tender age of eleven.

He wrote his first novel (based upon his experiences working at one of his grandfather's casinos in Las Vegas) at the age of seventeen; his third completed work, *Less than Zero*, was published in 1987 whilst he was a student at Bennington College – a very expensive progressive establishment, blessed with no formal entrance requirements. There he formed a band (The Parents), took acting classes (eventually discovering that he was 'way too private') and somehow found time to write amongst a blossoming hedonistic lifestyle. His creative writing teacher, Joe McGinniss, sent examples of his early work to his agent in New York, and the heavily-edited *Less than Zero* (famously written in only eight weeks) was the result. He noted his influences at the time as Joan Didion, the Ernest Hemingway of *The Sun Also Rises*, Stephen King, and perhaps rather bizarrely, James Joyce's *Ulysses*; the novel was a surprise word-of-mouth success, and Ellis found himself heavily promoted as American letters' foremost *enfant terrible*. Most critics assumed that both the novel and its follow-up, *The Rules of Attraction* (1987), set in a thinly-disguised Bennington-substitute, were straightforwardly autobiographical, an assumption which, given the amoral, nihilistic material, Ellis has spent the rest of his career strenuously denying. He turned down the opportunity to translate *Less than Zero* into a screenplay, and subsequently saw his novel transformed into a slick, Brat-Pack, rock-video monstrosity, a fate, which for all of Ellis's genuine horror, is entirely in keeping with the cultural assumptions of his fiction.

After graduating, Ellis moved to New York, and took for his next subject the burgeoning Wall-Street yuppie scene. Later he noted, 'I made an enormous amount of money and moved to Manhattan and I sort of got sucked up into this whole yuppie-mania that was going on at the time . . . I think in a lot of ways, working on *American Psycho* (1991) was my way of fighting against slipping into a certain kind of lifestyle.' Certainly the book appears motivated by a palpable sense of self-loathing: 'I cried a lot, I drank a lot, I did a lot of drugs during this period, I was a real mean son of a bitch . . . I felt I deserved to be writing a book like that,' he later noted. The book was also intended as an exorcism of his ultra-materialistic father, who died the following year, leaving behind debts of over ten million dollars. Whatever Ellis's motivation, the result was one of the great literary scandals of the decade. The book was dropped by his publisher, Simon & Schuster, on the eve of publication, after a number of key employees had threatened to resign if the book ever saw the light of day. When *American Psycho* was finally picked up by Vintage, influential critic Roger Rosenblatt described it as 'the most loathsome offering of the season', and the book was subsequently targeted in a series of campaigns by outraged womens' groups. Tammy Bruce of NOW called it 'a how-to manual on the torture and dismemberment of women', whilst, for his own part, Ellis maintained that the finished work was 'virtually a feminist tract'. Once again, the autobiographical status of the book was pushed to the fore, the common assumption being that something must have been seriously wrong for Ellis to have come up with such material in the first place. Interviews conducted in Ellis's tomb-like, all-black minimalist apartment, the author appearing at times as lobotomised, logo-conscious and inarticulate as his creation hardly helped; but Ellis has continued to argue that the book was clearly satirical, and that he should by no means be held morally accountable for Patrick Bateman's fictional crimes. Needless to say, such notoriety ensured that the book was a huge financial success, and one indication of its eventual rehabilitation and acceptance into the critical fold is suggested by the number of college courses on contemporary fiction which now employ it.

The Informers (1994), a return to the LA settings of *Less than Zero*, once again divided the critics, as has *Glamorama* (2000), his longest and most complex work to date, a sprawling conspiracy-thriller, which demonstrates a newfound debt to Don DeLillo and Thomas Pynchon. Mary Harron's witty film adaptation of *American Psycho* (2000) has led to a critical reappraisal of Ellis's most infamous work, whilst the sheer number of web-sites dedicated to discussions of his work – 1,048 at last count – testify to his continuing degree of (counter?) cultural influence.

ELLIS ON ELLIS

God, I hate the word 'literature' and all that it implies.

Now, in the overall culture books play a much smaller role in people's lives. Even people who don't read books, who don't touch books, I think at one time were touched by the way certain books had an impact on the culture. Now it seems to be very rare.

On *American Psycho*: I also think that the book was informed by a severe depression and black period I was going through, and I still maintain that it's the most autobiographical of all my novels because the mood of the book completely mirrored the mood I was in in the three years it took to write it... I was fairly down on myself so I felt I deserved to be writing a book like that. I felt I really deserved it.

On *Glamorama*: Models are so annoying and it's horrible how obsessed our culture is over them that I made a connection between models and ... terrorists. The models in this book were going to be terrorists. And I started to back down and have second thoughts because that's a pretty loopy theory and I knew I had to be very careful in order to bring it off. I had to ask myself 'are you sure you want to invest this much time in writing a book about this?' And in the end I did.

Q. Do you think that human beings are inherently evil?
A. Yes.

JEAN BAUDRILLARD (from *America* (1988))

On Los Angeles: Things seem to be made of a more unreal substance; they seem to turn and move in a void as if by a special lighting effect.

This soft, resort-style civilization irresistibly evokes the end of the world.

Everything is so informal, there is so little in the way of reserve or manners, that you feel anything could blow up at any minute.

Life is so liquid, the signs and messages floating, the bodies and cars so fluid, the hair so blonde, and the soft technologies so luxuriant, that you dream of death and murder, of orgies and cannibalism, to counteract the perfection of the ocean, of the light, of that insane excess of light, to counteract the hypocrisy of everything here.

In the very heartland of wealth and liberation you always hear the same question: 'What are you doing after the orgy?' What do you do when everything is available – sex, flowers, the stereotypes of life and death? This is America's problem, and through America, it has become the world's problem.

LINKS TO OTHER AUTHORS

Don DeLillo: The notion of simulacra are central to both writers' work. Both are interested in that moment when reproduction overtakes production, but whilst DeLillo's prose positions itself in opposition to this logic, Ellis makes his work a symptom of the Postmodern condition. The end of individualism, and a concurrent emptying out of discourse also links their fictional praxis.

Paul Auster: A loss of identity, and the fear of becoming trapped in an assumed role, connects Auster to Ellis.

Douglas Coupland: Both writers are concerned with surfaces, the mediascape and the absolutely artificial. Both Coupland's sentimentality and Ellis's cynicism can be seen as responses to Postmodernism's waning of affect, a loss of feeling or emotion due to the numbing logic of reproduction.

BIBLIOGRAPHY

Primary Works

Less than Zero (1985), New York: Simon & Schuster.
The Rules of Attraction (1987), New York: Simon & Schuster.
American Psycho (1991), New York: Vintage.
The Informers (1994), New York: Borzoi.
Glamorama (1999), New York: Knopf.

Critical Sources

Abadi-Nagy, Z. (2000), 'The narrational function in minimalist fiction', *Neohelican*, 27 (2), Summer, pp. 237–48.
Annesley, James (1998), *Blank Fictions*, London: Pluto.
Baudrillard, Jean (1988), *America*, London: Verso.
Brooker, Peter (1996), *New York Fictions*, Harlow: Longman.
Caputi, Jane (1993), 'American psychos: the serial killer in contemporary fiction', *Journal of American Culture*, Winter, pp. 101–12.
Frecarro, C. (1997), 'Historical violence, censorship and the serial-killer, and Bret Easton Ellis: the case of *American Psycho*', *Diacritics*, 27 (2), Summer, pp. 44–58.
Gerrard, Nicci (1994), 'Bret and the beast in the corner', *The Observer*, 16 October.
Iannone, Carol (1991), 'PC and the Ellis affair', *Commentary*, July.
Price, D. W. (1998), 'Bakhtinian prosaics, grotesque realism and the question of the carnivalesque in Bret Easton Ellis' *American Psycho*', *Southern Humanities Review*, 32 (4), Fall, pp. 321–46.
Freese, Peter (1990), 'Bret Easton Ellis, *Less than Zero*: entropy in the "MTV" novel?', in Reingard Nishik and Barbara Korte (eds), *Modes of Narrative: Approaches to American, Canadian and British Fiction*, Wurzburg: Konighausen & Neumann.
Kaplan, E. Ann (1987), *Rocking around the Clock: Music Television, Postmodernism and Consumer Culture*, London: Methuen.
Mailer, Norman (1991), 'Children of the Pied Piper', *Vanity Fair*, March.
Rosenblatt, Roger (1990), 'Snuff this book: will Bret get away with murder?', *New York Times Book Review*, 16 December.
Sahlin, Nicki (1991), '"But this road doesn't go anywhere": the existential dilemma in *Less than Zero*', *Critique* 33, Fall, pp. 23–42.
Tyrnauer, Matthew (1994), 'Who's afraid of Bret Easton Ellis?', *Vanity Fair*, August.
Udovich, Mim (1991), '*American Psycho*', *The Village Voice*, 19 March.
Walsh, John (1991), 'Accessories before the fact', *The Sunday Times*, 21 September.

Weldon, Fay (1991), *'American Psycho'*, *The Guardian*, 10 April.

Young, Elizabeth, and Caveney, Graham (1992), *Shopping in Space*, London: Serpent's Tail.

Zaller, Robert (1993), *'American Psycho,* American censorship and the Dahmer case', *Revue Français d'études Americaines*, July, pp. 317–25.

DOUGLAS COUPLAND[1]

⟋⟍⌀⊂⟍⟍

Ty'Unlike our grandparents, we live in a world that we ourselves made. Until about fifty years ago, images of Nature were the key to feeling in art. Nature – its cycles of growth and decay, its responses to wind, weather, light, and the passage of the seasons, its ceaseless renewal, its infinite complexity of form and behaviour on every level, from the molecule to the galaxy – provided the metaphors within which almost every relationship of the Self to the Other could be described and examined. The sense of a natural order, always in some way correcting the pretensions of the Self, gave mode and measure to pre-modern art. If this sense has now become dimmed, it is partly because for most people Nature has been replaced by the culture of congestion: of cities and mass media. We are crammed like battery hens with stimuli, and what seems significant is not the quality or meaning of the messages, but their excess. Overload has changed our art. Especially in the last thirty years, capitalism plus electronics have given us a new habitat, our forest of media.'
Robert Hughes[2]

Leaving aside his Canadian citizenship for a moment, in what sense does Coupland deserve to be taken seriously as a great, even canonical, American writer? After all, and despite his own protestations to the contrary, it certainly seems as if Coupland has set out to chronicle the experiences of his own 'lost' generation, just as Fitzgerald did in the '20s, or Kerouac in the '50s. His central theme – the longing to escape an overly complex and materially corrupt civilisation, to 'light out for the territories' and thereby rescue a sense of selfhood amongst the solitude of Nature – is, in a sense, *the* great American theme; indeed, the essential origin-myth of America itself. When Coupland talks of 'Emallgration' as a 'migration toward lower-tech, lower-information environments containing a lessened emphasis on consumerism' (*X*, 173), he is simply applying a patina of jargon to America's seemingly inexhaustible pastoral ideal; the idea of the wilderness as redemption, salvation from the corrupting influence of civilisation. But whilst his themes may be traditional, the form of his work most certainly is not. Coupland's novels are compendiums of pop-art cartoons, throwaway slogans, kooky aphorisms and sound-bite sketches; literary Post-it notes for what Michael Brockington calls the 'leisure-challenged or easily distracted'; 'literature-lite' intended for an audience without the time or inclination to wade through conventional prose.[3, 4] An assumption of Attention Deficiency Syndrome is built into Coupland's work, which is as giddy as a sugar-rush and edited like a music-promo, 'prose as easy to read as it is to watch TV'.[5] Little wonder then that 'serious' critics are wary. For them, his 'fortune-cookie philosophy' attains the aesthetic stature of a T-shirt or fridge-magnet; fiction for a post-literate generation, dumbed-down to the same vacuity of the media buzz it purports to criticise.[6] Easily consumed, instantly forgotten, this is literature as fast food: instantly gratifying but in no sense nourishing.

Coupland's defence of his fictional practices is particularly interesting, however. His aesthetic sensibility, he argues, is informed by the visual arts much more than conventional modes of story-telling; his idols are Warhol, Lichtenstein and, in particular, Rosenquist, whose billboard collages of advertising-copy, comic-strips and kitsch intimations of nuclear disaster, come closest to capturing the spirit of Coupland's work. Indeed, Richard Hamilton's famous Pop Art Manifesto of 1957 in a sense defines Coupland's essential universe:

Popular (designed for a mass audience)
Transient (short-term solution)
Expendable (easily forgotten)
Low-cost
Mass-produced
Young (aimed at youth)
Witty
Sexy
Gimmicky
Glamorous
Big Business.[7]

The fact that such sentiments are already over forty years old, suggests the tremendous cultural lag of fiction, still caught up in an orthodox realism which regards such notions as heresy, rather like a collector of prim Victorian watercolours suddenly presented with a Rauschenberg. Coupland's work exists within an accelerated culture which lacks the luxury of the considered critical reflection which was once the hallmark of literary activity. Now it must compete in a leisure-market alongside other commodities, and to do so it must stand out amongst the glut and glare, adapt itself to the slick parade of consumer-enticements. The form of Coupland's work therefore suggests an accommodation to the dominant-culture, a willingness to play its own game – but, of course, there are risks involved in such an operation. Pop Art can only retain its critical edge via irony – appropriating cultural artifacts in order to read them against the grain, substituting the message of the image (buy this!) for a knowing appreciation of the trade-off involved. In a sense, Pop Art is about being happily hood-winked; one knows that the advertising copy is there to instigate a sense of want, but the surface pleasures involved – a delight in the kitsch vitality of advertising, its larger-than-life pitch-making and formal design, the colours, shapes, and complex play of desire – makes being taken for a ride worthwhile. Pop Art wants its food laced with sugary flavour-enhancers, prefers the arresting billboard to the boring landscape behind. It retains no nostalgia for the real or the natural, but rather is at home in a wholly artificial, manmade sphere – the ubiquitous shopping mall a kind of vast Pop-Art installation. It knows that advertising is all about commerce rather than art, but this very knowingness rescues it from gross materialism – it's not about wanting the good or product, but about enjoying the transaction, appreciating the complex interplay of signs which get consumers salivating. In comparison to say, Cormac McCarthy or E. Annie Proulx, it prefers a world of plastic to a world of mud.

But does Coupland? There is a constant tension between the pop-surface of his prose – the disposable one-liners, cartoon characterisations, and style-magazine polish – and his deeper spiritual yearnings, his melancholy sense of disappointment and regret. One might think of Kurt Vonnegut, who also sugar-coats his deeply pessimistic pills, but Coupland's prose is more schizophrenic than that; the tension in his work is a productive one, disrupting the shiny, primary-colour surface of his prose. In a sense, Coupland, like Bret Easton Ellis, turns his own art into a symptom of the general cultural condition, but there is little of the self-loathing which is Ellis's most striking characteristic. Instead, one gets the impression that Coupland could go either way; one can just as easily imagine him attending an anti-capitalist rally as shopping in a designer-goods store. After all, this is a writer who once vowed that he didn't own a TV set because he 'wanted a nineteenth century brain', and yet whose knowledge of disposable pop-trivia is encyclopaedic; a satirist who defined marketing as 'feeding the poop back into diners fast enough to make them think they're getting real food' (*X*, 27), and who recently offered his services to any publisher who could edit his work to make it more slickly commercial. And it's in this manner that Coupland illuminates the essential dilemma of the Postmodern condition.

How should an artist, in whatever medium, respond to the barrage of signs, images, messages and codes which makes up our daily, mediated environment? Repudiate it utterly as a deadening of the senses, a falsification of experience, something banal, maddening, even corrupt? But if one simply closes one's eyes, then does art run the risk of irrelevancy, obsolescence, and denial? After all, this is where most of us live, amongst a forest of signs which reflect our own desires (no matter how distorted) back at us. Admittedly, there is a sense that these signs have somehow proliferated and run wild, becoming less recognisable, less explicable, less tame, so that even our manmade world now seems alien: but can one really remove these signs from the picture (like an earlier generation airbrushing out the railroads and the logging-dumps) and still stay true to contemporary reality? What, then, if one chooses the path of least resistance and incorporates the mediascape into one's work? Here the worry is that one simply ends up duplicating the general malaise and erasing the critical function altogether. As Robert Hughes has said of Pop Art, it only makes sense in the museum; if juxtaposed with real billboards, advertising copy and TV screens, it is simply crushed by its more aggressive cousins.[8] Artists can choose between accommodation or flight, but both manoeuvres seem equally doomed; what is most interesting (and problematic) about Coupland's work is that it attempts the two things simultaneously. In purely literary terms the results may be deeply flawed, but nevertheless, as with Ellis, it is these very flaws which make Coupland's fiction so consistently interesting.

To what extent does slacker-culture represent an attempt to resist the cultural imperatives of a monolithic, soullessly commercial, corporate America? Discuss.

Coupland's best known work, *Generation X* (1991), is concerned with the question of whether it is still possible to drop out of society, to find some space uncontaminated by target-marketing, media-buzz, and the corporate lifestyle. His slackers, bohemians and losers – all disaffected, middle-class twenty-somethings – eke out marginal lives on the periphery of society, drifting through a series of 'McJobs' (low-pay, service-sector drudgery) either unwilling or unable to take up the white-collar futures which college and advertising agencies have promised them. Whether through conscious choice or dismal failure (and this is a key distinction in the book) Coupland's protagonists have to deal with the idea of having less; of 'downsizing', curtailing desire, leading smaller lives. Crucially, the novel is the product of recession and economic downturn, of a deeply uncertain business climate where notions of job security or stable employment are things of the past. The baby-boom years of prosperity are now long gone, and Generation X sees itself (whether rightly or wrongly) as the first generation which has to deal with having less than its parents. Alongside the desire to escape from the ever more stringent demands of the commercial sphere, there is a sense of being duped, of having the rug pulled out from under their feet. Because of their middle-class backgrounds, Coupland's characters have always assumed they'd be okay, that their sheer normality would protect them from the ferocity of the market-place. Like a small child whose security blanket has just been torn away, they respond with equal parts bewilderment and resentment; unsure and disorientated, Generation X displays an equivocal desire either to crawl back into the womblike mother-ship or else to reject the untrustworthy system entirely.

The nostalgia of Coupland's work thus has a peculiarly bitter flavour. When the novel's narrator, Andy, gazes wistfully at the desperately unhip group-portrait of his family taken back in the 1970s, he is staggered by the 'corn-fed optimism, the cheerful waves of shampoo, and the air-brushed teeth-beams' (*X*, 133) which the photograph emits. Now, fifteen years later, after the bad marriages, drugs, divorce, empty unsatisfying jobs, unsavoury apartments and faded possibilities; with a sense of growing duller, increasingly tired, increasingly defeated, Andy's *cri de coeur* captures the despairing tone of the novel: 'Oh, Mr Leonard, how *did* we all end up so messy? We're looking hard for that *fromage* you were holding – we really are – but we're just *not* seeing it any more. Send us a clue, *please*'. (*X*, 136)

There is, I feel, something specifically American about this sense of being fleeced of the future. America, after all, is the only country where the right to be happy is enshrined in the constitution, whose essential sensibility is predisposed toward the future, personal and social improvement, a dream of progress and perfectibility. Generation X feels tricked by a million happy endings of a million TV movies, duped by America's ingrained optimism; they are the post-Vietnam, post- Watergate, post-OPEC demographic, suspicious of what awaits them, queasily aware that the past has been used up.

In one sense, of course, Coupland's intense nostalgia for the '70s represents a desire to be a kid again, to shrug off any sense of adult responsibility. His characters eat kiddie-snacks, avidly consume cartoons and comic strips, and hang onto retro-fashions, in an attempt to preserve some sense of the innocence and security of childhood. 'I'd never be able to find refuge again in Saturday mornings spent in rumpus rooms,' admits the narrator, 'itchy with fibreglass insulation, listening to Mel Blanc's voice on the TV, snacking on chewable vitamin C tablets and tormenting my sister's Barbies' (*X*, 27). Hence the 'bed-time stories' which Andy and his friends obsessively invent are explicitly regressive, set in a world ('Texlahoma' (*X*, 39)) where it is perpetually 1974, *Scooby Doo* is on TV, and all is right with the world – from a child's point of view, anyway (the irony being, of course, that the '70s marked the beginning of global economic recession – but what do kids know or care of such things?). This nostalgia is also for a stable family unit; for a time before divorce, unemployment, and the meltdown of the nuclear family. In one chapter, 'Remember Earth Clearly', each member of the slacker-circle is asked what memory they would seek to recall at the last second of nuclear destruction (the threat of the bomb underpinning the sense of futurelessness which is central to the novel). In each case, their chosen flashback revolves around a sense of family cohesion, a time when parents were young rather than old, and a deep-seated desire for parental approval which is strikingly at odds with the novel's ostensibly rebellious tone. The most significant is Dag's tale of trying to fill the car with gas for the first time; when he slips and petrol sprays everywhere, his normally authoritarian father is unexpectedly benign. 'Hey, Sport. Isn't the smell of gasoline great?' he asks. 'Close your eyes and inhale. So *clean*. It smells like the *future*' (*X*, 94). The key date of 1974 is still innocent of ecological catastrophe, of the concept of diminishing resources, and the need to conserve and replenish. It still believes in bigger, better and faster cars, in plastic and plutonium, in a modernity which will eventually wind up clogging the planet's biosphere for thousands of years to come. A smouldering rancour thus disrupts Coupland's nostalgia, a rage against the irresponsibility of previous generations who believed that they could consume and consume without ever having to pick up the tab. Of his parents' generation, Andy notes: 'Sometimes I want to tell them that I envy their upbringing, that was so free of *futurelessness*. And I want to throttle them for blithely handing over the world to us like so much skid-marked underwear' (*X*, 86).

Instead of material plenty and a life of middle-class security, the twenty-somethings in the novel inhabit a dilapidated housing project on the edge of Palm Springs, 'a bleached and defoliated Flintstones cartoon' (*X*, 10) whose main industries are detox centres and liposuction plants (one of the novel's most arresting images is of stray dogs licking at canisters of yuppie-fat (*X*, 4)). Palm Springs itself underpins the resentment of the young toward the old; this is where the wealthy go to live out their retirement, Generation X reduced to low-paid jobs fetching drinks or carrying out colonic irrigation. But the desert-space beyond also proffers some faint glimmer of redemption; throughout the novel there is a sense of the crumbling 1950s architecture being reclaimed by the land – by lizards, insects, flowers, odd bits of flora and fauna existing amongst the cracks in derelict nuclear test-sites and failed hotel complexes. The desert also suggests a site outside of the system, a blank space in which to empty out the thoughts which other people have put inside your head.

For whilst their impecunious state has been foisted upon them, Generation X is also on the run from yuppiedom, the corporate mentality, which, as the narrator notes, 'is something that all of us might become in the absence of vigilance' (*X*, 80). They dread becoming photocopied identikit images drawn from advertising campaigns and target-marketing, their apartments glossy brochures (think of the IKEA sequence in David Fincher's *Fight Club* (1999)), their existence no more substantial than the slick images of a life-style supplement. The novel's satire is particularly acute when it comes to Coupland's critique of the office-grind and mission-statement mentality; his evocation of 'veal-fattening pens' and 'sick-building syndrome' (*X*, 20) is instantly recognisable to anyone who has ever worked in call-centres or tele-banking. The recirculated germs, cancer-inducing VDU's, the wooden partitions which creep ever closer with poor performance quotas – all are captured in their soul-shrivelling banality. Andy's moment of career-induced crisis comes when his boss furtively reveals his most 'valuable thing', the treasured possession which is the key to his soul – a photograph of Marilyn Monroe's pubic hair ('black as the ace of spades if you must know' (*X*, 58)), a kind of holy relic of Post-modernism, a convergence of celebrity culture, ghoulish prurience and mediated desire. It is at this point that Andy knows he must flee this Warholian culture of reproduction and dissemination, that he must seek out real things, save himself by recourse to the authentic. 'So I came down here [to the desert]' he notes, 'to breathe dust and walk with the dogs – to look at a rock or a cactus and know that I am the first person to see that cactus and that rock' (*X*, 59). Andy's flight thus articulates the central concerns of this book; the search for originals, for reality, an innocence of perception freed from the logic of simula-tion and replication omnipresent in our over-mediated world. The blankness of the desert – a notion central to both McCarthy and Proulx – thus represents an escape from cultural overload, a clean slate, an uncontaminated space. But does such a thing really exist?

Though Coupland takes Andy's flight seriously, his work constantly reiterates the failure of the nomadic quest – one might also think of Marco Fogg's failure to find Effing's cave in Auster's *Moon Palace* (1989) or DeLillo's parody of desert asceticism and flagellation in *End Zone* (1972). Over and over again in Coupland's work, the faithful pilgrim returns from the wilderness disappointed and unenlightened – Linus in *Girlfriend in a Coma* (1998), Johnson in *Miss Wyoming* (2000) – only *Life after God* (1994) hints, albeit tentatively, at some kind of pastoral revelation. Generation X tries desperately to generate some sense of natural epiphany – a silver fish brought by a passing Pelican (*X* , 173), the unselfish love of a busload of disabled children (*X* , 179), contact with the real via the clawmarks of a swooping creature (*X*, 178) – but the sheer number of epiphanies smacks of creative desperation. Like any good populist text, *Generation X* strains to deliver the happy ending its readership demands, but Coupland himself seems aware that his longing for virgin space will never ultimately be satisfied, that the source of contamination lies within. Even at his most stridently affirmative, a faint whiff of depression is never far away in Coupland's work.

Generation X remains lonely, introverted, uptight, obsessed by a popular culture they ostensibly disdain. As Will Blythe puts it, Coupland's characters demonstrate 'the sardonicism of people who have spent a lot of time talking back to commercials'; the raw material of their 'bed-time stories' remains the detritus of trash culture, the soap-opera plots and sit-com profundity.[9] Generation X longs to create rather than either copy or passively consume, but they cannot wholly escape the culture of reruns and the already said. Having seen all the scenarios of adult life endlessly played out on TV, every ending is known in advance; they are jaded of emotions they haven't even experienced, too knowing to speak without the benefit of speech marks.[10] Little wonder then that Coupland's world is so loveless.

Andy believes that he inhabits 'a land so empty that all objects placed under its breathing hot skin become objects of irony' (X, 16). To pluck a consumer good from its usual habitat and place it in the Mojave desert is akin to Marcel DuChamp positioning a urinal in an art gallery; the object is freed from its function and becomes aesthetic rather than utilitarian. Its existence seems comically incongruous, at once banal and curiously heightened; to play with a space-hopper in the middle of the desert is both to indict the banality of consumer culture but also to admit to its ubiquity. Coupland's characters seek out the unfashionable, the unhip, the farthest from the designer culture that they can go, but this inverse consumerism is still consumerism – it is perhaps a telling irony that the novel was raided by marketing departments and style gurus in search of the rebellious grunge market of the early '90s. The social theorist Pierre Bordieu has argued that the signs of consumer-culture are not fixed but open to interpretation, that the signals of late capitalism, rather than being homogeneous, are contested by various social groups. 'Consumer goods lead a double-life: as both agents of social control and as objects used by ordinary people in constructing their own culture,' Bordieu writes; Generation X appropriates the references, the retro-fashions, the advertising slogans, but there is no political agenda beyond a sense of implied superiority (what Blythe calls 'a sneaky way of separating themselves from the uninitiated, for whom stupidity is merely stupid'), or declaration of hip independence.[11, 12] They still need these things – albeit in an ironic sense – to define a sense of identity. They may reverse the meaning but are still reliant on the system.

Only one character, Elvissa, takes this cultural abstinence further, relinquishing her last ties to language and meaning by relocating to a mysterious nunnery somewhere in the desert waste. Even this asceticism cannot be taken wholly seriously though; the nunnery advertises its wares via glossy flyers and slick advertising, its silence compromised and commercial. Moreover, the desert is not a wholly positive environment in the novel. Its trackless space is continually linked to the nuclear ground-zero which haunts Generation X's dreams, its allure linked to a desire to erase everything, the same 'craving for terrible things' which informs DeLillo's *White Noise* (1984).[13] This etiolated emptiness exists at the opposite pole from Andy's belief in the pastoral, but both are central to the novel's tone.

Certainly, Coupland is keenly aware of the faux-minimalism of the slacker-life. There is an ever-present sense of playing at being poor, an act of cultural slumming performed in full knowledge of that great middle-class safety net – going home to Mom and Dad. On some level this is voluntary pauperism: a denial of adult responsibility, the decision deliberately to fail before failure is imposed upon you. There is also some truth to James Annesley's description of Andy's gang as 'characters who would like to own a house but can't afford to'.[14] The tension between choosing to have less on ethical grounds and simply responding to the economic downturn is never wholly resolved; Dag's indignant jealousy of the bourgeoisie and Andy's high-minded search for the 'real' are both integral to the novel, but they still remain unreconciled at its end. As Annesley points out, it's hard not to feel that slackerhood is simply another lifestyle choice, complete with its own fashions, commodities and consumer-goods.[15] Its implied superiority can grate; its holier-than-thou assumption that material deficit necessarily produces a spiritual windfall. But for all of that, is there an undeniable force to Andy's arguments? Certainly, he believes himself to be wiser than his younger siblings who have been taken in by the glib merchandising of the image-doctors. Of the next generation, he writes:

They're *perky*. They embrace and believe all the pseudo-globalism and ersatz racial harmony of ad campaigns engineered by the makers of soft drinks and computer-invented sweaters. Many of them want to work for IBM when their lives end at the age of twenty-five (*'Excuse me, but can you tell me more about your pension plan?'*). But in some dark and undefinable way, these kids are also Dow, Union Carbide, General Dynamics, and the military... If their AirBus were to crash on some frosty Andean plateau, they would have little, if any, compunction about eating dead fellow passengers. (*X*, 106)

Although Coupland remains too politely middle-class to say it, surely this 'dark and undefinable' connection is capitalism. Designer trainers imply Indonesian children in sweat-shops; smart new sports cars lead inexorably to drilling for oil in Alaska. After all, economic prosperity necessitates political, and occasionally military, action; buying counter-cultural goods – bongs, *Rage Against the Machine* albums, retro-punk fashion – is still implicated in Wall Street, the futures market, the vast global market-place. In this sense, everything is connected. It is hard not to feel that on some level Coupland would dearly love to embrace the Postmodern, to accept its spectacle, its stimulation, its simulated pleasures, just as Pop-Art did in the '60s. This 'Pop' Coupland seems profoundly bored by his earnest, anti-consumerist twin (just as Pop Art was bored by the romantic intensity of abstract expressionism) whose search for the 'authentic' is perpetually doomed to failure. But the political ramifications of this assimilation leave an unpleasant taste in the mouth; in accordance with a kind of economic chaos theory, what we buy on the high street is bound up with ecological disaster, Third-World debt, covert CIA operations, and, perhaps most obviously, the veal-fattening pens of the working life.

Given Andy's speech, it is thus perhaps surprising that Coupland's second novel, *Shampoo Planet* (1992), which deals with the much-despised 'Generation Y' is so equivocal. Children of the hippie generation (rather than *X*'s baby-boomers) 'they react by loving corporations, and they don't mind wearing ties. To them, Ronald Reagan is emperor. I'm actually quite in love with them. They're so much more optimistic,' Coupland admitted at the time.[16] Of all of Coupland's works, *Shampoo Planet* is the one which falls apart most spectacularly under the conflicting pressures of Coupland's views. Given the counter-cultural slant of *Generation X*, one begins the novel knowing full well that the logo-obsessed, ultra-consumerist, would-be corporate exec Tyler is heading for a fall, that the novel will map his (painful) begetting of wisdom, his understanding of the emptiness of his 'mallspeak' existence. But Coupland offers no such thing; by the end of the novel, Tyler has gained his dream position to work with the mysterious Donald Trump-cum-Bill Gates-corporate-head, and his absurd proposition to turn landfill sites into literally trashy theme parks is his making as a businessman. As Julian Evans wrote in *The Guardian* at the time, 'If this is parody why should we care, and if it's not, why is this world . . . so empty?'[17]

The key scene here is the extended comedy sequence where Tyler travels to meet his burnt-out hippie father, now living in a dank hovel and permanent acid haze, amongst the Californian red-woods. After a weekend of tie-dyed humourlessness and tree-hugging piety, Tyler and his girlfriend can't get back to the inauthentic fast enough:

> We can't eat enough chemicals: '*Caffeine – caffeine – caffeine*,' I chant to the waitress.
> 'NutraSweet!' adds Stephanie.
> 'Edible oil products!'
> 'White Sugar!'
> 'Now!' (*Shampoo*, 202)

After a shower and change of clothes, all they want to see is the future, 'any future' (*Shampoo*, 202) – branded goods, synthetic fibres, endless cable channels, as many E-numbers as possible. Who wants the real? Postmodernism is better than the real. But this reverse-epiphany sits uneasily with an earlier trek to the mountains which Tyler undertakes with his more earnest girlfriend, Anna-Louise, where they arrive at the woods of Glen Anna only to find 'the forest is gone and there are no words I can say' (*Shampoo*, 78). All that remains is a 'prairie of gray mud and stumps' and the diesel fumes of logging trucks (*Shampoo*, 78). And who is to say that Tyler's beloved corporation, Bechtol, or one of its subsidiaries, isn't to blame? Bechtol isn't just luxury hotels and benign consumer-durables, but mining, weaponry, genetic engineering, what Tyler's father would no doubt call 'the system'. What's most interesting about the book is Coupland's uncertainty of tone, the combination of Luddite suspicion and geeky enthusiasm he displays in regard to our technology-irradiated future:

> 'Fair's fair,' added Anna-Louise. 'I mean, if we're supposed to learn all of the new information people are inventing, we have to

throw old information out to make way for the new stuff.' I guess history and geography are what's being thrown away. But then what is geography to Harmony or Pony or Davidson, who speak to people all over the planet every day all at once on their computer nets and modems? Or what is history to Mei-Lin or Gaia, who receive seventy-five channels on their families dish-TV systems? Anna-Louise is right: fair's fair. And my friends are better prepared mentally than anybody else for the future that is actually going to arrive. Nature always prepares her babies for what they'll need. Me and my friends are throwing-out consultants. Wish us all luck; we'll send you resumes and kisses. (*Shampoo*, 70)

It's probably too simplistic to draw some kind of schematic division between Coupland's Vancouver-set fiction (*Life after God* (1994), *Girlfriend in a Coma* (1998)), which tends towards the anxious, angst-ridden and pessimistic, and the more playful, cartoon-like comedy of his American texts – *Generation X* wouldn't fit into this schema for a start – but there is a perpetual sense of competing influences in his work. Even the much perkier *Shampoo Planet* is still tinged by slacker sentiments. The slogans which Tyler and Stephanie felt-tip onto dollar bills appear oddly out of character; dislocated trace elements of Coupland's earlier book. Coupland even engineers another 'natural epiphany' to conclude the novel, when the ceiling above Anna-Louise collapses, depositing her eccentric neighbour's entire menagerie (budgies, puppies, carp and kittens) onto Tyler's bed: '"Anna-Louise, wake-up," I say. "Wake up – *the world is alive*"' (*Shampoo*, 282). Are we to take this, then, as the return of a repressed natural order of things? But Coupland's fiction (like Ellis') is full of zoos, pet-shops, cages. Nature is tame; now it's culture that's running wild.

'Soil isn't a Document.'

(*X*, 14)

In this sense, Coupland's work is also reminiscent of one of the key fore-runners of Pop Art, Grant Wood (1891–1941), whose landscape paintings of agrarian America in the '30s create a strange toy-town vision of nature: impossibly sculpted hills like mounds of mashed potato, round shapes and primary colours, cookie-cutter farms and jelly trees.[18] If not for its date, one could believe this was Nature as designed by a committee of computer programmers, slotted into place at the click of a mouse – Nature perfected, turned into a theme park. Coupland's landscapes are also Pop-Art creations (one can imagine Lichtenstein painting the dots), a Legoland created in man's image. One of the most striking characteristics of his prose is that the natural is always described in terms of the artificial. In Coupland's work, the artificial always comes first, is privileged as the norm. Spring mornings smell like air-freshener, the night sky a giant screen-saver, sunrise 'a line of Vegas showgirls bursting over the stage' (*X*, 4). At times, Coupland extends his metaphors to breaking point – 'bald eagles hanging out in the updrafts like preteens massed in a video arcade' (*Shampoo*, 176) or a tree's branches 'like a mother weeping for her kidnapped child, holding forth samples of her missing child's pyjamas to the CNN cameras' (*Shampoo*, 142) – thereby parodying any notion of the virgin real. *Microserfs* (1995) offers the most extreme examples of this, replacing all biological metaphors with their computerised equivalents: ill bodies 'crash', emotions are 'rewired' by mood-enhancing drugs, bad memories deleted. But still some vestigial longing for Nature remains.

The stories in *Life after God* (1994) are accompanied by a series of felt-tip doodles, naïve children's illustrations which provide a sad, nostalgic contrast to Coupland's tales of failed marriages, drug dependency and the quiet desperation of the working life. Coupland's inspiration is presumably Kurt Vonnegut's *Breakfast of Champions* (1974), whose scribbles also work to defamiliarise the ordinary, to break things down to their most basic shapes and lines – a Martian view of the world akin to Craig Raine's poetry, or a child's primer on the ugliness of modern life. In *Life after God*, Coupland uses the picture-book sketches to represent his characters' longing for the pure, the natural, the real; but the cartoon sketches are fuzzy, indistinct, a half-remembered Disney version of the landscape. In 'Little Creatures', the narrator tries to explain human nature (he is separated from his wife) to his child through animal behaviour, but his analogies get increasingly bitter and strained – Squirrelly the Squirrel, the failed artist; Clappy the Kitten with too many bills on her MasterCard; Doggles the alcoholic dog (*God*, 19). Both adult and child are fascinated by the animals and birds they pass as they drive from Vancouver to Prince George, past the vast mountains and the snow-filled valleys, but the natural remains distant, separated by glass and air-conditioning: a cartoon.

Life after God also registers an important shift in Coupland's work. From this point on, 'Nature' is important less as some kind of metaphysical ideal, but rather as a synonym for natural feelings, genuine emotions, authentic responses. Whilst *Generation X* sought to gain some distance from mass culture through irony, his later works seek salvation through sincerity. 'I'm trying to escape from ironic hell' states one character in *Life after God*; 'Cynicism into faith; randomness into clarity; worry into devotion' (*God*, 231).

As we have seen, 'irony' is a way of reading signs against their intended meaning, freeing oneself from the commercial by knowingness, playing the game for its own sake rather than as a mindless consumer. But isn't such irony itself built into the system – from 'ironic' advertising (much more prevalent now than the simple hardsell) to the knowing wink to camera which characterises so much Postmodernism? We might know that every social transaction is financial, that all artworks are consumer goods, that the signifiers of Hollywood romance bear little relation to real feelings – but what good does such cynicism do us? In *Life after God* and *Girlfriend in a Coma*, Coupland seeks out the opposite extreme, deploying sentimentality to counter soullessness, unfashionable religious yearnings in an utterly secular world, uncomfortable honesty in place of the glib one-liner – what Coupland calls 'knee-jerk irony' (*X*, 150), symptom of a perpetual adolescence. Of course, such sincerity may well be more than a little embarrassing and, as a defence against the Postmodern, can be seen as apolitical, anti-intellectual and twee. Irony may be Postmodernism's great cultural prophylactic – turning everything into parody, play, a game without consequences – but our screens are still awash with simulated sentimentality, as Coupland's recurrent references to Princess Di make clear. Is Coupland just faking sincerity? Certainly, his latest novels – *Miss Wyoming* (2000) and *All Families are Psychotic* (2001) – suggest that the device is not without its risks; the outrageous wish-fulfilment endings of both novels (*All Families are Psychotic* ends with its lead characters being cured of AIDS and cancer respectively!) are so self-conscious, their sentimentality so artificial, that the novels become examples of the very banality which Coupland professes to critique. The tension between the real and the artificial, between Coupland's anguished demand that there must be more to life than this, and the diminished aesthetic resources he uses to express such yearnings – his cartoon alienation – seems ever more unstable here.

The result has the emotional content of Lichtenstein's images of lovelorn teenagers and maudlin lovers taken from '50s romance comics: feelings blown up to the size of billboards, but whose very scale cause these emotions to vanish imperceptively amongst the endless forest of signs.

NOTES

1. Abbreviations and page references refer to the following editions of Coupland's work: X (*Generation X*, London: Abacus, 1992), *Shampoo* (*Shampoo Planet*, London: Scribner, 1999), *God* (*Life after God*, London: Scribner, 1999).
2. Robert Hughes (1991), *The Shock of the New*, London: Thames/Hudson, p. 324.
3. Michael Brockington (1996), 'Five short years: half a decade of Douglas Coupland', *The Vancouver Review*, Fall, p. 8.
4. Elizabeth Young (1999), 'Postscript', *Shampoo Planet*, London: Scribner, p. 283.
5. Nicholas Lezard (1998), 'I know it's serious', *The Guardian*, 14 November.
6. Julian Evans (1999), 'Emptiness of a lonely planet', *The Guardian*, 27 October.
7. Richard Hamilton, quoted in Hughes, p. 344.
8. Hughes, p. 354.
9. Will Blythe (1994), 'Doing laundry at the end of history', *Esquire*, March.
10. Ibid.
11. Pierre Bordieu, quoted by James Annesley (1998), *Blank Fictions*, London: Pluto, p. 92.
12. Blythe, p. 72.
13. Don DeLillo (1986), *White Noise*, London: Picador, p. 123.
14. Annesley, p. 124.
15. Ibid., p. 123.
16. Douglas Coupland, quoted by Kate Muir (1992), 'To label lovers everywhere', *The Times*, 17 August.
17. Evans, *The Guardian*.
18. See, for example, Grant Wood's painting of *Stone City, Iowa*, 1930 (Joslyn Art Museum, Omaha).

BIOGRAPHY

Douglas Coupland was born in 1961, on a Canadian military base in Germany. His father was a doctor, whilst his mother studied comparative theology, though Coupland is at pains to stress that he was raised without any formal religious observance at all. The third of four sons ('I am Peter Brady'), Coupland's upbringing was stable and undramatic. His family moved to Vancouver in 1965, and this remains Coupland's spiritual home, a city of glass gazing out at the icy-green immensity of Horseshoe Bay, 'the most idiosyncratic city in America' (he professes not to know what the word Canada means. 'I suppose it's an Indian thing,' he notes).

He studied sculpture and industrial design, first in Vancouver, then in Hawaii, Milan, and Japan, where he also completed courses in Japanese Business Science. After a brief venture into high finance (the inspiration for the 'veal-fattening pens' of *Generation X* (1991), he returned to Vancouver and 'the art-life', supporting himself through 'McJobs' (pumping gas, copying blue-prints), whilst exhibiting his first sculpture show, 'The Floating World', at the Vancouver art gallery in 1987.

After a local editor was amused by a postcard he'd written from Japan, he was asked to write a number of journalistic pieces on the US and Canadian art scene. *Generation X* was initially commissioned as a non-fiction riposte to the recently released *Yuppie Handbook*, but Coupland turned in a novel instead, an extension of his work with Vancouver cartoonist, Paul Leroche. In no sense a slacker in terms of his own life, in the decade since Coupland has published ten books, ranging from novels to essays (*Polaroids from the Dead* (1996)), an 'ironic' city guide to Vancouver (*City of Glass* (2000)), and a coffee-book study of *Lara Croft and the Tomb Raider Phenomenon* (1998).

In a moment of apparent candour he described writing as simply a way of making money, and money as 'just another art-supply'; certainly, visual art informs his work much more than any explicit literary sources. His eccentricities are well-known (he only owns furniture which he makes himself, shuns mass-produced products, and keeps only art objects, personal letters and meteorites in his minimalist Ron Thom-designed home), and fiercely guards his personal life. Both *Life after God* (1994) and *Girlfriend in a Coma* (1998) came out of long periods of depression, but of late he has professed himself bored of 'handknit sweaters and earnest dining' and reinvented himself as a multimedia conceptualist via his astonishingly slick web-sites ('You think they're slick? Good!') and new editor and publisher. The plotlessness of his early work has been replaced by a shiny, commercial sheen, but Coupland remains a profoundly contradictory figure. Despite his reputation as the Pope of Pop culture, he has admitted to not owning a TV for most of his life ('I wanted a nineteenth-century brain'), and for all his attempts to spell out the *Zeitgeist* via aphoristic sound-bites, maintains that 'I speak for myself, not for a generation. I never have.'

COUPLANDISMS

Dead at 30, Buried at 70.

Shopping is not Creating.

New Zealand Gets Nuked Too.

Purchased Experiences Don't Count.

Simulate Yourself.

Nostalgia is a Weapon.

Adventure without risk is Disneyland.

You disguise your laziness as pride.

You pretend to be more eccentric than you actually are because you worry you are an interchangeable cog.

You are unable to visualize yourself in a future.

We're all theme-parks.

Technology favors horrible people.

Let's just hope we accidentally build God.

LINKS TO OTHER AUTHORS

Don DeLillo: When Bell in DeLillo's *Americana* (1971) compares his small-town upbringing to the bizarre technological and terminological excesses of the Postmodern city, he questions 'what impossible distance must be traveled to get from here to there, what language crossed, what levels of being' – a sentiment and sensibility close to Coupland's art. In the same novel, the crazed Vietnam vet, Brand, notes 'One of the things I've figured out for myself out here in exile is that there's too much slang in my head'; exile, asceticism and the paring away of 'manufactured passions' (DeLillo) connect both writers' early work.

Paul Auster: If you could somehow set yourself adrift from your culture, abdicate all responsibilities, cut yourself free from all the things that determine your cultural role, give yourself up to chance, fate and the random nature of the cosmos, would you find yourself or lose any last vestige of identity?

Cormac McCarthy: Both authors use the metaphor of desert space to play off notions of nature and civilisation in what threatens to be a wholly artificial world.

E. Annie Proulx: Coupland's middle-class tourists, culturally slumming in search of the authentic, get pretty short shrift in Proulx's prose.

Bret Easton Ellis: One could read Ellis's world as a kind of nightmare vision of everything Generation X fears it might one day become: wholly absorbed in the buying and selling of image.

Thomas Pynchon: The idea of the wilderness as blank space, a clean slate which permits at least the possibility of original or personal inscription, underpins many of the novels studied in this book.

BIBLIOGRAPHY

Primary works
Generation X (1991), New York: St Martin's Press.
Shampoo Planet (1992), New York: Simon & Schuster.
Life after God (1994), New York: Simon & Schuster.
Microserfs (1995), New York: ReganBooks.
Polaroids from the Dead (1996), New York: ReganBooks (essays).
Girlfriend in a Coma (1998), New York: ReganBooks.
Miss Wyoming (2000), New York: Pantheon Books.
All Families are Psychotic (2001), New York: Pantheon Books.

Critical sources
Abcarian, Robin (1991), 'Boomer backlash', *Los Angeles Times*, 12 June.
Annesley, James (1998), *Blank Fictions*, London: Pluto.
Bernstein, Fred (2000), 'Entertaining Mr X', *The Independent*, 27 February.
Blythe, Will (1994), 'Doing laundry at the end of history', *Esquire*, March.
Brockington, Michael (1996), 'Five short years: half a decade of Douglas Coupland', *The Vancouver Review*, Fall.
Clark, Alex (2001), 'Wacky families', *The Guardian*, 8 September.
Eshun, Ekow (2000), 'Generation games', *The Observer*, 27 February.
Ettinghausen, Jeremy (2000), 'A flash in the pan who ran and ran', *The Daily Telegraph*, 8 March.
Evans, Julian (1999), 'Emptiness of a lonely planet', *The Guardian*, 27 October.
Lambrose, R. J. (2000), 'The abusable past', *Radical Historical Review*, 77, Spring, pp. 162–6.

Lezard, Nicholas (1998), 'I know it's serious', *The Guardian*, 14 November.

Lohr, Steve (1994), 'No more McJobs for Mr X', *New York Times*, 29 May.

McGill, R. (2000), 'The sublime simulation', *Essays on Canadian Writing*, 70, Spring, pp. 252–76.

Muir, Kate (1992), 'To label lovers everywhere', *The Times*, 17 August.

Wheelwright, Julie (2000), 'Douglas Coupland – talking about which generation?', *The Independent*, 12 February.

Useful Websites

http.//www.coupland.com

http.//www.geocities.com/SoHo/Gallery/5560/index.html

CONCLUSION:
THOMAS PYNCHON'S *MASON & DIXON*

———————⟿⟾———————

'Two things fill my mind with ever new and increasing wonder
– the starry firmament above me and the moral law within me.'
Immanuel Kant[1]

'All plots tend to move deathward . . . We edge nearer death every
time we plot.'
Don DeLillo[2]

One of the central themes of American literature has always been the
loss of Eden, an elegaic sense of irretrievable dreams, promises and
possibilities. This sense of loss provides the melancholy counterbalance
to America's apparently boundless optimism, energy and youth; Utopia
can be positioned either in the future or in the past – in what will come
to pass or what could have been.

In mythic terms, America (and more specifically the West) signifies a
sense of limitless possibility, freedom and bounty; America as the great
unmeasured continent, endless and inexhaustable. Indeed, American
culture ceaselessly returns to that seminal first landfall, the first sight-
ing of the continent's generous contours and fertile abundance, the
notion of America as a promised land. Here one could begin again,
become somebody else; here one could find freedom from persecution
and corruption, a chance to build a perfect civilisation, released from
the pernicious inequalities and tyrannies of Europe. Central to this
utopian conception of America was the notion of space; land enough
for all to harvest, room for all beliefs, expanses which could never be
plumbed. Diligence and hard work would be required to tame the
wilderness, but this would in turn cure its inhabitants of the laxity of
corpulent living. The earth would make you good; the sky would make

you free. Ultimately, however, this hour of infinite plenitude was a fleeting one. After all, the land was also there to be grabbed first, annexed and apportioned, legally and physically fought over. All must be measured, divvied up, cut down, the mirage of inexhaustibility merely exacerbating the rapaciousness of its inheritors. Until, of course, everything is gone, and one finally grasps the true meaning of history: the transformation of what might have been into what, irrevocably, is.

A sense of exhaustion and consumption underpins much of the writing in this book, and this notion of the posthumous is central to Thomas Pynchon's prodigious historical satire, *Mason & Dixon* (1997). Indeed, *Mason & Dixon* encapsulates many of the key themes of this study: map making as a means of talking about representation; a concern with what lies at 'the fringes of readability' (*M&D*, 287) or language; the relationship between ideas and things, abstraction and matter; or as the cod-eighteenth-century prose of *Mason & Dixon* has it, 'Stars and Mud, ever conjugate, a Paradox to consider' (*M&D*, 724). But it is the novel's concern with the terminal measurement of the world – everything now documented, catalogued, the complete figuration of the landscape – which tallies most closely with Postmodernism's sense of built-in obeselescence.

As every American schoolchild knows, Mason and Dixon were the British surveyors responsible for the calculation of the boundary line between Pennsylvania and Maryland, and thereby also responsible for the demarcation between North and South. Although the Royal Charter commissioning the survey would be rendered irrelevant by the War of Independence only eight years later, the line would eventually prove crucial as the dividing point between free and slave states before the Civil War, the duo's arbitrary abstraction transformed into a crucial border.

Pynchon, however, begins the novel with Mason and Dixon's first commission together, when they travel to Cape Town in the southern hemisphere to observe the Transit of Venus – the passage of Venus across the sun. This employment is by no means a matter of pure scientific enquiry, however – such measurements are intended to aid in the gauging of the distance between the earth and the sun and thereby to lead to the calculation of standardised time-zones to be inscribed upon the globe. It is commerce, rather than disinterested astronomy, which requires the pair's work: the laws of capital require quantifiable properties, agreed-upon transactions, calculable costs and variables.

Pynchon's central premise here is that the Age of Reason has more to do with filthy lucre than Euclid. The market stretches everywhere; every discovery, record or expedition possesses a mercantile value, every assignation is ultimately commercial. Dixon, hoping to find in the wilds of Africa a sense of liberty and adventure, is disappointed; are there, he asks 'Markets that never answer to the Company, gatherings that remain forever unknown . . . I'd be much oblig'd if we might roam 'round together, some Evening, and happen we'll see' (M&D, 69). But the various factions of the East India Company, the Dutch Company or the Royal Society run every last outpost, no matter how seemingly remote or destitute. The surveyors feel themselves subject to some 'Invisible Power . . . Something richer than many a Nation, yet with no Boundaries – which tho' never part of any Coalition, yet maintains its own great Army and Navy' (M&D, 140), a vast interlocking system, whose tentacles stretch everywhere, threatening to submerge the world beneath 'oceanik Waves of ink' (M&D, 140). Despite Mason's repeated protestations that he's 'not in the market' (M&D, 696), both men have taken 'the King's money' (M&D, 693), their observations and representations profoundly implicated in the assertion that 'Charter'd Companies may indeed be the form the world has increasingly begun to take' (M&D, 252).

Such notions, of course, bear a striking contemporary relevance. The flow of data, the systemisation of the world, and the regulation of its codes and descriptions – all these lie at the heart of descriptions of the Postmodern. Indeed, *Mason & Dixon* is on one level a kind of eighteenth-century conspiracy novel, involving mysterious corporations, complex commercial interests, Jesuit spies (who communicate via a mysterious telegraph which sends out encoded signals and images via the night-sky) and a dizzying array of counterfeiters, cabbalists and French, English, Spanish and Chinese secret agents who frequently swap disguises (and roles) in mid-sentence. As in Pynchon's other novels, the entire landscape seems encrypted with secret meanings, messages and codes: rock formations, the loop of rivers, ley-lines. Cartography becomes the translation of 'a secret Body of Knowledge' (M&D, 487), the tracing of a mysterious typography, but rather than penetrating some divine mystery, its transcription seems to place the world ever more securely in the hands of the authorities, the shadowy keepers of esoteric knowledge. In one deeply unsettling scene, Mason and Dixon come upon a secret Masonic lodge whose members all appear to be wax figures – unless the figures 'were not Effigies at all, but real people, only *pretending* to be effigies' (*M&D*, 291). Readers of DeLillo or Auster will immediately recognise this sense of disorientation and uncertainty, whereby every description appears a potential booby-trap, clue or trick. On the one hand, the world is growing increasingly classified and administered; on the other, Mason and Dixon feel the complexities of the situation slipping away from their grasp.

And at the heart of all this is the Mason–Dixon Line. In order to take accurate measurements, the surveying party must hack a ruthlessly straight line through the wilderness, carving their geometry through forests, swamps, rivers and settlements. Even though the veracity of the line is frequently called into doubt depending on how drunk, stoned (Indian hemp is in plentiful supply) or bad-tempered the team are on any given occassion, the calculations must always add up; indeed, it is the invisible calculations rather than the tangible undergrowth which constitute legal reality. Needless to say, there is something deeply unnatural about forcing the earth to conform to a irrefutable line, as straight as a ruler. Tractless nature becomes authorised property whilst distinct boundaries divide and segregate: suddenly one is either on one side or the other. By the time of the Civil War, this line would, for many, demarcate freedom and slavery, and references to slavery permeate the text. Indeed, in a sense, servitude and bondage is the dark secret at the heart of the commodity market; people as things, goods to be bartered. Everything is connected in the market-place, even the honest calculations of the fiercely anti-authoritarian Dixon. As he blunders through another fetid marsh, encrusted in muck and darkness, his observations are nevertheless being fed into a ferociously abstract but efficent system, a system which ultimately envelops everything. What can be said to lie outside it? The straight lines the duo are drawing are the bars of what Max Weber calls 'the iron cage of reason', the conscription and assimilation of all variables – or possibilities.[3]

This antipathy toward the straight line or the official account underpins the eccentricity of the book. In the place of logic and order, Pynchon substitutes wild, absurdist humour (including, but by no means limited to, a love-lorn mechanical duck, an enormous sentient beetroot, thinking-clocks, ghosts, a dragon and the world's largest cheese). Against the documented annals of history (another straight, chronological, line), he posits an anachronistic chronicle:

tended lovingly and honorably by fabulists and counterfeiters, Ballad-Mongers and Cranks of ev'ry radius, Masters of Disguise to provide her the Costume, Toilette, and Bearing, and Speech nimble enough to keep her beyond the Desires, or even the Curiosity, of Government. (*M&D*, 350)

Several of the indigenous tribes Mason and Dixon encounter regard insanity as a 'holy state' (*M&D*, 674), and the image of the holy fool resonates throughout the novel. In their human bungling of the line – distracted by women, taverns, or simply the love of a tall-tale – Mason and Dixon are redeemed from the ruthless efficiency of their enterprise; one might think of Charlie Chaplin in *Modern Times* (1936), disrupting the factory production-line by his human need to scratch, idle or dream. Clumsiness and stupidity suggest the human element which cannot be erased from the system, the novel's extended vaudeville act (complete with musical numbers) the antithesis of the Age of Reason. At one point the narrator holds forth regarding the notorious wedge at the corner of Maryland, its northeasternmost extremity omitted from any map due to a geometrical inconsistency (*M&D*, 469): here there 'remains an Unseen World, beyond Resolution, of transactions never recorded' (*M&D*, 470). This mythical space, beyond the grip of the commercial, the represented, or carefully precalculated, acts as a kind of fictional ideal in the novel: the West as possibility; unmarked land.

A preference for fecund disorder above sterile logic, fancy over history, confabulation above the official account; Pynchon, however, is too subtle and complex a novelist for this to be the whole story. Like Huck Finn fleeing 'civilizin'' in Twain's novel, the further the pair travel from order or reason, the more violent and dangerous the terrain becomes. The endless internecine feud between the Shepherdsons and the Grangerfords in *Huckleberry Finn* (1884) is reproduced in *Mason & Dixon* in the form of several scenes of lawless slaughter, although, in a Postmodern twist, these sites of bloodletting are already starting to beget official tour-groups and museums. Concerning Pynchon's novel, Tony Tanner quotes Crèvecoeur's observation that 'our first trees [were] felled, in general, by the most vicious of our people', and McCarthy's *Blood Meridian* (1985) also comes to mind; the opposite of order is not necessarily benign, and blank spaces can also terrify and appall.[4]

Moreover, Pynchon also draws upon the classical motif that the journey westwards is a trope for death, 'as to journey west,' notes the Reverend Cherrycoke, 'is to live, raise Children, grow older, and die, carried along by the Stream of the Day' (M&D, 263). The westwards horizon marks the setting of the sun and thereby man's own twilight, for the night 'takes back ev'rything committed upon the Land that Day, without appeal, dissolving all in Shadow' (M&D, 585). The West marks the passing of all things, the border between this world and the next. The natural landscape is rendered as a vale of shades throughout the work, America the home of both the first things and the last. The natural is also the mortal, Pynchon reminds us; the 'vacancy' (M&D, 709) of the nocturnal forests or the infinitude of the stars metaphors of extinction. One might think of the poetry of Robert Frost here: does the night sky signify some sense of celestial order and plan, or merely denote a vast emptiness, twin to that other mortal nothingness, endless and silent? Freud has argued that all dreams of journeys are ultimately dreams of death and such imagery undercuts the 'Jolly Theatrikals' of the novel:

> What Machine is it . . . that bears us along so relentlessly? We go rattling thro' another Day – another Year, – as thro' an empty Town without a name, in the Midnight . . . we have but Memories of some Pause at the Pleasure-Spas of our younger Day, the Maidens, the Cards, the Claret, – we seek to extend our stay, but now a silent Functionary in dark Livery indicates it is time to re-board the Coach, and resume the Journey. Long before the Destination, moreover, shall this Machine come abruptly to a stop . . . gather'd dense with Fear, shall we open the Door to confer with the Driver, to Discover that there is no Driver, . . . no Horses, . . . only the Machine, fading as we stand, and a Prairie of desperate Immensity. (M&D, 361)

The abiding image of the novel is of some dilapidated tavern perched in the middle of nowhere, a flickering light in an immense darkness. Outside lies Eternity, Stygian and impenetrable, but Pynchon would rather linger with his heroes, tell another tall-tale, sing another tavern-ballad, sup another ale; anything to put off the moment of having to venture outside into the tractless night. It is perhaps significant that the novel is narrated by the loquacious Reverend Wicks Cherrycoke, who is permitted to stay within his hosts' house 'for as long as he can keep the children amused' (*M&D*, 6). Like Scheherezade, he spins endless confabulation, designed to postpone the moment of leave-taking for as long as possible. Ultimately, the novel places its faith not in the natural, authentic or eternal, but in the common pleasures of the ale-house: banter, company, invention. One might think of Jerome Klinkowitz's metaphor of structuring the void here, but the physical, mortal facts are not so easily decried *in absentia*.[5] At the end of the Line (in every sense), Pynchon realises that he must accede to historical fact and send his heroes home to their deaths, but for several pages he resists. Suppose they went on, he intimates, suppose the journey continued – for several pages, his prose refuses to give in to the inevitable. He lets his heroes linger a little longer, pour another drink, launch into another endless shaggy-dog story. But, eventually of course, their carriage awaits.

In the final analysis, the writers gathered here are concerned less with the authentic or the eternal, than with the search for such things – which is to say, a stress on the act rather than the thing. Whilst those discontented with the Postmodern may seek out vestiges of the natural or essential, it is the attempt to describe these things – rather than success or even the things themselves – which *post*-Postmodernism pins its hopes on. Language, as opposed to the unworded remains the vessel of salvation; but only by reaching for something outside itself, something not yet said, can language remain vital or alive. As Paul Auster writes in *Moon Palace* (1989), 'We find ourselves by looking to what we're not.'[6] We need a sense of something beyond the artificial, something not a copy of a copy of a copy, to strive for; but ultimately it is our own stammering tongue, and not the world-in-itself, which counts. Indeed, it increasingly seems that a renewed faith in language as expression – rather than naïve mimesis – is the way out of the Postmodern dead-end. It's the individual voice – and not real things – which might save us from the world we've made for ourselves.

'When the tremulous radiance of a summer night fills with twinkling stars and the moon itself is full, I am slowly drawn into a state of enhanced sensitivity made of friendship and disdain for the world and eternity,' wrote Kant: a fitting epigraph for Pynchon's masterpiece.[7]

NOTES

1. Immanuel Kant, quoted by Bohumil Hrabal (1993), *Too Loud a Solitude* (transl. Michael Heim), London: Abacus, p. 49.
2. Don DeLillo (1986), *White Noise*, London: Picador, p. 26.
3. See Douglas Tallack (1991), *Twentieth Century America*, London: Longman, pp. 11–12.
4. See Tony Tanner (2000), *The American Mystery*, Cambridge: Cambridge University Press, p. 226.
5. See Jerome Klinkowitz (1992), *Structuring the Void*, Durham: Duke University Press, pp. 1–14.
6. Paul Auster (1990), *Moon Palace*, London: Faber, p. 154.
7. Kant, quoted by Hrabal, p. 50.

BIBLIOGRAPHY

Baker, Stephen (2000), *The Fiction of Postmodernity*, Edinburgh: Edinburgh University Press.

Boyle, T. Coraghessan (1997), 'The great divide', *New York Times*, 18 May.

Kakutani, Michiko (1997), 'Pynchon hits the road with Mason and Dixon', *New York Times*, 29 April.

Mars-Jones, Adam (1997), 'How a Quaker gets his oats', *The Observer*, 15 June.

Moody, Rick (1997), 'Surveyors of the Enlightenment', *Atlantic Monthly*, July.

Moony, Ted (1997), '*Mason & Dixon*', *Los Angeles Times*, 10 May.

Quan, A. (1998), '*Mason & Dixon*', *Antioch Review*, 56 (3), Summer, pp. 375–6.

Siegel, M. (1998), '*Mason & Dixon*', *Journal of Pop Culture*, 31 (4), Spring, pp. 176–7.

Tanner, Tony (2000), *The American Mystery*, Cambridge: Cambridge University Press.

Wood, Michael (1998), '*Mason & Dixon*', *Raritarian*, 17 (4), Spring.

THEMATIC INDEX

249

INDEX BY AUTHOR

253